MANAGEMENT ACCOUNTING

MANAGEMENT ACCOUNTING

European Perspectives

Edited by

ALNOOR BHIMANI

OXFORD UNIVERSITY PRESS · OXFORD
1996

Oxford University Press, Walton Street, Oxford OX2 6DP
Oxford New York
Athens Auckland Bangkok Bogota Bombay
Buenos Aires Calcutta Cape Town Dar es Salaam
Delhi Florence Hong Kong Istanbul Karachi
Kuala Lumpur Madras Madrid Melbourne
Mexico City Nairobi Paris Singapore
Taipei Tokyo Toronto
and associated companies in
Berlin Ibadan

Oxford is a trade mark of Oxford University Press

Published in the United States
by Oxford University Press Inc., New York

British Library Cataloguing in Publication Data
Data available

Library of Congress Cataloging in Publication Data
Data available
ISBN 0–19–828966–9

1 3 5 7 9 10 8 6 4 2

Typeset by Hope Services (Abingdon) Ltd.
Printed in Great Britain
on acid-free paper by
Bookcraft Ltd.
Midsomer Norton, Somerset

CONTENTS

Foreword vii
Anthony Hopwood

List of Contributors x

List of Figures xvi

List of Tables xvii

Introduction xix
Alnoor Bhimani

1. Management Accounting Changes: The Belgian Experience 1
Werner Bruggeman, Regine Slagmulder, and Dominique Waeytens

2. Management Accounting in Denmark: Theory and Practice 31
Poul Israelsen, Michael Andersen, Carsten Rohde, and Poul Erik Sørensen

3. Drivers of Management Accounting in Finland 54
Kalervo Virtanen, Teemu Malmi, Juhani Vaivio, and Eero Kasanen

4. Management Accounting Practice in France 74
Michel Lebas

5. Management Accounting: A German Perspective 100
Gerhard Scherrer

6. A Survey of Management Accounting Practice in Greek Firms 123
Apostolos Ballas and George Venieris

7. Management Accounting in Italy: Evolution within Tradition 140
Maria Bergamin Barbato, Paolo Collini, and Alberto Quagli

8. Managing Costs in The Netherlands: Past Theory and Current Practice 164
Tom L. C. M. Groot

9. Management Accounting in Spain: Trends in Thought and Practice 180

Angel Saez-Torrecilla, Antonio Fernandez-Fernandez, Joaquin Texeira-Quiros, and Mercedes Vaquera-Mosquero

10. Cost Management in Sweden: From Modern to Post-Modern 199

Urban Ask, Christian Ax, and Sten Jönsson

11. Management Accounting in the United Kingdom: Reflections on Research, Practice, and the Profession 218

Alnoor Bhimani

Index 243

FOREWORD

Anthony G. Hopwood

Europe has a rich and deep tradition of research and practice in the areas of cost and management accounting. Early approaches relating economic thought to accounting action emerged in Germany early in the century, and have resulted in sophisticated traditions of both theorizing and practice. The British theoretical approach to costing which emerged at the London School of Economics in the 1930s provided a powerful critique of prevailing practice which subsequently had an enormous influence in both academic and practising communities. The Italian tradition of *Economia aziendale* provided a way of conceiving the linkages between internal accountings and the more general functioning of the enterprise, not least its strategic posture and its relationship to wider competitive pressures in the market-place. Danish research in the post-war era further illuminated the relationships between cost and management accounts and the wider aims and objectives of the organization. Alongside other Scandinavian research, it also created the basis for a more applied tradition of research that delved into the actual organizational functioning of accounting systems and highlighted the significance of careful explorations of accounting in action. Even in some of the countries of Eastern Europe, the remnants of earlier German approaches to cost accounting theory and practice remain, providing a quite sophisticated basis for examining the contributions which wise accounting can make to organizational efficiency and improvement in the new market era.

One could go on outlining other equally significant contributions which long traditions of European thought and practice have made to what is now considered management accounting. Interestingly, however, the perspectives which together might constitute a European view of the subject have remained poorly documented and fragmented. Most of the relevant literatures have remained national in orientation. Relatively few descriptions have appeared in different languages, not least in English. No attempts have been made to pull together the diverse traditions of economic inquiries into cost and management accounting. The result is that even in Europe there is a relatively limited consciousness of past traditions and achievements, and the potential that these might have for casting light on the complex problems which face management accountants trying to recouple their practices to changing business conditions and organizational forms. Ideas about management accounting in Europe seemingly remain diverse, fragmented, and poorly articulated.

An enormous potential is thereby lost. Although a great deal of effort has been invested in recent years in probing the management accounting condition, most of the major problems and difficulties remain. Designing flows of information on organizational costs that can relate to shifting decision contexts and problem formulations remains a major issue. Relating information on financial performance to patterns of devolved managerial responsibility and accountability is still an important problem. Mobilizing accounting so that it can have an impact on organization action is a concern that requires much more than a reformulation of the bureaucracy of costing. It requires a very different set of insights into how information relates to action in organizational settings, how different competitive and strategic conditions shape the possibilities for accounting influence, and how important economic and financial messages can be brought to bear on managerial decisions by means of accounting reports.

Indeed, putting the problem agenda in such terms illuminates the highly constrained nature of some of today's agendas for management accounting research and practical reform. Although the original organizational diagnoses which underlay the so-called new management accounting research of the late 1980s and early 1990s were rich and insightful, the resultant fascination with a single bureaucratic remedy—activity based costing—must surely be increasingly seen as very partial. Sharing so many of the organizational and managerial characteristics of the costings of old, it seems highly unlikely that it can provide a significant basis for responding to the much deeper questions and worries about the state of management accounting that have emerged both from practical concerns and research explorations. Rather than focusing on ascertaining *the* cost, surely the need is for a much deeper understanding of the multiplicity of often quite different questionings of cost that occur in managerial decision processes. Instead of trying to incorporate very diverse aspects of the economic and operational life of the organization into relatively few indicators, surely the need is for a better understanding of the multiple ways in which notions of costliness can infuse organizational discourse and action. Compared with such alternative thoughts, the conceptions of organizational and economic action that are built into so much of the so-called new management accounting seem very limited and very inadequate.

If this prognosis is correct, then there remains an urgent need for both research and practical inquiry into management accounting that is grounded in a wider understanding of the economic and organizational functioning of the enterprise. It is here that the variety of European approaches to research and action offers some potential. Together they have sustained a continuing tradition of serious economic analysis of forms of cost accounting. Over the years they have provided bases for critically examining the relationship of management accounting to different strategic and competitive configurations. Equally importantly, they have continued to emphasize the need for both research and practice to comprehend the complexities of organizational practice. Often committed to a tradition of grounded inquiry, and sometimes even practical experimentation, many European traditions of research have provided their own systems of checks and balances on the dangers of overly abstract inquiry that incorporates too simplistic notions of how accounting functions in practice.

By bringing together a collection of essays which focus on European practices and understandings of management accounting, the present volume performs an important service to the community of both scholars and practitioners. By mapping out both the diversity and the commonalities of the European tradition, it provides an insight into the possibilities for alternative understanding of both action and inquiry.

LIST OF CONTRIBUTORS

ANDERSEN, Michael, M.Sc., Ph.D., is Senior Lecturer at Copenhagen Business School. His research field is management accounting, with a special emphasis on the control of profit centres, from both an empirical and a theoretical point of view. In addition to teaching at Copenhagen Business School, he also teaches at Aälborg University. He has close links with Danish industry, where he acts partly as consultant and partly as lecturer.

ASK, Urban, is a Ph.D. student of accounting and finance at the Göteborg School of Economics and Commercial Law, University of Göteborg, Sweden. His thesis is on cost accounting practice. He has co-authored, with Christian Ax, *Cost Management—Developments in Costing and Management Control* (in Swedish), articles published in Swedish journals, and papers presented at international conferences.

AX, Christian, is a Ph.D. student of accounting and finance at the Göteborg School of Economics and Commercial Law, University of Göteborg, Sweden. His thesis is on cost accounting practice. He has co-authored, with Urban Ask, *Cost Management—Developments in Costing and Management Control* (in Swedish), articles published in Swedish journals, and papers presented at international conferences.

BALLAS, Apostolos, is an Assistant Professor of Accounting at the Athens LBA. He was educated at the Industrial School of Thessaloniki, the LSE, and the London Business School, where he obtained his Ph.D. He has previously taught at the University of Macedonia. His current research interests include the development of valuation models which use accounting data, management culture as a determinant of accounting policy, and the influence of government policies in accounting development.

BERGAMIN BARBATO, Maria, is a full-time Professor of Accounting and Management Control at University Ca'Foscari in Venice. Professor Bergamin Barbato previously taught financial accounting and cost accounting at the same university. She is director of the doctoral programme in business economics and management at Ca'Foscari University, and she teaches at both graduate and undergraduate levels. Her main areas of research are cost management, performance measurement within organizations, and organizational aspects of control.

BHIMANI, Alnoor (Al), is a Senior Lecturer in accounting and finance at the London School of Economics. He was educated at King's College (London), Cornell University, and the London School of Economics, and qualified as a certified management accountant in Canada. He has previously held teaching positions at the universities of York and Western Ontario in Canada. His research interests include the relationship between technology and management accounting practices, the social analysis of accounting change in different organizational contexts, and international management accounting issues. He is co-author of *Management Accounting: Evolution not Revolution* (1989) and *Management Accounting: Pathways to Progress* (1994), and publishes widely in academic and professional journals.

BRUGGEMAN, Werner, is Professor of Management Accounting and Control at the Faculty of Economics and the Vlerick School of Management of the University of Ghent, Belgium. He is principal of the Vlerick School of Management and head of the Accounting Department. He is author of *Management Accounting in the New Production Environment* (1992), and has published articles in the *International Journal of Production Economics*, the *British Journal of Management*, and the *International Journal of Production and Operations Management*. His research interests include activity-based cost management and contingency models in management control.

COLLINI, Paolo, is a full-time researcher in management at Ca'Foscari University in Venice, where he teaches accounting. He holds an MBA from Boston University and a research doctorate (Ph.D.) in business economics and management from Ca'Foscari University. His main areas of research are cost management, manufacturing accounting, and strategic cost management.

FERNANDEZ-FERNANDEZ, Antonio, is a full Professor in the Economics and Business Sciences Faculty of Extremadura University. He has previously taught at Seville University and is also a certified public accountant in Spain. He is a member of ACODI, ASEPUC, and the AECA Council for Management Accounting Normalization. Presently he is researching management accounting in the new technological environment, including activity-based management systems, quality cost management, and strategic management. He is co-author of three books on management and cost accounting, and has contributed to five edited books on management accounting in the new manufacturing context.

GROOT, Tom, is Professor of Management Accounting at the Vrije Universiteit of Amsterdam. He was educated at the University of

Groningen and wrote his Ph.D. thesis on university management. He worked as management consultant in Central America for the Ministry of International Co-operation, and afterwards held academic positions at the University of Limburg and the Open University. He has co-authored books, and written numerous articles about financial management of non-profit organizations and the relationship between management accounting and management control. He is co-editor of two Dutch journals, and his current research interests include the behavioural aspects of budgeting and performance evaluation systems and, more generally, the design and implementation of cost management systems.

HOPWOOD, Anthony, is Professor of Management Studies at the University of Oxford, where he also is deputy director of the School of Management Studies. Previously he was on the staff of the London School of Economics and the London Business School. He is also Visiting Professor of Management at the European Institute for Advanced Studies in Management, Brussels, and a past president of the European Accounting Association. He is editor-in-chief of the international research journal *Accounting, Organizations and Society*.

ISRAELSEN, Poul, is Professor of Accounting at the Southern Denmark Business School. He has an M.Sc. (Econ.) from Aarhus University, and has previously held teaching and research positions at Aalborg University and the Aarhus School of Business. He has also been a Visiting Professor at the University of Wisconsin (1982/3). His current research interest is the construction of multi-functional cost management systems. He is the author of *Activity versus Variability-Based Management Accounting*.

JÖNSSON, Sten, has been, since 1976, a Professor of Accounting and finance at the Göteborg School of Economics and Commercial Law, University of Göteborg, Sweden. He has spent his entire academic career at the University of Göteborg. Previous research includes strategy formation, the regulation of accounting practices, accounting support for operational improvement in different kinds of organizations, and, lately, managerial style as competitive advantage. He is editor of the *Scandinavian Journal of Management*.

KASANEN, Eero, is a Professor of Finance at the Helsinki School of Economics. He obtained doctorates from Harvard Business School and Turku School of Economics. He has published in various scholarly journals, including *Financial Management* and *Managerial Finance*, and has written chapters for international textbooks on capital budgeting. His current research interests include issues in cost accounting, earnings management, hedging, and mutual fund performance measurement.

LEBAS, Michel J., is Professor of Management Accounting and Management Control at the HEC School of Management (*Groupe HEC*) in Jouy-en-Josas, near Paris. He was educated at HEC in France, at the Amos Tuck Graduate School of Business at Dartmouth College and the Stanford Graduate School of Business in the United States. He has been Academic Dean of his French *alma mater*. He has held visiting professorships at the University of Washington in Seattle, the Darden Graduate School of Business at the University of Virginia, the Helsinki School of Economics International Centre and Bocconi's SDA. He is a free-lance consultant, a CAM-I academic associate, and represents the French Ordre des Experts Comptables as a member of both the Financial and Management Accounting Committee of the International Federation of Accountants and the Management Accounting and Controlling Working Party of the Fédération des Experts Comptables Européens (Fee). He is a member of the 'management accounting concepts working party' of the Conseil National de la Comptabilité. His publications include several books and numerous articles on management accounting, management control and performance management in French and international journals.

MALMI, Teemu, works as a Researcher in the Department of Accounting and Finance at the Helsinki School of Economics, and is engaged in doctoral work. His current research interests include management and cost accounting, especially Activity Based Costing.

QUAGLI, Alberto, is a full-time Researcher at the University of Pisa, where he teaches accounting. He holds a research doctorate (Ph.D.) in business economics and management from the University of Pisa. His main areas of research are management accounting and accounting for intangible assets.

ROHDE, Carsten, M.Sc., Ph.D., is Senior Lecturer at Copenhagen Business School. His research field is management accounting, and his special interest is in the problems and opportunities of designing analysable income statements in trading and manufacturing companies. In addition to teaching at Copenhagen Business School, he also teaches at Aalborg University. He has close links with Danish industry, where he acts partly as consultant and partly as lecturer.

SAEZ-TORRECILLA, Angel, was a full professor at the Open University in Madrid. He had previously taught at the Complutense University and at Seville University. He had written many textbooks on financial management and cost accounting. He was a member of the editorial board of *Management Accounting Research* and *Revista Española de Financiacion y Contabilidad*. His research focused on activity based cost and management systems. Professor Saez-Torrecilla died in July 1995.

SCHERRER, Gerhard, is a Professor of Accounting and Auditing at the University of Regensburg, Germany. He received his Ph.D. from the University of Munich and habilitated at the University of Hamburg. He has published books on management accounting (*Kostenrechnung*, 1992) and on financial reporting in Germany (*D-Markeröffnungsbilanz*, 1991; *Liquidationsrechnungslegung*, 1990, together with B. Heni), including a recent textbook on consolidated accounting (*Konzernrechnungslegung*, 1994). His current research interests include management accounting and the financial reporting of enterprises in liquidation. He is editor of a commentary on German accounting legislation.

SLAGMULDER, Regine, is a doctoral Research Fellow in the Department of Management Accounting and Control of the School of Economics and the Vlerick School of Management of the University of Ghent, Belgium. She has an M.Sc. in engineering and a Master's Degree in Industrial Management. She was a visiting scholar at INSEAD (France) and at the School of Management of Boston University (USA). She is co-author of the book *Management Accounting in the New Production Environment* (1992), and has published articles on investment decision making in the *International Journal of Production and Operations Management* and in *Integrated Manufacturing Systems*. Her current research interests include management control for strategic capital investments.

SØRENSEN, Poul Erik, is Senior Lecturer in Management Accounting at the Aarhus School of Business. He worked eight years in banking before starting his university studies. He graduated from Aarhus University with an M.Sc. (Econ.) in managerial economics, and has since taught management accounting at several Danish business schools. He has been active in the introduction of new approaches to management accounting in Denmark. His current research interests include cost management, performance management systems, and the historical development of management accounting in Denmark.

TEXEIRA-QUIROS, Joaquin, holds a Ph.D. in economics and business sciences, and has been teaching at the Extremadura University for over a decade. He is researching activity based costing and quality costs in Extremadura manufacturing companies. He has published many papers in the main Spanish journals, and has been a speaker at many workshops, congresses, and conferences on cost and management accounting.

VAIVIO, Juhani, is a Research Assistant in the Department of Accounting and Finance of the Helsinki School of Economics. He is current preparing a Ph.D. in management accounting, and his research interest lies in the organizational and managerial aspects of non-financial management accounting measurement.

VAQUERA-MOSQUERO, Mercedes, is a Lecturer in cost and management accounting in the Economics and Business Faculty at the Extramadura University. She has been researching activity based costing systems generally, and is presently studying the application of new management and cost accounting tools in hospitals. She has published many papers in professional journals, and has been a speaker at many national and international workshops, congresses, and conferences on cost and management accounting.

VENIERIS, George, is Professor of Accounting at the Athens University of Economics and Business. He obtained his B.Sc. at that institution, and pursued his graduate studies at the University of Birmingham, where he obtained his M.Sc. as well as his Ph.D. He has previously taught, as a visiting professor, at the University of York in Toronto. His current research interests are the capital structure of Greek companies, comparative studies of accounting in the EU, and the determinants of share prices of companies listed on the Athens Stock Exchange.

VIRTANEN, Kalervo, is Professor of Management Accounting at the Helsinki School of Economics. His research interests and publications are in the areas of capital investment, acquisitions, and management control. He is also an authorized public accountant.

WAEYTENS, Dominique, is a doctoral Research Fellow in the Department of Management Accounting at the Vlerick School of Management of the University of Ghent, Belgium. He is currently working on his doctoral degree, for which he studied at the Graduate School of Business Administration of the University of Colorado at Boulder. His research deals with the evaluation of the social, behavioural, and economic effects of activity based management systems. He is co-author of *Management Accounting in the New Production Environment* (1992), and has published articles on activity based costing for continuous improvement in the *International Journal of Production Economics*.

LIST OF FIGURES

2.1.	The Danish model for recording cost accounting data	39
4.1.	Cost characteristics as described in the 1982 *Plan Comptable Général*	80
4.2.	Cost flow diagram of the *méthode des sections homogènes*	83
4.3.	The diversity of methods used for the attachment of head-quarters overhead to the various units in a group	87
4.4.	The performance causal model	89
4.5.	An illustration of the components of customer satisfaction that need to be managed to guarantee performance of the organization	91
4.6.	The deployment of objectives, copy of the causal model	92
4.7.	An illustration of an indicator of the status of the customer portfolio in terms of real profitability	92
4.8.	The schema of information flows in the 'nesting' of *Tableaux de Bord*	94
4.9.	An integrated view of the five logics of information management	96
5.1.	The subdivision of the total process time	111
5.2.	The system of reference figures	113
7.1.	Overhead allocation structure	155
9.1.	The evolution of cost accounting normalization	190
9.2.	Types of companies	191

LIST OF TABLES

1.	Qualified accountants in Europe	xix
1.1.	Frequency distribution of the hurdle rate (minimum required rate of return)	5
1.2.	Frequency distribution of the maximum pay-back period	6
1.3.	Frequency distribution of the expected IRR for the CIM investment	6
1.4.	Frequency distribution of the expected pay-back period for the CIM investment	7
1.5.	Elements other than the expected financial results that played an important role in the investment decision about CIM technology	7
1.6.	Methods used for risk analysis in evaluating CIM investments	8
1.7.	Responsibility for capital investment decisions delegated to divisional managers	9
1.8.	Use of post-implementation audit for capital investments	9
1.9.	Use of ABC/ABM approaches in Belgium	15
1.10.	Types of barrier	21
2.1.	Planned or considered changes of accounting systems among companies which are dissatisfied or only partly satisfied with their present system	46
3.1.	Principles, methods, calculations, and novel applications used in product costing in Finland	64
3.2.	Applications of ABC in Finland	65
5.1.	Published articles on cost accounting in the German journals *Betriebswirtschaftliche Forschung und Praxis, Controlling, Die Betriebswirtschaft, Der Betrieb, Kostenrechnungspraxis, Zeitschrift für betriebswirtschaftliche Forschung*	102
5.2.	The use of cost accounting systems in Germany	103
5.3.	Classification of industries in Becker 1985	103
5.4.	Classification of industries in Hauer 1994	103
5.5.	Use of imputed costs in German enterprises	105
5.6.	Use of cost variance analysis in German enterprises	106
5.7.	Operating profit per unit	119
6.1.	Management accounting accounts in HGAP	126
6.2.	Aggregates of companies interviewed	129
8.1.	Use of current value and historical costs for capital budgeting and performance evaluation	170

8.2. Use of current product costs and historical product costs for pricing decisions 170
8.3. Critical success factors considered most important by Dutch enterprises 173
8.4. Performance-evaluation indicators most widely used in The Netherlands 174
8.5. Principles of valuation used by Dutch firms in 1986 and 1994 175
9.1. Analysis of articles in journals published since 1950 182
9.2. Analysis of papers presented at congresses since 1981 184
9.3. Analysis of Ph.D. theses since 1970 185
9.4. Research evolution in the different branches of accounting 186
9.5. Evolution of Spanish teaching texts 188
9.6. Types of costing systems 192
10.1. Usage of costing methods 207
11.1. Trends in capital appraisal techniques in United Kingdom companies 225
11.2. Choice of allocation bases 226
11.3. The existing and future use of ABC 226
11.4. The implementation of ABC 227
11.5. The adoption of ABC 227
11.6. Different uses of activity-based techniques in eleven companies 228
11.7. Use or planned use of cost management techniques 228
11.8. Types of cost information used in decision making 229
11.9. Importance of standard costing systems for different purposes 229
11.10. Extent to which performance is measured 230
11.11. Performance measures to board and executives 230
11.12. Use of different investment appraisal methods 231
11.13. Use of different appraisal methods 231

Introduction

Alnoor Bhimani

Just as Europe consists of countries with different languages, cultures, histories, wealth levels, and systems of jurisprudence and exhibits a mosaic of differences in tastes and preferences, so do accounting's roles and functions differ widely across European countries. Certainly, the number of qualified accountants varies considerably from one European country to another (see Table 1). More significantly, divergent frames of reference in accounting generally and in management accounting specifically are prevalent. This is all too evident when one considers the range of perspectives and prognostications aired by Europeans attending academic and professional seminars

Table 1. Qualified accountants in Europe

Country	Accountants per 10,000 population[a]
United Kingdom	23[b]
Germany	8[c]
Italy	7.5
Sweden	5.1[d]
Denmark	5
France	4
Finland	3.5
The Netherlands	3.0
Belgium	2.5
Spain	1.0
Greece	0.8

[a] Figures taken from Thorp and Kipfer 1991 unless otherwise noted.

[b] Figure includes accountants employed in industry, financial services, and professional firms as tax advisers, auditors, and management consultants.

[c] Figure includes 40,000 *Stewerberaters* specializing in taxation.

[d] Based on the number of certified public accountants and approved public accountants in 1990 as published by Statistics Sweden (figures kindly provided by Urban Ask and Christian Ax).

[e] Based on the number of authorized public accountants (KHT) and approved accountants (HTM) in 1995 (figures kindly provided by Juhani Vaivio).

in accounting. In the literature, differences between management accounting practices and control approaches between European countries are likewise widely reported (Ahrens 1994; Bromwich and Bhimani 1994; CIMA 1993; Euske *et al.* 1993; Horovitz 1980; Löning 1994; Sheridan 1995; Strange 1991), and, increasingly, the focus of interrogation is no longer on whether there is variety but its extent and form.

In considering European variety in management accounting, it may be asked what historical factors have conditioned management accounting wherever and in whatever form it exists? Are there links between management accounting research and practice? Are there competing theories within the field which are nation-specific? To what extent is the implementation of emergent cost management approaches evident within companies? What trends, if any, are discernible in management accounting thinking generally? Such issues are addressed in the pages that follow. Beyond this, the intent of the book is to provide some basis for exploring national specificities in management accounting, while also offering room to ponder its commonalities. To enable this, the brief to authors was to provide a historical perspective on management accounting research and practice in their country, complemented by a discussion of salient *raisons d'êtres* for present practice and thought in the field. Given that this is a tall order by any standard, the guide-lines to authors were purposely left fairly open-ended. It was desired from the outset that there should be minimal risk of inadvertently inflecting either the direction of substantive discussion or the style of presentation, both of which are relevant in bringing into relief national characteristics.

An initial concern was the use of the term 'management accounting', which is not pan-European. Although the term recurs throughout the volume, individual contributors have attempted to ground its usage contextually. In most cases, research traditions, practices, and techniques are discussed so as to bring the implied national 'reality' of management accounting to the fore. The term is the only one which overarches the volume by editorial intent, so as to provide a linchpin linking together the different chapters. The contributors have otherwise had a free hand and, indeed, have been encouraged to use the terminology of their choice, identifying, where relevant, original terms alongside their English translations in order not to eschew local significance.

The authors were asked to give a sense of whether modern management accounting approaches now increasingly articulated in the applied literature were evident in enterprises within their country and to substantiate arguments empirically wherever possible. Consequently, all chapters present findings of empirical investigations, some of which stem from secondary sources, though in a number of cases the studies reported upon were undertaken specifically for the contribution to this book.

It should be recognized that any commentary on the state of knowledge or practice in any field cannot be fully comprehensive. For the essays collated here this has two important implications. In terms of author choice, no perspective is impartial, and, no doubt, expert opinions will always vary. Thus, rather than purport to give *the* view, each chapter offers *a* view. The intent is that the discussions which follow will engage other accounting commentators to further refine, expand, or perhaps even refute the contentions made. Ideally, what is not aired here will find expression elsewhere because of its gaping absence. This volume is also partial in that it omits coverage of many European countries. This should not be looked upon as a judgement on which countries warrant inclusion. The limited number of countries represented reflects the editor's knowledge of European commentators in the area during the planning stages, their potential availability as contributors, as well as stipulated limits on the size of the book. Countries not included here will, it is hoped, find representation on appropriate future platforms, so as to contribute to the knowledge landscape that is starting to take shape in internationally focused studies of management accounting.

The chapters which follow each point to a diversity of features of management accounting thought and practice in the countries covered, and provide a useful starting-point for comparative observations. Although a great many differences in outlook exist within Europe, commonalities, and even signs of convergence, abound in some respects. Just as Europeans have been said not to 'feel European. They feel Italian, Spanish or Dutch . . . though there is an undeniable continent-wide tendency towards unification' (van der Meer 1991: 1), so management accounting in Europe might be seen to exhibit similar tensions between the specific and the general, as well as between the particular and the universal. Possibly within management accounting, as has been said of organizational activity more generally, we are witnessing 'the internationalization of local patterns in a global world, and the superposition of an integrative culture and institutions upon a world which remains nationally, societally or culturally specific' (Sorge 1994: viii).

It would be inappropriate in this Introduction to attempt to delineate the differentiating characteristics of each country as outlined in the chapters, but it is worthwhile to briefly comment on certain distinguishing features that suggest commonalities. One characteristic point which has significance across all chapters concerns activity based costing as a technical approach. All contributors have thought it appropriate to comment upon its relevance alongside coverage of more traditional management accounting concerns such as overhead cost allocation, inventory valuation, and full- versus direct-costing approaches. Certainly, aspects of the technical underpinnings of activity based costing have, in a number of countries, been articulated prior to the emergence of the term. It is nevertheless noteworthy that a non-European term which was effectively non-existent a decade ago has, in one way or another, come to provide a linguistic category permeating conceptual accounting discourse across the European countries covered here.

Another issue which is worthy of mention is that almost all the chapters mention the role of the State in affecting management accounting practices. The influence was unanticipated in some instances but more direct in others, with links, for instance, to changes in government policies, tax regulations, standardization of commercial practices, the passing of wartime legislation, and the implementation of industrial price controls. In each case, the State 'effect' seems to have been linked to country-specific changes affecting management accounting in distinct ways, even though, at times, its mobilization appears to have been tied to a concern with achieving some form of harmony with a foreign accounting framework.

Finally, it is notable that almost all the contributors have commented on the existence of action in some quarters to alter management accounting such that it conforms more closely to the precepts of general prescriptive models. The search for 'best practice', and the pursuit of 'world class' management accounting systems by some, might suggest that the future holds more universal elements of management accounting. However, the prior course of management accounting change seems to have engendered in the main an element of national distinctiveness. Whereas the future outlook of management accounting practice may suggest forms of converging effects increasingly at play, the field's past reflects, in large part, a sustained level of divergent peculiarities.

Questions have always been raised as to the technical propriety of particular approaches in management accounting, and to an extent these are explored in this collection of European perspectives. Those questions that require delving into the potentially multi-faceted and diverse origins of economic representations of organizational activities are only now being posed. Although this volume also addresses some of these issues, there is still much that remains to be uncovered as to the reasons for the diversity in management accounting in different European countries, let alone explanations of similarities. It might be asked by what means the applicability of particular management accounting mechanisms gain legitimacy in organizations within one country but not another. In what diverse ways do extra-organizational changes alter the internal functioning of enterprises, and how do transformations in national political agendas, social institutions, and economic arenas affect organizational accounting practices? Does the use of like management accounting techniques across countries imply similarities in the functions they play in organizations, and does the existence of unlike management accounting practices imply that organizations in different countries pursue different strategies? It is to be hoped that this book will reinforce the legitimacy of such questioning, and perhaps even incite further explorations along these lines. It will have proved worthwhile, however, if it only provides a preliminary entrée to management accounting trends, issues, and concerns in Europe.

References

Ahrens, T. (1994), 'Accounting for Which Outside? Contrasting Perspectives on Strategic Conceptions of Action in Britain and Germany', paper presented at the Workshop in Accounting, Strategy and Control at the European Institute for Advanced Studies in Management held in Brussels, 15–17 Sept.

Bromwich, M., and Bhimani, A. (1994), *Management Accounting*: *Pathways to Progress* (London: CIMA).

Chartered Institute of Management Accountants (1993), *Management Accountancy in Continental Multinational Enterprises* (London: CIMA).

Euske, K. J., Lebas, M. J., and McNair, C. J. (1993), 'Performance Measurement in an International Setting', *Management Accounting Research*, 4: 275–300.

Horovitz, J. H. (1980), *Top Management Control in Europe* (London: Macmillan).

Löning, H. (1994), 'Une Approche culturel de l'utilisation des systèmes d'information comptable et de gestion: l'example de la France et de la Grande-Bretagne', Ph.D. diss., HEC, Jouy-en-Josas, France.

Sheridan, T. T. (1995), 'Management Accounting in Global European Corporations: Anglophone and Continental Viewpoints', *Management Accounting Research*, 6: 287–94.

Sorge, A. (1994), Editorial, *Organization Studies*, 15: i–x.

Strange, N. (1991), 'Management Accounting and Competitive Advantage: A Comparison of British and German Management Accounting', paper presented at the Management Accounting Research Group Conference held in Birmingham, 12 Sept.

Thorp, J., and Kipfer, J. (1991), 'The French Approach to Management Accounting', *Management Accounting*, 68 (Dec.), 32–6.

van der Meer, J. B. H. (1991), 'Introduction', *The Business of Europe*: *Managing Change* in R. Calori and P. Lawrence (eds.) (London: Sage), 1–8.

1
Management Accounting Changes
The Belgian Experience

Werner Bruggeman, Regine Slagmulder, and Dominique Waeytens

Introduction

During the last years we have seen many innovative practices and new methods in the field of management accounting. For different subject areas it was advocated that existing concepts and techniques were obsolete and create dysfunctional behaviour. It has been suggested that the so-called traditional systems should be replaced by new approaches.

In capital budgeting, there is a call for strategic investment appraisal instead of traditional discounted cash flow methods. In cost accounting, activity-based costing is becoming popular. Also, new concepts and theories are being sought for measuring performance.

In this chapter we describe the main trends in management accounting in Belgium. The paper focuses on the following questions: How do Belgian companies evaluate investment projects? How are Belgian companies implementing activity-based costing and activity-based management, and what changes are being made to their performance measurement systems? Our analyses are based partly on questionnaire research results and partly on case-studies. Before discussing the various studies, we briefly describe the historical background against which Belgian management accounting practices can be better understood.

Background

Management accounting is a very young discipline in Belgium. In the 1950s and the 1960s cost accounting witnessed considerable influence from the Netherlands. Dutch authors such as J. van der Schroeff (1956) and J. L. Mey (1960) were leading commentators and writers in the field. The accent was on the design of an 'analytical cost accounting system', which received much interest in Belgium. The purpose of such a system is to make a detailed analysis of all the costs of a firm by assigning them to the cost centre in which they occur. The idea is that if one wants to calculate accurate product costs, one should recognize that many expenses are direct in relation only to the expense centre, not to the products for which the costs are incurred. For this reason, as well as to get more relevant information about where in the company certain costs arise, all costs are traced to their most direct cost centre. Subsequently, all costs from the so-called indirect expense centres (e.g. administration, maintenance, storage, buildings) are apportioned to the direct expense centre (e.g. manufacturing), using allocation rules based on causal relationships. For example, machine maintenance costs are often assigned to their respective manufacturing centres based on the number of machine hours in those centres. Costs of buildings are assigned based on the area occupied by the cost centres. Finally, when all costs have been assigned to the manufacturing cost centre(s), the product cost is calculated by dividing the total manufacturing cost by the output of the cost centre. To support the analytical cost accounting system, companies have specific software available, which, in many cases, is integrated into the general ledger system. Some companies have developed their own customized systems.

In the 1970s and the 1980s the influence of the US and the UK literature increased. During the 1960s many multinationals started separate divisions in Belgium, and more Belgian managers and employees were involved in the implementation of US types of accounting and reporting systems. Discounted cash flow calculations and high hurdle rates became part of the investment decision processes, and variance reporting was widely used in performance evaluation. In academia, some cost accounting scholars adopted the Horngren and Foster textbook. This created a certain openness to a US management accounting frame of reference.

Dissemination of information on new trends in management accounting has taken place mainly through universities, business schools, and consulting firms. Belgium has no specific professional organization for management accounting. However, there is the Institute of Accountants (IDAC), which has a primarily financial (non-managerial) orientation. Also there is a second professional body, the Institute of Auditors (IBR). The distinctive task of the IBR auditor is to certify financial statements for companies above a certain size. Companies that are not legally obliged to have an IBR auditor can use an IDAC accountant to certify financial statements and prepare financial reports. The position of the IDAC accountant has been clarified by the law of 21 February 1985. Among the tasks of the accountants are controlling the books and the accounts, providing expert opinions on the fairness and completeness of the financial statements and books, advising on the administrative and accounting organization of the company, performing bookkeeping activities, and providing tax advice. The admission requirements for the IDAC accounting profession have been stated in the law of 21 February 1985 and the Royal Decision of 20 April 1990. After passing an admission exam, in which diverse areas of technical knowledge are tested (bookkeeping, control, tax, business law, civil law, social law, consolidation, finance, etc.), newly qualified accountants undertake a three-year apprenticeship guided by a mentor who is already an acknowledged IDAC accountant. After that period, a practical examination must be passed, and a positive report must be provided by the mentor before entry to the profession.

Despite the fact that Belgian management accountants are not led by a separate Institute of Management Accountants, the practice of cost and management accounting is rapidly changing. The change process is strongly influenced by the US and UK literature. A significant proportion of the Belgian companies are small and medium-sized, many of them family-owned (in the textile and the metal component manufacturing industry). The management in these companies is very entrepreneurial, and accounting systems in many cases are not well developed. These companies are now gradually positioning themselves as more global competitors, and are increasingly instituting modern forms of management accounting and control systems.

We believe that management accounting change in Belgian companies is characterized by two features: first, an openness to experiences of foreign countries, especially the United States and the United Kingdom; secondly, a high concern for the practical relevance of new accounting information, which may be due to the entrepreneurial spirit of many Belgium enterprises. Given this background, we analyse below the observed change patterns in more detail.

Evaluation of Strategic Capital Investments

Problem Definition

The literature reports a growing dissatisfaction with the traditional capital budgeting techniques such as discounted cash flow. Many authors claim that the obsolescence of accounting-based investment evaluation methods leads to myopic investment behaviour and creates a bias against strategic investments, such as the adoption of advanced manufacturing technology (AMT) (Hayes and Garvin 1983).

The accounting methods have been criticized for not providing the information needed to evaluate and support strategic process innovations, because they place too much emphasis on short-term returns. Part of the problem is due to the use of excessively high hurdle rates (Kaplan and Atkinson 1989; Hayes *et al.* 1988). Moreover, discounted cash flow (DCF) calculations often do not capture the full range of benefits, because strategic benefits from new production technologies (such as better quality, increased flexibility, and options for future growth) are more difficult to quantify than traditional cost savings. These alleged weaknesses are seen as evidence of the inappropriateness of financial appraisal when evaluating strategic investments.

In reaction to the increasing dissatisfaction with the accounting-based budgeting methods, more attention has been given to the strategic aspects of investments in manufacturing (Goldhar and Jelinek 1983; Hill 1985; Hayes *et al.* 1988). Some authors argue that strategic investments must be exempted from the control of accounting systems. For instance, Hayes and Garvin (1983) are in favour of an 'acts-of-faith' approach—i.e. the conviction that decisions about strategic investments are rooted in managers' beliefs rather than in analytical procedures. Others advocate a systematic strategic analysis and planning, based on the investment's expected contributions to long-term competitiveness and profitability, as a more solid base for appraising prospective process innovations (Bromwich and Bhimani 1991).

Some authors of the accounting literature consider financial evaluation as still valuable, but advocate a more proper use of capital budgeting techniques. According to Kaplan (1986), investment justification of AMT should not be based on faith alone. He believes it is the task of top management to assess whether or not intangible strategic benefits outweigh the shortfall in a DCF calculation. Finnie (1988) comes up with similar arguments against abandoning financial appraisals in the capital expenditure decision, stating that the pursuit of broad strategic goals (such as increasing market share) does not overcome the issue of whether satisfactory financial results can be achieved.

Opinion is thus divided as to which approach to evaluating capital investments is most appropriate. In this empirical study, we are interested in investigating how Belgian companies evaluate strategic investments in manufacturing plant and equipment. The key question is whether Belgian managers rely mainly on accounting-based appraisal techniques or whether the financial analysis is overridden by strategic considerations. Our survey and field research in a number of Belgian manufacturing firms has yielded some interesting observations, which are presented below.

Survey Results

A survey of capital budgeting practices for computer integrated manufacturing (CIM) technologies was conducted in collaboration with INSEAD (France). It was part of a research project aimed at getting a better insight into the current state and planned future developments of CIM technologies in Europe. Part of the survey focused on the investment decision practices for CIM technologies. Data were collected from 42 European firms that had been recently involved in investments in CIM technology. The firms in the sample represent a variety of industries, including electronics, metal processing, chemicals/pharmaceuticals, textile, food processing, and telecommunications. The data were collected by means of a questionnaire which was mailed to plant managers, CIM managers, and controllers in manufacturing companies that were selected from several databases on the grounds of the likelihood that they had undertaken investments in CIM technologies in the past. Seventeen of the 42 respondent companies were based in Belgium.

The investment projects contained in our sample required an average capital outlay of 1.9 million ecus, ranging from 100,000 ecus to 10 million ecus. Most related to the adoption of leading edge technology (e.g. computer-aided design (CAD), computer-aided manufacturing (CAM), flexible manufacturing systems), and represented a major innovation for the adopting companies. About 80% of the projects under consideration were perceived as successful in financial terms. We give below a summary of the main results for the Belgian sample, and compare them with the European data.

Capital budgeting practices for evaluating investments in CIM technologies

Finance theory states that each investment project should be evaluated at its opportunity cost of capital, the so-called hurdle rate. In practice, methods of determining the hurdle rate and its numerical value vary widely. The average hurdle rate used for evaluating investments in the sample was 23%. The average cut-off point for the pay-back period specified was 2.2 years. These results are close to the European averages of 22.3% hurdle rate and 2.5 years pay-back respectively. A frequency distribution of the minimum required rate of return and the maximum pay-back period are given below (Tables 1.1 and 1.2).

About 12% of the Belgian respondents specified a minimum required rate of return as the single financial criterion used for investment evaluation (compared to 8% for Europe), whereas another 12% (13% for Europe) set an upper limit on the pay-back period, but did not use any hurdle rate to

Table 1.1. Frequency distribution of the hurdle rate (minimum required rate of return)

Hurdle rate (%)	% respondents*
≤ 15	25.0
15–30	37.5
≥ 30	12.5
n.a. (confidential)	25.0

* Includes only those respondents who reported that a hurdle rate was specified, which represents about 47% of the total number.

Table 1.2. Frequency distribution of the maximum pay-back period

Maximum pay-back period (years)	% respondents*
≤ 1	12.5
>1–3	37.5
≥ 3	25.0
n.a. (confidential)	25.0

* Includes only those respondents who reported that a maximum pay-back period was specified, which represents about 47% of the total number.

delineate what constituted acceptable investment proposals. Of the Belgian companies, 23% specified cut-off levels for both criteria (13% for Europe). It is interesting to note, however, that a fairly large number of respondents (41%) did not specify either a minimum acceptable rate of return or a pay-back criterion. The hurdle rate was higher for investments in CIM technologies than for other investments in 38% of the Belgian cases (20% for Europe).

It is interesting to compare the pre-set hurdle rate and pay-back period to the computed *ex ante* internal return of return (IRR) or pay-back period for the investment in CIM technology (see Tables 1.3 and 1.4). The average expected IRR is 21% (when we disregard one outlier of 260%), which approximates the average hurdle rate of 23%. The average expected pay-back period is 3.3 years, which exceeds the average maximum pay-back period of 2.2 years. We note that in one-third of the companies where the expected IRR and/or pay-back period of the CIM investment was computed, no formal criteria for these financial measures were specified.

Although 65% of the companies responded that they treated strictly the required minimum rate of return or maximum pay-back period as a pass/fail hurdle, more than 80% (75% for Europe) admitted to using these financial

Table 1.3. Frequency distribution of the expected IRR for the CIM investment

Expected IRR (%)	% respondents*
≤ 15	0.0
>15–30	44.4
≥ 30	11.1
n.a. (confidential)	44.4

* Includes only those respondents who reported that the expected hurdle rate was computed, which represents about 53% of the total number.

Table 1.4. Frequency distribution of the expected pay-back period for the CIM investment

Expected pay-back period (years)	% respondents*
≤ 1	8.3
> 1–3	33.3
≥ 3	25.0
n.a. (confidential)	33.3

* Includes only those respondents who reported that the expected pay-back period was computed, which represents about 71% of the total number.

criteria rather loosely when evaluating strategic investments. That is, an investment whose expected return does not meet the pre-set requirements can still be accepted for strategic reasons. The same phenomenon was observed in 75% of the European respondents.

Other elements that played a role in the decision to acquire CIM technology when the expected return did not meet the minimum require rate of return are listed in Table 1.5, in decreasing order of importance.

Table 1.5. Elements other than the expected financial results that played an important role in the investment decision about CIM technology

Other key elements in decision making	Average score	
	Belgium*	Europe
The fact that the investment fits with the firm's well-defined competitive strategy	6.00	5.9
Long-term strategic vision of top management	4.75	5.3
Technological know-how of top management	4.13	3.9
Fact that there was a committed project champion	3.63	4.1
Pressure to stay in business	3.25	3.6

* Includes only those investments whose expected return did not meet the minimum required rate of return, which represents about 47% of the total number of investments included in the sample.

In more than 60% of the cases, the most likely cash-flow scenario was used in the financial justification of the CIM investment. Three-quarters of the respondents reported that the 'base case' assumptions underlying the calculation of the investment's expected return related to the cost structure, often in combination with increased income. It is also interesting to note that two-thirds of the Belgian respondents (38% of the European companies) admitted that there was a tendency to introduce an overly optimistic bias in the cash-flow estimates in order to get an investment project approved by top management.

Risk in the context of capital budgeting is usually perceived by executives as the probability of not achieving a given target return or the degree of downside deviation from the expected return. Surveys indicate that many firms rely on intuitive judgement to account for risk, although more sophisticated models are finding increasing usage (Gurnani 1984). The frequency distribution of the most commonly used techniques for risk analysis in our sample is presented in Table 1.6. Over half the respondents reported that they did not use any method for incorporating risk in the investment appraisal.

Table 1.6. Methods used for risk analysis in evaluating CIM investments

Method used for risk analysis	% respondents	
	Belgium*	Europe
Risk was not taken into account	52.9	45.2
Shortening required pay-back period	17.6	16.7
Increasing required hurdle rate	5.9	9.5
Subjective adjustment of cash flows	5.9	7.1
Sensitivity analysis	11.8	7.1
Comparative analysis of different cash-flow scenarios	5.9	7.1
Probability analysis (simulation)	0.0	0.0
Other	5.9	7.2

The extent to which responsibility for capital investment decisions was delegated to divisional managers is shown in Table 1.7. The results indicate that divisional managers in 44% of the companies are allowed to decide autonomously about individual investments up to a certain capital expenditure limit. Approval from corporate headquarters is required in more than half the companies.

Approximately 47% of the companies (43% for Europe) reported that the proposal for the CIM investment had emanated as a local initiative, and was subject to formal approval by top management. A similar number of respondents (41% versus 43% for Europe) described the investment as being primarily top-down mandated as a corporate policy, while lower levels in the organization participated to some extent in the decision making. In one case, the final authorization by top management was seen as a mere formality, because the investment proposal had gained support from a large part of the organization as it progressed up the management hierarchy. The above results suggest that senior management has a strong influence on the investment decision-making process for CIM technologies.

Some companies use post-audit procedures to follow up on capital invest-

Table 1.7. Responsibility for capital investment decisions delegated to divisional managers

Responsibility for capital expenditures	% respondents	
	Belgium*	Europe
Approval from corporate headquarters required for all capital investments	56.3	40
Ceiling on capital expenditure for individual projects	43.8	57.2
Divisional managers allowed to spend within the limits of their budgets; no limit for individual projects	18.8	2.8
Divisional managers can spend without restriction, provided they can find the necessary funds	0.0	0

* Includes only those companies which have a divisional structure, which represents about 94% of the total number of respondents.

ment projects after their implementation, in order to find out whether the original estimates of costs and benefits are realized. Table 1.8 shows the extent to which post-implementation audits are performed by our survey respondents. From these results we conclude that Belgian companies are somewhat lagging behind other European companies.

Table 1.8. Use of post-implementation audit for capital investments

Post-audit of capital investments	% respondents	
	Belgium*	Europe
No post-completion audit done	41.2	32.5
Post-audit done for some investments	35.3	40.0
Post-audit done for all investments	23.5	22.5

Sample Case-Studies

Field research in six Belgian manufacturing companies has revealed some of the key characteristics of the investment decision process and the accounting systems that affect it (see also Slagmulder and Bruggeman 1992).

The first case-study concerns a producer of hardside cases and attaché cases (company A). The plant's manufacturing strategy is focused on low-cost production of a medium variety of standard cases with short through-put times. Plant managers intend to implement just in time (JIT), and are continuously looking for opportunities to invest in manufacturing flexibility which fit within this JIT concept. Flexibility is defined here as the capability to produce with shorter throughput times using work stations that are capable of performing different successive operations. All investment projects are screened financially, using the internal rate of return (IRR) criterion with a 25% hurdle rate. Every project should be justified on the basis of cost savings and/or incremental sales.

One investment project concerned the adoption of a flexible computer-controlled robot cell for assembly (investment of 5.5 million Bef). The robot was originally intended to assemble a variety of sub-assemblies, but was eventually focused on assembling the wheels and wheel handles of the cases. It was linked with a transfer system that consisted of a rectangular base with parallel rails, upon which eight shuttles moved between different operational positions.

The investment was justified mainly on a strategic basis. The adoption and implementation of the robot would give the company a first mover advantage, and create the opportunity to learn about the integration of flexible technologies in manufacturing. The mix- and design-flexibility of the robot were expected to be very high, as the robot would be capable of assembling new parts in the future. However, this advantage turned out to be of no value whatsoever, because the company did not compete on design-flexibility.

The investment could be justified financially by the estimated labour savings, with a 26.6% return. However, manufacturing engineers were aware of other automation alternatives that could provide more labour savings but offered less design-flexibility. At present, the design-flexibility capability is not being used, and the robot cell assembles the wheels in mass-production mode.

Another investment in company A entails the adoption of a CNC laser-cutting system for magnesium frames. The need for a laser cutter arose because a new product design had been developed. Cutting the frames on conventional punchers would cause tremendous change-over times, and would require production in large batches. This would increase inventory and lower machine utilization and productivity. The laser-cutter, on the other hand, was able to produce smaller lot sizes, and also allowed more design-flexibility. The total investment amounted to 13.5 million Bef. The investment appeared to be more reactive than pro-active: it was needed because of a lack of design-for-manufacture, and the justification was not based on a clear strategic goal. As in the first project, the company was engaged in investing in design-flexibility, without knowing whether this type of flexibility could really create a competitive advantage. The DCF calculation resulted into an estimated IRR of 30.5%. Eventually, the project was considered a moderate success. The laser-cutter provided the expected design-flexibility, but this advantage was not part of a focused strategy. The prospective cost savings were not realized, because the actual cutting speed was too low. As a result, the cutting machine lost capacity, and frequently became a bottleneck in the production process.

In textile company B, an investment in advanced technology for continuous dyeing was investigated. The continuous dyeing line offers the capability of continuous transition from light to dark colours without any interruptions and with automatic cleaning. The initial capital expenditure for the purchase of the dyeing machine was 114 million Bef, and an additional investment of 55 million Bef was required for a new building. The proposed investment seemed to provide a solution to the unlimited diversity in market demand and the need for fast delivery, which required shorter throughput times and fewer machine set-ups. As the customer was not willing to pay a price premium, the company felt the need for new equipment which would allow them to combine cost-efficiency with flexibility. A high quality level was also considered important. A spreadsheet model was used as a guide-line for the financial justification, which allowed simulation of optimistic, pessimistic, and most likely scenarios. The minimum required rate of return used in the calculation of the net present value (NPV) was 10%. Under these circumstances the NPV appeared to be slightly positive. However, the quantitative analysis was poor, and showed some serious deficiencies: the capital outlay had been seriously underestimated because the costs incurred in other divisions for this investment project had not been taken into account, and the learning effect had also been underestimated.

At the time of the interview, the investment in the continuous dyeing process was considered a failure, because it caused serious perturbations of the entire production process. The company had been facing technical transition problems for over a year, which caused problems of poor quality and delays in delivery and thus negatively affected its competitiveness. The main reason for these problems was the lack of an integrative vision in the decision making. Top management realized that the effects of the introduction of the new technology on all previous and subsequent operations should have been analysed in advance. This would have revealed that the factory layout had to be adapted because the new equipment changed the production flow. They were convinced, however, that these problems would only be transitory, and that eventually the desired competitive advantage of greater diversity and shorter throughput times would be achieved.

Top management very closely monitors the financial performance of the company's investment policy. Two variables are reported in this regard:

Capital intensity = \f(total balance sheet—short-term debts, sales turnover)
Productivity = \f(value added, resources used (wages, salaries, interests, depreciation))

During the past two years, the company had pursued a policy of actively investing in AMT. Consequently, capital intensity had increased, whereas productivity did not rise, hence the company's return on investment (ROI) decreased. This observation led top management to the conclusion that they should limit product diversity, because investing in unlimited mix-flexibility may not pay off in the long run.

Company C in our field research is a large truck assembly company which competes on low-volume production, high diversity, high quality, and low cost. The company has a clearly defined manufacturing strategy, and decisions about investments in advanced technologies are based mainly on strategic arguments. The company adopted a flexible manufacturing system for the production of axle-bodies, which was capable of executing the different operations in sequence. The investment project was expected to help shorten throughput times, lower set-up times, and increase diversity.

An NPV calculation was prepared, based on the expected cost savings due to lower set-up times and less material handling compared to the existing production technology, on the assumption that product diversity would increase in the future. The IRR of the project hardly met the target of 25%; nevertheless, top management made the decision to go ahead with the investment because of the strategic benefits. The company's philosophy is that financial considerations can never be a barrier for strategically attractive investments.

Top management finds it very difficult to estimate the project's *ex post* financial performance. They feel, however, that there is a real danger of investing too much capital in unlimited flexibility, because enhanced flexibility is hardly reflected in the bottom line, due to the high level of competition in the industry. This is due to the fact that truck manufacturers actually run 'stuck-in-the-middle' plants: they produce standard trucks, substandards, and specials, all using the same production process. Investments in flexible technology in these plants hardly pay off, because the capacity of the flexible technology is also used to produce standard parts, for which no flexibility is required.

Strategic Fit: The Key Issue

We conclude from the empirical study that Belgian companies still rely on traditional DCF techniques in evaluating strategic investments in manufacturing technology. However, the majority of the companies use the financial criteria rather loosely. A key consideration in the decision making is whether the investment fits with the firm's competitive strategy. Investments whose expected return does not meet the minimum financial requirements are often accepted if there are important compensating strategic factors.

One general finding from our field research is that the quality of the strategic analysis is a critical success factor in the decision about strategic investments. Quality of the strategic analysis contains the explicit formulation of the firm's competitive advantage as well as the analysis of fit of the investment with the strategy pursued. If, for instance, top management has not clearly defined the type of manufacturing flexibility they want to develop, engineers or marketing people might lead the plant to invest in a type of flexibility that is not a strategic priority for the firm (e.g. company A).

The explicit definition of company goals and strategies also contributes to the effectiveness and the relevance of the financial justification, because the strategy to be pursued in the future determines the base case for the DCF analysis. Indeed, we note that many investments in manufacturing technology are justified on the basis of cost savings and/or increases in contribution output, which are based on strategic assumptions about the desired production features (e.g. flexibility) and the market requirements. For example, the truck assembly plant C justified its investment on the basis of the savings in change-over costs that could be realized, assuming that product diversity would increase significantly in the future.

As stated above, sound strategic analysis is a prerequisite for effective investment decision making. The question remains as to whether strategic considerations are sufficient to justify the huge capital expenditure involved in major investments, such as the acquisition of AMT. From our case-studies, we observe that in industries facing high competition, where investments in AMT are crucial to sustaining the firm's competitive position, strategic arguments dominate in the investment justification decision. The continuous dyeing system in the textile company B and the flexible manufacturing system (FMS) in the truck assembly plant C are examples of investments that have been initiated because the fierce competition in the industry forced them to be more flexible. Both companies felt that they would soon be out of business if they decided *not* to invest in AMT. In this regard, the moderate expected financial return that followed from the cash-flow analysis played no significant role in the decision making.

Even though most companies make a fairly detailed DCF or pay-back calculation for their investments, the outcome of the financial analysis is not considered to be the key decision criterion in all cases. We note that some companies go ahead with a project even if the calculated return is lower than the hurdle rate. This does not mean, however, that traditional capital budgeting analysis has become totally irrelevant. Our study shows that financial return is still used as the key decision criterion in certain situations, depending on manufacturing strategy. For instance, in a 'high volume, medium variety, low cost' environment (e.g. company A), strategic investments in AMT are intended to decrease throughput times, lower set-up times, improve the production flow and productivity, decrease inventory holding costs, eliminate bottlenecks, increase contribution output of the factory, etc., all of which represent easily quantifiable benefits. In the following section we turn our attention to another trend in Belgian management accounting systems: changes in cost information and management systems, with a special focus on the adoption of activity-based costing systems (ABC).

Activity-Based Cost Systems

Traditional cost systems have been severely criticized. Case-studies have shown that these cost systems cause managers to make incorrect strategic product-mix decisions because of their inability to accurately assign overhead costs to products and to customers. This is primarily because traditional cost systems use volume-driven allocation bases. Cooper and Kaplan (1988) propose to use activity-based costing systems (ABC), which enable companies to link the costs of performing activities to the product and customers for which these activities are performed. This is done by first assigning resources consumed to the activities and later apportioning the activity costs to the cost objects (products or customers) by using cost drivers (such as the number of labour hours, number of set-up hours, number of orders, etc.). ABC can be used in the accounting system to better allocate (historical) indirect costs to products. However Cooper and Kaplan (1988) consider ABC more as a (stand-alone) resource-consumption model to be used in decision making, e.g. product-profitability analysis for strategic decision making, estimating the cost of activities, estimating the impact of operational improvements on the cost of the activities, and motivating people to change their behaviour. We describe below the main trends in ABC implementation in Belgium.

ABC Implementation in Belgium

Belgian companies can be classified into two groups: divisions of foreign multinationals and (mostly family-owned) small- and medium-sized companies. The implementation of ABC in divisions of multinationals is largely controlled by the corporate headquarters. Local companies make their own cost/benefit analysis of the ABC system.

Some companies traditionally have a so-called analytical cost-accounting system in place. This system assigns different costs to cost centres and to cost objects (products). Usually the system uses a large number of allocation bases (not only direct labour hours) to allocate costs of cost centres to other cost centres and to allocate costs of the cost centres to cost objects. These companies consider ABC to be a method for obtaining more accurate cost allocations. Other companies run a 'direct costing' system that collects direct costs of production orders. In these systems, overhead is not allocated. Users of direct costing consider ABC to be a method to better track overheads and to improve the profitability information of products and orders.

In Belgium, managers are given many opportunities to attend seminars and short courses on ABC organized by universities and consulting companies. The effect of these seminars is that managers have become aware of the shortcomings of their traditional systems, and have favour ABC implementation. More and more companies are beginning to redesign their cost systems using the activity perspective.

A questionnaire study carried out by Ernst and Young Belgium (1994) indicated that of eighty-eight Belgian companies included in the survey, 19.5% had some form of ABC system in place, 49.5% planned to change to ABC, and 31% reported that they were not interested in ABC. In 62% of the applications, the purpose of the project was to improve the accuracy of the product costs. In 30% of cases, the purpose was to increase the company's understanding of cost behavior. Only 17% of the companies reported that they had a cost-reduction motive.

The Ernst & Young study also shows that 13.8% of the companies perform some form of activity-based management (ABM), 26.4% plan to introduce it, and 59.8% are not considering it. Activity-based budgeting (ABB) is operational in 13.8% of the companies, 27.6% are planning to introduce it, and 58.6% are not considering it (see Table 1.9).

Table 1.9. Use of ABC/ABM approaches in Belgium

	Not under consideration (%)	Planned (%)	In operation (%)
Activity-based costing	31	49.5	19.5
Activity-based management	59.8	26.4	13.8
Activity-based budgeting	58.6	27.6	13.8

Source: Ernst & Young 1994.

In 65% of the cases, companies apply ABC to all departments of the company; 30% use it only in specific departments; 4% apply it to specific processes only. The introduction of ABC involved a top management decision in 71% of the cases. In 29% of the companies, department managers took the decision. The study also indicated that most companies used the ABC/ABM literature and attended ABC/ABM seminars as their main sources of information.

In general, we see that companies are reluctant to integrate activity accounting with their analytical cost-accounting system. Changing from 'cost centre thinking' to 'activity thinking' is very difficult. It is not just a mental change, but most companies are afraid that activity accounting will increase the complexity of the accounting system, and that the increased costs of information will not outweigh the benefits.

When we study the implementations in more detail, we find different types of so-called ABC systems in place: quick fixes of the traditional cost-accounting system (by increasing the number of overhead allocation bases), *ad hoc* ABC analyses for product/customer profitability analysis, computer-based stand-alone ABC resource-consumption models with simulation capabilities, and activity costs and cost driver studies to support continuous improvement processes.

In the following sections we consider the latter three approaches to ABC. We do so by briefly discussing case-studies of Belgian companies which have experimented with these different types of ABC.

Sample Case-Studies

Ad hoc ABC studies for product/customer profitability analysis

An example of this type of ABC analysis was found in a Belgian plant in the electronics industry, producing a wide variety of light bulbs. Plant management became interested in ABC because it felt that many of the problems associated with traditional costing systems were present in the company. In particular, top management suspected that the costing system would systematically overcost large orders of standard products and undercost small orders of complex, customized orders. The costing system was believed to place excessive reliance on volume-based overhead allocation bases. Consequently the plant systematically attracted special orders, and its bids for large orders of standard products were always too high. Top management decided to analyse the costing system in one particular department in which the cross-subsidization problem was believed to exist. The spirals department was chosen, because two distinct product groups could be distinguished there: normal spirals, which were frequently ordered in large quantities, and special spirals, which were produced according to customer specifications. Both were produced in the same production facilities, basically using the same type of machines. However, the production hall for the spirals was organized as a focused factory, with groups of machines dedicated to the normal spirals line, and other machines dedicated to the small lot sizes of the special spirals. Most direct workers were also dedicated to specific machines, so their costs could be easily attributed to the different product groups. However, systematic costing distortions existed with the costs of production supervisors, engineers, technical staff, maintenance people, and production planning personnel. Most of these costs were covered in the direct machine-hour rate or in the direct labour-hour rate, which implied that large standard orders were allocated more of these costs than small orders of special spirals. In reality, however, the production supervisors had almost no work with the normal spirals production line, but were much more involved with the special spirals machines. The special spirals machines had to be frequently set up, scheduled and rescheduled, closely monitored, and well maintained. They also demanded much more attention from the engineers, technicians, and planning people. It was clear that the costing system could seriously misallocate these cost categories to products, and that product complexity had to be taken into account.

It turned out that a good proxy for product complexity was the number of steps on the product routing. The complex special spirals generally had more routing steps than the normal standard spirals. Also, within the normal spiral category, variation in product complexity (and attention required of the production overhead people) was pretty well captured by the number-of-routing-steps variable. This correlation was not really verified statistically, but many people could confirm that there should be a high correlation indeed. So, rather than establish two cost centres (one for the special spiral machines, one for the normal spiral machines—which would not really be straightforward) and continue working with the machine—and man-hour rates, the division identified 'the number of routing steps' as an important cost driver for much of the production overhead activities. Other cost drivers were found to be the number of production orders and the number of products (codes). Other adjustments to the costing system were a recalculation of the machine- and man-hour rates based on more homogeneous cost pools and an identification of department- and plant-related overhead, which in the new costing system were not allocated but covered by the contribution margin.

This ABC analysis in the spiral department lasted for about one month in 1991. The project was carried out by a special team of the management control department, assisted by two academics with experience and knowledge in the ABC domain. The study confirmed top management's belief about cross-subsidization. Since the plant was part of a large multinational electronics company, it could not independently decide on a complete redesign of the accounting system. The results of the study, however, were used to reassess the profitability of certain products and customers, so as to make more informed product and customer decisions.

Computer-based stand-alone ABC resource-consumption models with simulation capabilities

We have assisted in two ABC analyses with software implementation in medium-sized Belgian companies in the textile industry. One was a carpet manufacturer, the other a mattress ticking company. In both cases the objective was to build a customer order cost simulation tool which could be used to evaluate the profitability of new orders prior to acceptance. Both companies carry so many possible combinations of product specifications that virtually every order becomes a unique product. This short-case description is based on the mattress ticking company, which produces the covers of mattresses. Customers can choose from a multitude of different designs, in different colours, different materials, different qualities (number of picks per cm), different sizes, different treatments (water-resistant, fire-resistant, etc.), and with different delivery times, destinations, etc. Given this variety, it is almost impossible to work with standard costs, because every order is unique. Therefore a computerized cost simulation tool had to be built. All the determinants of the order cost had to be identified, and the

ABC philosophy turned out to be a useful approach (even though many of those determinants were situated on the direct cost level).

Important cost determinants (cost drivers) were found to be the number of colours in the design, because this was correlated with set-up time on the Jacquard looms. Also, the type of thread used was found to be an important determinant of the number of machine interruptions. The sophisticated production control system enabled us to statistically correlate the number of machine breakdowns with the type of thread used. It turned out that certain types of thread were much weaker than others, and therefore broke much more easily than others. Stronger threads, on the other hand, were associated with fewer loom interruptions. For each type of thread we calculated a coefficient of machine interruptions, so as to better allocate the costs of breakdowns to the type of thread used. The cost pool associated with this cost driver consisted essentially of the cost of the weaver who had to repair the broken thread and the cost of the machine during the time of breakdown. An opportunity cost of non-production was also calculated, although its inclusion in the order cost was optional. Maintenance activities were split into preventative and curative maintenance, the first being driven by the number of machine-hours, the latter by the number of technical machine breakdowns. Many overhead activities in sales and order administration were found to be related to the number of customer orders. A cost per customer order, independent of volume, showed the relatively high total cost of small orders as compared to large volumes. This was known intuitively, but the study provided a workable basis for order acceptance and pricing decisions.

After the ABC analysis, we designed a series of flow charts that depicted the simulation and query capabilities that the computer model should have. Together with the programmers, we discussed the translation of the written report into software. It was decided to integrate this software into the existing computer information system. The ABC order cost simulation model is an additional choice in the main menu available to the accounting department. For each potential new order, the accountant answers a number of questions about the cost determinants of the order: volume, design, number of colours, number of picks per cm, type of material, etc. On request, the model calculates a direct cost or a full cost at a historical or standard valuation.

Activity costs and cost driver studies to support continuous improvement processes

An attempt to build an ABC model for continuous improvement was made in a Belgian company in the textile machines industry (a complete analysis of this case can be found in Waeytens and Bruggeman 1994). In 1991, this company became increasingly aware of the pressures of a declining market and increased competitiveness in the business. By the end of 1991, top management decided to lay off a large number of people. At the same time it felt the need for more relevant management information in order to find opportunities for cost reduction and improvement initiatives. In June 1991, the company engaged one of the world-leading consulting companies for a project with two objectives: first to develop an activity-based costing model of the firm (analyse activities, assign costs to activities, analyse cost drivers of the activities, etc.); and second, to assist in the continuous improvement programme, based on the activity information. Three groups were formed to supervise and manage the project on different levels:

1. The Strategic Group developed the objectives of the study, and decided the length and cost of the project. The Strategic Group was formed by the top management and the major functional directors, such as sales and marketing, finance, production, purchasing, and personnel. This group was periodically kept informed on the progress of the project.
2. The Project Group was formed by division managers, who were assigned to steer the project on a more operational level.
3. The ABC team was formed by the consultants and 2 people from the management accounting department who were fully assigned to the project. The ABC team conducted the interviews for the activity and cost driver analysis, and periodically provided feedback to the Project Group and the Strategic Group.

The consultants used a standard methodology for the project, involving 13 stages (from first contact to final report and recommendations), with considerable importance attached to the engagement of top management, committing and motivating people for the project, assuring consciousness of the project throughout the whole company at all levels, and planning and designing the project. Information sessions were organized for all middle managers, and they were all formally asked to collaborate.

In order to make the model appropriate for both product costing and continuous improvement, the ABC team decided to work with two categories of cost drivers: a logical driver and a cost-calculation driver. The calculation drivers were used for product-costing purposes, while the logical drivers were used to encapsulate the actual cost behaviour of the resource categories and to provide insight into how to control costs. In practice, however, it was very difficult to work with these two types of drivers, and it made the model very complex. The ABC team could not find an acceptable degree of detail, and finally the model ended up with more than 300 cost drivers, 20 to 30 of which were effectively used for product costing.

The project ended by mid-1992 with an official report and an ABC model presented in written form as well as in preliminary software. The software enabled reports of activities to be generated, grouped by division, cost-driver information linked to activities and to departments, and types of costs linked to activities. Management information was included in the model by the use of 'attributes', which are key words such as 'quality', 'standardization', 'safety', 'transport', 'value-added', 'engineering changes', and which grouped all costs related to those attributes. The next step was to use this information to identify, quantify, and prioritize opportunities for improvement.

The model turned out to be very complex, and top management was hesitant to implement it formally on definitive software which would replace the existing accounting information software. However, top management also felt that they had invested a lot of money in the system, and they wanted to turn the model into improved profitability through cost management based on the ABC information. In order to give the improvement project a new launch, they invited a well-known professor to a meeting with over 50 people of top and middle management and some staff people from accounting and marketing. He made those people aware of the need for cost reduction and continuous improvement in general, and explained how ABC could help them to identify opportunities for improvement and to effectively manage their costs. They were very enthusiastic about this meeting, and appreciated the simplicity the professor mentioned and the focus on cost management rather than cost calculation. Together with top management, the professor committed those people to identify and formulate initiatives of cost reduction and improvement in their divisions, based on the ABC approach. The managers were to accomplish this within 2 months. The professor recommended the implementation of a small-scale ABC analysis within their department. The existing ABC model was kept available for all managers, for reference when necessary.

Ultimately, no manager was able to offer any improvement initiative, and they did not succeed in identifying real savings and improvement opportunities. Top management subsequently decided not to continue with ABC, and the project came to an inglorious end. Further research will perhaps reveal the minimal conditions for a successful transition to an ABM philosophy. Certainly this case-study sheds some light on the barriers people raise to resist the new accounting information system. The classification of barriers is based on Harvey (1990: 34–45), and for each barrier we provide a representative statement heard in the company (see Table 1.10).

This case illustrates again that the design of accounting systems rests upon complex contingencies entailing environmental, organizational, and individual elements (Bhimani 1994). We learned from this example that accounting change is as much a process of change as any other organizational change, and that it should be carefully planned. It cannot be decoupled from the people who will have to use it. In the following section we consider performance measurement as a third area of Belgian management accounting changes.

Table 1.10. Types of barrier

Type of barrier	Representative statement
Lack of top brass support	Top management did not consider this project as a priority. We were not explicitly asked to co-operate, and we were not motivated to do so.
Burdens	We are already involved in several other projects, such as the ISO 9001 programme. We can't really manage our department: we are too involved in daily operations, and we don't have the authority to flexibly manage our costs. We had no time. A formal implementation would create an enormous maintenance effort for the ABC model.
Lack of benefits	We can't influence our costs in the short run. There are more structural problems that have to be solved first. Our department is too small to find any significant improvements. The ABC system would provide information too late. The project had a wrong focus: too much detail, too much centred around production instead of the real overhead activities.
Insecurity	We already lost people last year; we can't lay off people again. A formal implementation of the ABC model would create a revolutionary change in the company.
Boredom (lack of excitement about the change)	Our people were not enthusiastic about the approach.
Lack of control (chaos)	We were not guided in our attempt to identify opportunities for improvement.
Superiority (the impression that 'experts' know what's wrong with the company, and that everybody just has to do as they are told)	We were forced to take the ABC approach.

Performance Measurement Systems

Introduction

Recent literature on operations management and management accounting describes situations in which accounting-based performance measurement systems generate dysfunctional behaviour in organizations, and lead to sub-optimal decision making (McNair *et al.* 1989; Goldratt and Fox 1990; Nanni *et al.* 1990). Problem areas identified are:

1. Too much independent control of responsibility centres.
2. Inadequate choice of performance criteria that are not in line with strategy.

Recent literature has proposed some new approaches to measurement: non-financial measures, throughput accounting, activity-based costing, etc.

We describe below some significant trends in performance measurement change in Belgian companies. We will illustrate these trends by a number of case-studies.

Performance Measurement Changes in Belgium

Many companies here implemented significant changes in their performance measurement systems. Volume-based performance measures (such as kg/hr) and a focus on the unit of products have created dysfunctional behaviour in the operations. However, in the change process, we do not see companies completely abandoning these measures. Few companies seemed to believe that emphasizing non-financial measures instead of financial measures solves the problem. Non-financial measures (such as quality and due date performance) have received increasing attention, but cost performance criteria are still very important. To eliminate dysfunctional behaviour, companies have changed their cost measures. For example, they have developed strategy-dependent cost targets, and used activity-based costing (and the cost driver information) to recalculate the targets. More attention is being paid to the time dimension of the controllability of costs. Cost-variance reporting is useful only for costs that are controllable in the short term. This is why the use of unit product cost as a performance measure creates dysfunctional behaviour. Many components of the unit cost are not controllable in the short term, so that, for a significant part of the cost, producing large quantities is the only way to decrease the product cost.

To induce more market- and output-oriented thinking in operations, companies have also started using the throughput accounting concept. By focusing people's minds on throughput, a cost-reduction mentality is transformed into a contribution-maximization orientation. The impact of the 'theory of constraints' is that operational people focus more on delivery and less on adding volume to inventory. Throughput accounting is viewed as a financial performance measurement system that is perfectly in line with strategic priorities such as delivery performance and time-based competition.

Sample Case-Studies

The following case-studies illustrate different types of dysfunctional behaviour observed in Belgian companies. In each study, we also describe the changes in the performance measurement system that the company is experimenting with.

Company A

Company A is a textile company producing toweling, bath robes, and ready-made clothing. Corporate sales turnover is 3 billion Bef. The company employs 1,000 people. Until about 1987, the strategic focus was on cost leadership: production volume was rather stable, efficiencies were very important, the product mix was limited, and quality was not explicitly measured. The production was evaluated on volume-related measures such as kg per direct labour-hour or pics per direct labour-hour and metres per direct labour-hour. In 1988, the company realized that the competitive environment had begun to change towards a more market-oriented philosophy. It was then no longer appropriate to produce volume. What really mattered was the right product mix at the right time. Consequently, set-ups became more frequent, machine efficiencies decreased, inventories increased, target volumes (kg per direct labour-hour) could not be achieved, and different types of dysfunctional behaviour resulted:

1. Manufacturing showed considerable resistance to change, because the new strategy caused serious problems in production as well as reduced performance.
2. The salespeople thought that within the new philosophy everything should be possible, and they accepted extreme orders without assessing the consequences for the manufacturing departments.
3. In the weaving department, the production foremen combined different orders from the current and the future planning week to reduce set-ups and to increase volume. As a result, delivery targets could not be achieved, and customers complained.
4. Due to time pressures and the emphasis on kg produced, quality received less attention.
5. Sequential interdependencies between the departments caused quality problems occurring earlier to be compounded later. Thus, lack of quality monitors earlier caused failure to meet volume targets later.

In discussions between marketing and production departments, people believed that the dysfunctional behaviour problem could be solved by fitting performance measures to the strategy. When a company changes its strategy from low-cost high-volume production to a differentiation strategy, the performance measurement system should no longer focus on productivity, but on diversity, quality, and lead times. However, when the company reduced its stress on productivity, company profits started to erode. This situation called for renewed attention to cost effectiveness and productivity. The controllers decided to design a productivity measurement system based on *strategy-dependent targets*. Therefore an activity-based costing system was developed, with the following objectives:

1. To detect the real cost drivers, so as to increase the accuracy of the product costs for the different products (mainly on the direct cost level).
2. To calculate the product line profitabilities and communicate to the salespeople the cost drivers which have an important influence on costs.
3. To calculate the expected productivity in terms of kg per direct labour-hour, given a certain expected product mix to be produced.
4. To provide a simulation tool suited to considering the effect of different planning situations and different lot sizes on the manufacturing costs.

The reaction of production and marketing to the new system was very enthusiastic. It was an attempt to stimulate more co-operation and goal congruence between top management, production, and sales. Dysfunctional behaviour in production was reduced, because the pressure of a fixed productivity target was reduced. Instead, production was evaluated on a (lower) variable productivity norm which was a function of the expected product mix. On the other hand, the salespeople became more conscious of the production consequences of certain product and order characteristics. They were asked to consider these consequences in their order booking, and price adjustments were made for extreme orders.

Company B

Company B is a manufacturer of plastic kitchenware sold in Europe, Asia, South Africa, and the United States. It has 4 manufacturing plants. Dysfunctional behaviour was identified at the levels of plant management and production management. Each plant was treated as a cost centre. The performance measure used was the full cost per carton. The plant manager was responsible for minimizing the variance between the actual cost and the standard cost per carton. One way to achieve this goal was to minimize idle time on the moulding machines. Because a large part of the costs was fixed, plant managers could improve their performance by producing unneeded quantities to stock.

Because of a shortage of cash, however, the company's top management wanted to lower the inventories of finished products. Plant managers and production managers resisted this policy, and did not achieve any improvement in this respect. Deeper investigation of the problem revealed that plant managers used the inventory as a buffer to control their performance. When it was discovered that the accounting-based performance measurement system was the main cause of the dysfunctional behaviour, a meeting was organized with corporate control to investigate the possibility of altering the performance measurement system. It emerged that at the corporate level, plant managers were formally evaluated not on the cost per carton but on the degree of achievement of strategic goals. Consequently, top management could not understand why dysfunctional behaviour occurred. However, after more detailed investigation, it turned out that although the cost per carton was not formally used as an evaluation criterion for plant managers, it was the primary criterion used in decision making at lower levels. New products were allocated to plants based on the full cost per carton. If a plant manager was able to show lower unit costs, the chances were higher that the central production planning would decide to source the production of next year's new products from his plant. Companies with unfavourable variances on product costs gradually earned a bad image in the group, and less production was sourced from them. So, in this case, dysfunctional behaviour was generated not by the formal performance evaluation system but by the criteria used in daily decision making. After identifying the problem, a working group tried to find out how the major decision-making processes could be altered. They found that dysfunctional behaviour had to do with finding optimal decision rules for allocating the production of a product to a plant. They stated that in taking allocation decisions, the criterion 'full costs per carton' may not be appropriate because most of the overheads are fixed costs. They are now considering the use of the criterion 'unit-driven costs per carton': this means that a new product will be allocated to the plant in which it drives less additional costs (direct labour costs and production overheads driven by the number of cartons). The plants, however, have no information about the overhead activities driven by the number of cartons. To solve this problem, they plan to start an activity-based cost project, although not everyone is convinced of the relevance of ABC for this type of problem.

A similar problem occurred in the decision about resource allocation to plants based on the full-cost-per-carton measure. Dysfunctional behaviour was also experienced in this area. Plants focusing primarily on simple products (in Spain and Portugal) showed a lower cost per carton compared to plants producing partly simple and partly complex products. So top management was reluctant to invest in additional machine capacity in the plants producing more complex products. Also, plants competing in flexibility showed a higher cost per carton, and therefore had more difficulty in getting their expansion programmes approved. The management control department believes that this type of dysfunctional behaviour can be solved by implementing activity-based costing. When product costs and the cost per carton can be calculated taking into account the right cost drivers, one can cost the products in relation to their complexity and the chosen competitive strategy.

Some believe that ABC (and activity-based performance measurement) will offer solutions to all problems. But not all managers are convinced.

Some think that even if allocation decisions are made on the basis of unit-driven cost per carton, plant managers will still be able to profit by producing excessive inventory, because the unit-driven production overhead is not variable in the short run. When the number of cartons to be produced decreases, plant managers cannot easily fire indirect workers to minimize cost variances! Some managers think that product-allocation decisions can be better made on the basis of short-term variable costs (direct labour costs). Plant managers should also be evaluated, however, on the productivity and the effectiveness of the overhead. Some managers think that overhead productivity is a separate problem. It should become a formal evaluation criterion for plant managers, and should not influence the production-allocation decision. Once overhead productivity becomes a separate evaluation criterion that is assessed each year, there is a need to know the behaviour of these costs. Therefore, one must know the cost drivers, so again ABC comes into the picture.

Company C

Company C is an international manufacturer of pharmaceuticals, a multinational group. Quality and innovation are the company's competitive strengths. It produces medicines in liquid form, in powders, and in pills. The company became a global competitor in the 1980s, and now consists of 33 plants world-wide. This multinational organization employs 10,000 people. Two sources of dysfunctional behaviour have been detected in the past: in relation to direct labour productivity and the objective of unit-cost reduction.

The direct labour productivity is measured as the quantity produced (kg, litres, units) divided by the number of direct labour-hours. In every report to top management, these productivity measures were strongly emphasized. Some managers believe that this resulted in sub-optimal product-mix decisions, giving priority to high-volume products to increase productivity. Another consequence was high-volume orders on the production floor designed to improve direct labour productivity, which resulted in decreased delivery performance, especially on the Belgian market (where delivery times are shortest). The second source of dysfunctional behaviour was the emphasis on full unit production cost. This stimulated the production of high volumes to decrease unit costs. Full unit production costs did decrease, partly due to sales growth. But inventories increased, and a conflict arose between production and marketing because marketing wanted more flexibility and product diversity. Too much volume- and mix-flexibility was not compatible with production's budget constraints. Department managers were not really measured tightly on budget variances, but at top management level these variances were still seen as a major global measure of performance.

Because of these problems, the company decided to redesign its budgeting system and to measure performance on the basis of controllable costs instead of full costs. If the market demanded flexibility, then costs should be assigned to departments as a function of the variables that really caused the costs to increase. Five cost drivers were identified: the number of batches, the number of machine-hours, the number of direct labour-hours, the number of work orders, and volume (which drives material costs). Annual budgets can be calculated on the basis of these cost drivers, and monthly performance can be measured on controllable costs only. Budgets are not reassessed every month, but the allowable costs are calculated *ex post* based on the real production volumes.

Surprisingly, inventory level did not decrease. Three reasons can be found to explain this:

1. Marketing has become more cost-oriented. Marketing managers know the impact they have on production costs, and they try to stimulate high-volume low-cost production. Moreover, salespeople are evaluated on profit contribution, and have therefore become cost-sensitive.
2. No one is held responsible for inventory or evaluated on the impact they have on inventory.
3. Logistical planning systems are not sophisticated enough to contain inventory. High inventories were caused not only by the performance measurement systems, but also by the lack of adequate master production scheduling systems.

Company D

Company D is a Belgian manufacturer of high-quality soft- and hard-coated suitcases, beauty cases, travel cases, etc. It has several production facilities in Belgium, France, and Hungary, and production agreements with other plants in Taiwan, Czechoslovakia, Bulgaria, etc. It is in the process of changing its performance measurement system towards theory of constraints principles. The company had a traditional budgeting system for expected volume, expected direct and indirect labour-hours and costs. Three variances are calculated on a monthly basis: cost variances, volume variances, and performance variances. The last is a measure of efficiency: inputs/outputs in costs, in hours, or in volume. Several factors inspired the company towards throughput management.

1. Top management felt that the budgeting system was too internally oriented. It focused on efficiencies and costs, and therefore production managers combined work orders, especially at the end of each month, to be able to present a better performance ('end-of-the-month-syndrome').
2. A shift in the market. In the past the company could sell everything it produced, but recently there had been a problem with market saturation.
3. The customer had become more quality-sensitive, and wanted a higher degree of service, especially short delivery times.

Dysfunctional behaviour was found in the combining of orders to obtain a better performance, to the detriment of delivery performance (service). Another example is what took place in the company in France, where production managers installed small plastic injection machines which were assigned less indirect cost (because they used fewer direct labour-hours). The cost-accounting system calculated a lower cost for the parts manufactured on these machines, because they were assigned lower overhead costs. As a result, the production managers could perform better on their cost budget by stimulating production on these new machines. This problem was solved by allocating indirect manufacturing costs on the basis of machine-hours rather than direct labour-hours.

These problems, together with changes in the market, stimulated some top managers to experiment with throughput measurement in the French plant in 1990. Based on the book *The Goal* by Goldratt and Cox (1990) and a Jonah course followed by two top managers, they are focusing now on throughput operating expenses, and inventory. To increase throughput, batch sizes were decreased, which had a negative effect on performance (efficiency). After one year, however, the company succeeded in increasing performance, shortening throughput time, performing better on due dates, and surprisingly also producing improved efficiency performance. The combination of smaller batch sizes, higher throughput, and greater efficiency was explained by two reasons:

1. The company trained multi-functional workers, who needed a period of time to learn their new tasks, but in the end succeeded in obtaining better efficiencies.
2. In the beginning the efficiency standards were probably set too low, because of the expected difficulties in the first period. Therefore the standards will be adjusted in the future.

Conclusions

Belgian companies, the majority of which are small- or medium-sized, are undergoing significant management accounting changes. Although in investment decision making for advanced manufacturing technology, they still use traditional DCF techniques, strategic arguments play a very important role, and are believed to be critical in the decision-making process. In cost systems design Belgian companies are gradually changing over to ABC, but in this process they tend to be pragmatic. They are attempting to balance the costs and the benefits of cost information. Many companies implement ABC as a quick fix for the overhead allocation system problems in their traditional analytical cost-accounting systems. In these 'quick fixes', the accent is on forming other cost pools, not on activities. More professional applications are *ad hoc* ABC-based product profitability analyses to support strategic decisions and stand-alone product cost simulation models. In many companies, ABC is also used to support continuous improvement processes, but a number of these projects have failed because of a lack of top management support, interference with other improvement projects, lack of controllability of costs by middle management, and fear for people lay-offs. Top managers of small- and medium-sized Belgian companies are mainly sales- and production-oriented, and have less interest in internal processes. Cost management is usually a very centralized process (power is concentrated at the top), such that there is little controllability of costs at lower levels in the organization.

In terms of performance measurement, Belgian companies place heavy reliance on volume-based measures. During the implementation of flexibility strategies and total quality management, these measures have created dysfunctional behaviour. Companies are changing their measurement systems, however, and non-financial measures and throughput accounting are increasingly put to use, especially in the area of manufacturing and logistics. But in reporting systems, cost-performance criteria are still very important. Nevertheless, the standard costing system and the productivity-measurement systems are enhanced with flexible strategy-dependent standards.

Changes in management accounting are mainly driven and initiated by training seminars and short courses throughout by universities, business schools, and consulting organizations. In these seminars, awareness of dysfunctional aspects of traditional systems is raised, and the value of new methods is demonstrated. The influx of new ideas comes mainly from the United States and the United Kingdom. In cost management, we see little that is evidently 'Belgian', except perhaps the so-called analytical cost-accounting system, a cost centre-based responsibility accounting system that is in place in many companies. This system creates a barrier when ABC implementation is being considered. It is difficult to change the system and bring in the activity concept. As a consequence, what is being done is limited to changing the allocation rules and the cost pools. This situation causes many ABC projects to be only quick fixes of the traditional system. In this sense, accounting antecedents are influencing the shaping of more modern approaches to management accounting in practice in Belgian companies.

References

Agarwal, R. (1991), 'Justifying Investments in Flexible Manufacturing Technology: Adding Strategic Analysis to Capital Budgeting under Uncertainty', *Managerial Finance*, 17/2–3: 77–88.

Bhimani, A. (1994), 'Modern Cost Management: Putting the Organization before the Technique', *International Journal of Production Economics*, 36/1: 29–37.

Bromwich, M., and Bhimani, A. (1991), 'Strategic Investment Appraisal', *Management Accounting*, 72 (March): 45–8.

Cooper, R., and Kaplan, R. (1988), 'Measure Costs Right, Make the Right Decisions', *Harvard Business Review*, 66 (Sept.–Oct.): 98–103.

Ernst & Young (1994), 'Activity-Based Costing as Survival Strategy', working paper, Ernst & Young Belgium, Marcel Thirylaan 204, Belgium.

Finnie, J. (1988), 'The Role of Financial Appraisal in Decisions to Acquire Advanced Manufacturing Technology', *Accounting and Business Research*, 18/70: 133–9.

Goldhar, J. D., and Jelinek, M. (1983), 'Plan for Economies of Scope', *Harvard Business Review*, 61 (Nov.–Dec.): 141–8.

Goldratt, E., and Fox, J. (1990), *The Goal* (Aldershot: Gower).

Gurnani, C. (1984), 'Capital Budgeting: Theory and Practice', *Engineering Economist*, 30/1: 19–46.

Harvey, T. R. (1990), *Checklist for Change* (Boston: Allyn & Bacon).

Hayes, R. H., and Garvin, D. A. (1983), 'Managing as if Tomorrow Mattered', *Harvard Business Review*, 61 (May–June): 71–9.

Hayes, R. H., Wheelwright, S. C., and Clark, K. B. (1988), *Dynamic Manufacturing* (New York: Free Press).

Hill, T. (1985), *Manufacturing Strategy* (Basingstoke: Macmillan).

Kakati, M., and Dhar, U. R. (1991), 'Investment Justification in Flexible Manufacturing Systems', *Engineering Costs and Production Economics*, 21: 203–9.

Kaplan, R. S. (1986), 'Must CIM be Justified by Faith Alone?', *Harvard Business Review*, 64 (Mar.–Apr.): 87–95.

—— and Atkinson, A. (1989), *Advanced Management Accounting* (Englewood Cliffs, NJ: Prentice-Hall).

McNair, C. J., Mosconi, W., and Norris, T. F. (1989), *Beyond the Bottom-Line, Measuring World Class Performance* (Holmewood, Ill.: Irwin).

Mey, J. L. (1960), *Leerboek der bedrijfseconomie* (The Hague: Delwel).

Nanni, A. J., Dixon, J. R., and Vollmann, T. E. (1990), 'Strategic Control and Performance Measurement', *Journal of Cost Management*, 4 (Summer): 33–42.

Noble, J. L. (1990), 'A New Approach for Justifying Computer-Integrated Manufacturing', *Journal of Cost Management*, 4 (Winter): 14–19.

Primrose, P. L. (1991), *Investment in Manufacturing Technology* (London: Chapman & Hall).

Ross, M. (1986), 'Capital Budgeting Practices of Twelve Large Manufacturers', *Financial Management*, 15/4: 15–22.

Slagmulder, R., and Bruggeman, W. (1992), 'Justification of Strategic Investments in Flexible Manufacturing Technology', *Integrated Manufacturing Systems*, 3/3: 4–14.

—— —— and van Wassenhove, L. (1994), 'An Empirical Study of Capital Budgeting Practices for Strategic Investments in C.I.M. Technologies', working paper INSEAD, Fontainebleau, April.

van der Schroeff, J. (1956), *De leer van de kostprijs* (Amsterdam: Kosmos).

Waeytens, D., and Bruggeman, W. (1994), 'Barriers to Successful Implementation of ABC for Continuous Improvement: A Case-Study', *International Journal of Production Economics*, 36/1: 39–52.

2

Management Accounting in Denmark

Theory and Practice

Poul Israelsen, Michael Andersen, Carsten Rohde, and Poul Erik Sørensen

Introduction

The industrial revolution arrived relatively late in Denmark. While most authorities place the beginning of industrial development in the 1870s, this was a very slow development at first, probably due to the lack of raw materials. As a result, industrial development in Denmark was largely related to two other important industries—agriculture and shipping. While the agricultural sector was for many years characterized by small, local industrial firms, larger firms—first and foremost shipyards—quickly became established in the shipping industry. Despite this, there were only a few large industrial firms up to the Second World War. In 1948, there were only just over 500 firms with more than 100 workers, employing a total of 140,000 individuals, or an average of 225 workers per firm. This possibly reduced the potential for a strong cost and management tradition. And while, in the 1890s, the engineering profession both argued for and proposed various cost accounting systems, the discussion was almost purely at the level of bookkeeping techniques.

However, the 1930s saw the start of a long period of development for Danish cost and management accounting. As mentioned above, the engineering profession was particularly active in arguing for systemizing cost accounting methods. Engineers recognized the need to break down the dividing line between technical matters and managerial economics, and at the same time establish a dialogue with managerial economists. This led to the publication of *Nordisk Tidsskrift for Teknisk Økonomi* (Nordic Journal of Technical Economics) in 1935, which was fortunate to have a brilliant editorial staff, including, from 1937, Ivar Jantzen (Dtech) and Erich Schneider (professor of managerial economics) as editors. Schneider was professor of the first Danish university degree course in managerial

The authors would like to thank Professor James M. Reeve, University of Tennessee (currently Visiting Professor at the Southern Denmark Business School) for his comments and suggestions to an earlier draft of this chapter.

economics, which started at Aarhus University in 1936. Up to and including the early war years, the journal was at the centre of intensive Nordic and international research and debate on the cost and management accounting problems of the time. The main focus in the early years was on standardizing the recording systems and calculation principles. Thus, in 1937, both Norway and Sweden introduced their own calculation principles. Similar developments had taken place in England, Germany, and United States, which also introduced industry-wide standards, though their calculating methodologies differed from those of both Norway and Sweden. In Denmark, a committee was formed under the Akademiet for de Tekniske Videnskaber (Academy of Technical Sciences), consisting of a group of people connected with the journal. The task of this committee was to propose Danish cost concepts and methods of product costing, since this was felt to be the best way to approach the main task of developing uniform principles for costing. Until then, the use and abuse of concepts, in both theory and practice, had led to confusion and imprecision, creating an overwhelming desire and need for mutual understanding through uniform concepts. This work continued throughout the war and beyond, sometimes with vehement debates between technicians and managerial economists, but to no avail. The two sides failed to overcome their differences. This also effectively barred any possibility of establishing uniform costing principles. Realizing this, many Danish machining firms chose instead to develop their systems on the basis of the Swedish Mekanförbund's uniform chart of accounts and Swedish costing principles.

Parallel with this debate, a number of textbooks were also published on the subject (the first actual textbooks on cost and management accounting were written by Riis (1932) and Schneider (1939, revised Danish version, 1945)). In 1939, Palle Hansen became associate professor at the Copenhagen Business School (CBS), and published a number of traditionally oriented textbooks (e.g. Hansen 1945), which replaced those of the late Riis. As a German national, Schneider was forced to leave Denmark after the war, and later became professor of economics at Kiel. This left Hansen (CBS), who, until the beginning of the 1950s, was alone in carrying out research in cost and management accounting, which was strongly influenced by the Danish post-war business climate of scarcity and price control. The law on price control was abolished in 1952; until then, the Price Commission had decided which costs could be included in a product's costs. Therefore, before this time, the only means an enterprise had of covering its costs was to convince the price-regulating authorities of the propriety of allocating fixed costs—this despite the fact that, ever since Ivar Jantzen's doctoral thesis in 1924 (including references to Clark 1923), there had been broad theoretical agreement as to the irrelevance of fixed costs in price determination.

The Foundation is Laid

The beginning of the 1950s marked a watershed, which had important consequences for future developments. One of the most important changes was the considerable easing of price controls in connection with the abolition of the price law and the consequently greater freedom to develop cost and management accounting systems on the basis of managerial economic criteria. At the same time, there was a surge in Danish exports of industrial goods. These were necessary conditions for change.

In 1951, Vagn Madsen, later professor at Aarhus University, published a doctoral thesis entitled *Bidrag til Belysning af Rationaliseringsproblemerne i Industrivirksomheder* (Keys to Understanding Rationalization Problems in Industrial Firms). This thesis owed a lot to a one-year stay in the United States, at both the Harvard Business School and MIT, in 1949/50, where Madsen became acquainted with William Goetz's criteria for non-arbitrary recordings, which he developed into 'variability accounting'. For his part, Hansen renounced his earlier stand-point on the full absorption principle, and became an impassioned advocate of the contribution margin principle—employing the 'du Pont' format (Hansen 1958). He too had been influenced by a stay in the United States in 1952/3 as part of a larger Danish delegation, financed by the Marshall Aid programme, during which he was able to visit a number of leading American enterprises.

Although there was no attempt to integrate Madsen's variability accounting and Hansen's contribution margin principle at all to begin with, each has had, in its own way, a pronounced influence on developments up to the present day.

In the years following his visit to the United States, Hansen taught extensively in Danish trade and industrial firms. By then, the basic principles of both the contribution method and managerial economics were sufficiently developed and precise to be used directly in the relatively numerous small- and medium-sized firms which characterized—and still characterize—Danish industry. There seemed to be little need of sophisticated methods initially, since the main aim was to convert managers and accountants to a new way of thinking, and thereby remove the last vestiges of the old full-cost systems from the price law era. Hansen was so successful in this that his version of the direct costing principle became the dominant one—to such an extent, in fact, that it also served as the guiding principle in Danish financial accounting. (This remained unaltered until the passing of the first Danish Financial Statements Act of 1981, which was based on the (then) EEC's fourth directive.)

Hansen's contributions to the field—which, among others, included the founding of his own journal, *Lederskab og Lønsomhed* (Leadership and Profitability, 1957–86), the editing of *Håndbog i Budgettering* (Handbook of

Budgeting, 1975), and a book on profit centre organization (Organization of Profit Centres, 1980)—have developed into three main corner-stones of Danish management accounting:[1]

1. The separation of a firm's costs into two categories: product-variable costs, also called 'unit costs', and capacity costs. The latter have completely different management and control characteristics, and should not under any circumstances be allocated to the product-unit level.
2. The control of product-variable costs should always be carried out in two dimensions: (i) as part of controlling manufacturing costs and (ii) as part of controlling profitability. The former are controlled by contrasting actual costs with standard costs, the latter through contribution margin budgeting in the firm's sales departments, where the cost side consists of variable *standard* costs.
3. The introduction of 'inspiration analyses' as an aperiodic tool with which the firm's management can identify those sales segments which produce extraordinarily high or low profits after the allocation of that part of the capacity costs which are used to serve the segment in question, provided that this allocation is based on *measurements* of the capacity used. This can easily lead to arbitrary allocation of capacity costs, which is also why this type of analysis is called 'inspiration analysis'—by which is meant a source of inspiration for management in identifying areas in need of sales/cost adjustment—as opposed to decision information, which observes the differential logic of managerial economics.

During the same period, Madsen developed principles for a new cost accounting system (which he called 'variability accounting') in his doctoral thesis and later work, where he stressed that the system must take the form of a pure cost database without arbitrary allocation, so that the resulting rudimentary and undistorted data can be used in analyses and report outside the recording system. His thinking was thus based on a fundamental distinction between a data-recording task, which is the function of variability accounting, and data-manipulation tasks, which occur outside the system, but with this as source. Thus, variability accounting does not lead to automatic, system-inbuilt solutions to specific accounting problems (e.g. calculation of profit, product costing, etc.).

Madsen's version of variability accounting is characterized by the following (based on Madsen 1951, 1959, 1970):

1. All costs are recorded, at the time of consumption, in three dimensions: (i) 'type of production factor', (ii) 'department', and (iii) 'objective for the use of resources', or 'objective' for short. Recordings occur simultaneously in these three dimensions.
2. In order to avoid the arbitrary allocation of costs in the department and objective dimensions, a hierarchy of superjacent, subjacent, and adjacent

accounts are established in both dimensions, where the principle for the attributability of costs is that they be placed as far down the respective hierarchy as a non-arbitrary assignment allows. It should be noted here that a large number of objectives other than the firm's products are also included in the objective dimension. (See Appendix A for an example of a hierarchy in these two dimensions.)

3. An additional criterion for attributability in the department and objective dimensions is that the costs must be direct—i.e. measured as being used in the respective dimensions—and that the costs in the objective dimension must be classified in relation to the non-monetary quantitative factor (per account) with which they vary approximately proportionately. These factors are designated 'variability factors' (V-factors).
4. Recording takes place solely in the form of statistical entries, without the use of the double-entry principle, and the detail of the account structure depends on the 'cost and benefit' of the information obtained, and is thus company-specific. The recorded costs appear as actual consumption at standard/budgeted prices.

The motivation behind the initial development of variability accounting (Madsen 1951, 1959) was a desire to have all the information necessary for making economically well-founded rationalization decisions aimed at a more efficient utilization of the firm's resource constellation. Madsen's rationalization studies were, among other things, aimed at the administrative processes, batch sizes in production, and methods for increasing the manufacturing share of throughput time. In these analyses, the cost information of traditional cost accounting systems was worthless—even misleading—because these systems distorted the original cost data through a number of arbitrary allocations.

Later Developments

Developments after the initial Hansen/Madsen era built further on the pioneering work of these two authors. Madsen's later research efforts were concentrated in adjoining areas—organization, budgeting, and the relation between budgeting and strategy—while others were left to implement and test the viability of variability accounting (see e.g. Polesie 1976). In his book on budgeting (Madsen 1970), Madsen built his organizational foundation on the work of Herbert Simon (1961) and Cyert and March (1963) in particular, while the accounting concepts are based on his own variability accounting system, which, as regards income and profitability, now also included contribution analyses of the firm's various sales segments, in the form of non-arbitrary contributions in several layers. As regards the latter, Madsen was allegedly inspired by the German *Einzelkostendeckungsrechnung*, which had been developed by Paul Riebel (1959, 1967), who had also been influenced by Goetz's work. The culmination of Madsen's work was an investigation of the interplay between budget and strategy (Madsen 1976; Madsen and Polesie 1981), which had the ostensible aim of 'introducing more culture into the firm's budgeting process and more economic realism into the firm's strategy' (Madsen 1976: 13).

At the Copenhagen Business School, the chief responsibility for carrying on the pioneering work of Hansen fell to his student and co-worker, Zakken Worre (now professor). In his dissertation (1958, published in 1966) Worre introduced the concepts of absolute and relative divisibility of costs. With these concepts, he argued that the distinction between variable costs and capacity costs for an activity is related to the divisibility of the sales activity to which the activity relates. Therefore, the distinction between variable and capacity costs cannot be categorized as one or the other until the sales activity has been specified. Naturally, this can mean that the same activity can be a capacity cost to one specification, but variable to another. For example, if the product unit is the defined sales activity, then set-up costs and costs of shipment to the customer are capacity costs. This is because set-up and shipping resources are not variable with regard to such highly divisible definition of 'sales'. Merely adding or subtracting a product unit will not cause resources for set-up and shipping activities to change. However, if the sales activity is defined in terms of a particular market, then the same costs are variable. This would be true if units of capacity for set-up or shipping must be either added or subtracted due to changes in the market served. In this case, the 'market' is sufficiently large to cause the underlying resource to become variable on this definition. Thus, the contribution principle becomes the key to evaluating incremental adjustments of resource expenditure to changes in sales. In addition, the degree of reversibility of capacity costs is introduced, which refers to the time-horizon within which existing capacities can be reduced.

In an unpublished book manuscript entitled 'Det styringsorienterede regnskabsvæsen i støbeskeen' (Management-Oriented Accounting in the Melting Pot), Worre (1970*a*) carried out an exhaustive analysis of existing accounting terminology, including that developed by Madsen. He found the current terminology imprecise, and specified four necessary and sufficient dimensions which the *ex post* data of cost accounting (and revenue accounting) must adhere to. He called these the 'production factor', 'process', 'information entrance', and 'objective' dimensions. As far as the present stage of Danish management accounting is concerned (see next section), it is especially worth noting that the two concepts 'costs' and 'revenues' are replaced by 'cost data' and 'revenue data', to indicate that the firm's *ex post* recordings can/should contain all possible non-monetary measurements which can contribute to an explanation of the observed actual costs and revenues. During the next few years, Worre concentrated his efforts on implementing and testing this model in a number of different types of firms (Worre 1970*b*, 1971, and 1972).

The impression throughout the 1970s and well into the 1980s was that management accounting systems led to widely different results, depending on whether they were based on Madsen's or Worre's philosophy. This was possibly due to the fact that Worre's work on management-oriented accounting systems remained unpublished. Notwithstanding, it can be shown that the two lines of thought are compatible, in the sense that one can extract the same information from the two authors' systems (cf. Israelsen 1989). This compatibility is due, not least, to the fact that both authors strongly advocate excluding arbitrary allocations in the basic accounting data and that they both adhere to the contribution principle. Thus, the two authors have developed different, but compatible, conceptualizations—though, with his concepts of absolute and relative divisibility and reversibility,[2] Worre has gone much further. In an updated version of variability accounting, Israelsen (1993) has taken account of both these elements and the possibilities inherent in modern relational database techniques.

One of Worre's latest contributions is a two-volume (1991) work, which Worre himself describes as both a textbook and a synthesis of all his previous writings. This is not strictly accurate, however, since it also includes an interesting new proposal for a general taxonomy of capacities, which is used to demonstrate how capacity costs can be controlled through the modelling of capacity networks (for a brief description in English, see Worre 1995).

Characteristics of Present Danish Management Accounting

Based on the above historical outline, present Danish cost and management accounting theory can be said to have the following characteristics:

1. The basic idea is that the firm's *ex post* recordings are carried out with a view to inspiration analyses and improved future decision making. Since the various inspiration analyses and specific decision models demand different processing of data, an enterprise's cost accounting system cannot be based on only one of these data processing tasks, as it would impede the chances of providing relevant data for other analyses and decision models. Therefore:
2. The cost accounts must serve as a database for measured resource consumption (without data manipulation), and must contain both quantitative, non-monetary, measured data concerning resource consumption and resource use (as regards the capacities) and monetary amounts.
3. Access to non-arbitrary data must be safeguarded. Thus, the database must include only non-allocated costs, which is ensured by recording

only those attributes of resource consumption/use which can be ascertained at the time of consumption. In this way, the database will contain only measured direct consumption.

4. The firm as a whole is seen as a system, in the form of an input, process, and output model. This general rule can be broken down to apply to any activity/action in the firm. Attributes are established in the recording system for each of these three dimensions in such a way that the cross-references between the three dimensions are retained. The terminology used for this characterization varies between authors, but the objective is the same.
5. In addition to the type of input (production factor), the absolute divisibility of the factors is also recorded. In the case of the firm's capacities, this means the number of capacity units per capacity type, which thus provides information on the possibility of varying the capacity. For variable inputs, the minimum order sizes in which they can be procured are recorded.
6. The input factors are also characterized by their degree of reversibility. This concerns terms of notice as regards employees, remaining period of service in relation to owned physical capacities, and eventual contractual renegotiation dates as regards variable inputs and leased equipment.
7. The actual capacity use is recorded, which, combined with knowledge of available capacity, allows for an assessment of the degree of capacity utilization.
8. The number of output units is recorded. In the case of organizational units directly involved in the firm's production, this naturally means the number of in-house components and finished products. For all the other departments and processes, other measures for the scale of activity must be found. Here, the terms 'variability factor' or 'capacity demand unit' are used, which are equivalent to ABC's 'transaction drivers' (Cooper and Kaplan 1991*a*: 279).

The above characteristics are summarized in Figure 2.1.

There is a further characteristic:

9. One of the recording attributes of the output is which department or subsequent process is the recipient (where it therefore appears as an input). Combined with the above description, this enables the system as a whole to reflect the total activity/capacity network (see Worre 1991; Israelsen 1993). For those activities which together, through purchasing, production, and delivery (including related support functions), are responsible for the realization of the firm's sales in the period, the system facilitates the calculation of capacity needed to realize the plan, and provides information about the reversibility of those capacities *not* needed to realize it.

It is also worth noting that, due to the connection between output, process, and input—and thus also costs—it is possible to carry out a

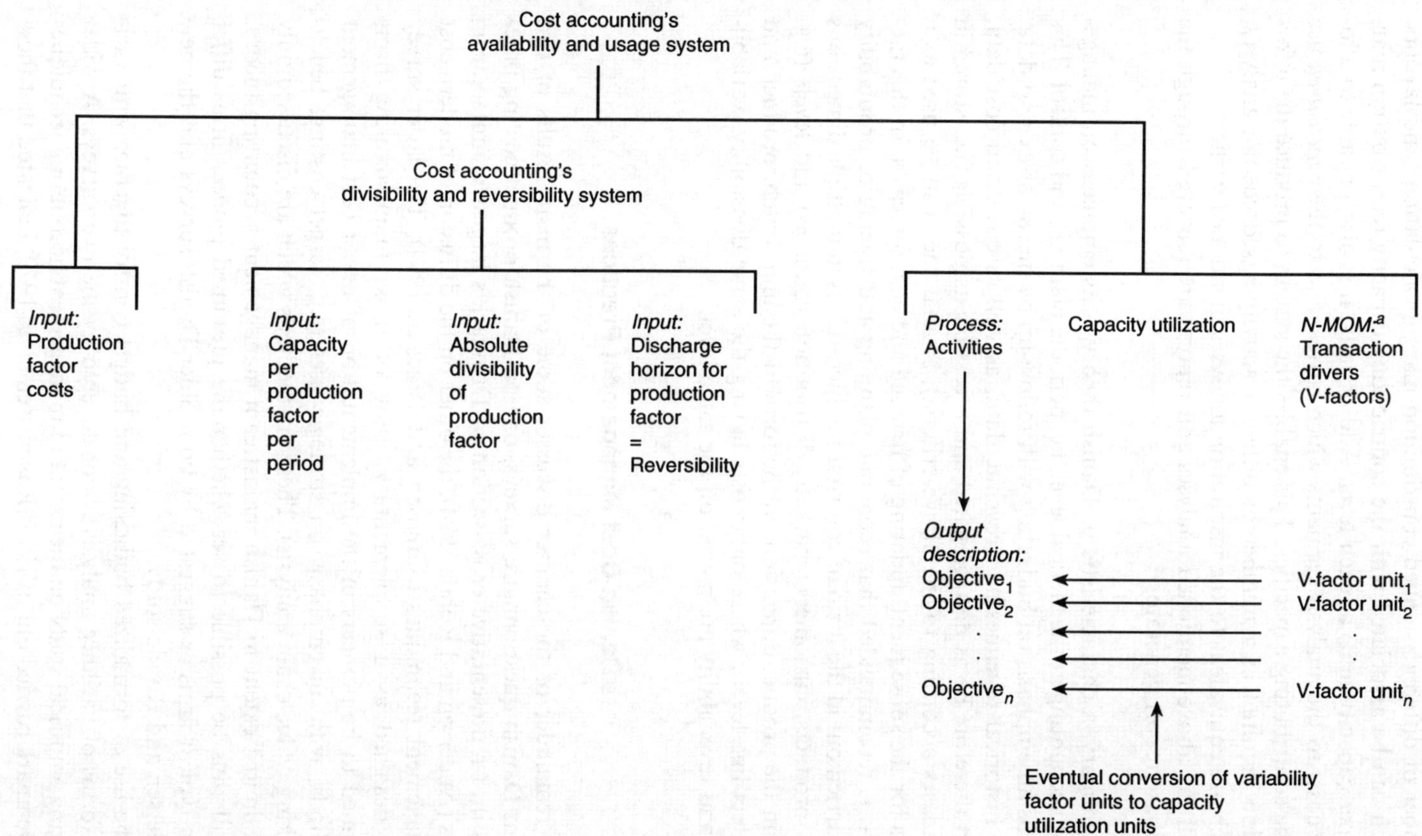

Fig. 2.1 The Danish model for recording cost accounting data ([a] = non-monetary output measure) (adapted from Israelsen 1993: 34)

number of different stepped contribution margin calculations and layouts, which can be associated with the contributing capacity (contribution margin per capacity unit) at each level. Additionally, it is also possible to allocate costs to the analysis segments which correspond to their *measured* use of the contributing capacities. This enables the system to produce the information required in a number of different activity-based costing analyses, which are equivalent to the inspiration analyses mentioned earlier.

All the above-mentioned analyses and reports are retrieved through the database report generator.

In summary, a characteristic of Danish theory is its emphasis on management accounting at the tactical level, i.e. periodic planning and control. This means an emphasis on budgeting with follow-up by means of *ex post* data. The historical revenues and revenue data, as well as costs and cost data, must therefore be as disaggregated and accessible as possible (i.e. stored in databases according to the above criteria), so that they can be used as a basis for the subsequent updating of revenue and cost forecasts. In this theory it is recommended that economic planning and tracing of profitability be carried out in the form of contribution hierarchies in multiple dimensions (e.g. products, customers, markets, distribution channels) and levels (e.g. within the product dimension, in the form of the unit, batch, product, and product-line level), where only costs having the same divisibility, variability, and reversibility are placed on the same level.

Danish Cost Management Practices

The remainder of the chapter discusses some of the main results of two recent Danish questionnaire surveys, one on Danish product costing practices in a representative cross-section of Denmark's largest manufacturing firms (Andersen and Rohde 1994), the other on the diffusion of modern cost management techniques (Sørensen and Israelsen 1994). The latter survey was designed as a supplementary study of those manufacturing firms assumed to be pioneers in the implementation of newer cost management methods, with an emphasis on strategic uses (e.g. target costing, benchmarking, value chain analysis). These are methods which are discussed only to a limited extent in Danish mainstream management accounting theory. It will thus be possible to see whether the presumed pioneer firms differ from typical firms as suggested by both older Danish surveys and the new Andersen and Rohde study.

The use of formalized budgeting and budget control together with various forms of variance analysis is not covered by the two surveys. A wide-ranging empirical study on the extent of management accounting techniques in Denmark carried out in 1977 (Rasmussen *et al.* 1979) indicated that these traditional management accounting instruments were well established in practically all manufacturing firms of a certain size (more than 100 employees). The new surveys have therefore mostly concentrated on assessing the extent to which the new ideas have influenced the design of the systems used, and whether they have been supplemented in the area of strategy.

Two Recent Empirical Studies: Content, Method, Delimitation, and Motivation

Both studies have been inspired by the intensive international debate on modern cost management methods of the past 10 years. However, the focus and choice of company populations is different in each study.

The *Product Costing Survey* (Andersen and Rohde 1994) focuses on the importance of the product cost calculation, including its content and structure, in different decision and follow-up situations, the aim of which is to discover whether the international debate has had an effect on practice.

The study was designed as a questionnaire survey of the largest manufacturing firms in Denmark. The survey population was restricted to firms (i) which operate under normal market conditions, (ii) which are of such a size that managing the firm's activities is a complex task requiring a certain degree of formalization, and (iii) which are mainly manufacturing firms. The latter stipulation was based on the assumption that it is in manufacturing firms that the most varied and complex calculation methods are used.

The survey was based on the 800 largest firms, measured by turnover in the latest official financial statement. For firms which are part of a group, it is the individual firm's turnover, not the group's, which determined its selection. Of the above-mentioned 800 firms, 105 were excluded from the survey because they failed to meet the above criteria. Of the remaining 695 companies, 118 returned usable answers, corresponding to a return rate of 17%.

The aim of the survey by Sørensen and Israelsen (1994) on the *diffusion of modern cost management techniques* was to assess the extent to which supposed progressive Danish manufacturing firms make use of the new cost management methods, e.g. revenue/cost segment analysis (including ABC, Cooper and Kaplan 1991*b*), target costing, strategic cost analysis, and benchmarking.

One of the first attempts to evaluate and incorporate the new ideas occurred in 1988/89, in a project initiated by the Danish Technological Institute involving five of the leading manufacturing firms in Denmark and researchers from various institutes of higher education. The principal aim of the project was to find new kinds of performance measures. A major source of inspiration was CAM-I's conceptual design (Berliner and Brimson 1988) and ideas from related concepts. This led, among other things, to a seminar at the start of 1990, where, for the first time in Denmark, Professor

Robert Kaplan of Harvard Business School presented his ideas on new cost management systems (Larsen 1990). The Institute for International Research (DK) has since held a number of seminars on the same subject. The survey population consists of those firms which have participated in one or more of these seminars, on the assumption that these must belong to the small group of pioneer firms in Denmark which are actively considering using the new cost management ideas. The approach used precludes some potentially interesting firms from being included in the survey. For example, a number of consultancy firms have been active in the area—e.g. as regards activity-based costing—and have been positively instrumental in the deployment of such new methods in some firms. It is also known that the corporate managements of some foreign groups have instructed their subsidiaries in Denmark to introduce new, company-wide, cost management systems including ABC systems. All in all, 190 manufacturing firms were sent the questionnaire, of which 47 returned usable replies—a response rate of 25%.

Some of the main results of the two surveys are discussed in the following two sections.

Use of Product Costing Methods in Danish Manufacturing Firms

Those parts of the survey by Andersen and Rohde (1994) discussed here are structured in the following way. (i) First, an account is given of the firms' disaggregation of their revenues, since this affects the firms' possibilities both as regards a differentiated price policy and segmented profitability analyses. This is followed by the relationships found between the firms' product costing calculation and the price-determination method, in as much as the main aim is to discover the extent to which firms use a mechanical price-determination method or a market-oriented approach. An account follows of (ii) the variable and fixed cost elements (both *ex ante* and *ex post*) contained in the product cost calculation, and how firms use them in price fixing and in profitability analyses of sales segments. Lastly, (iii) there is a discussion of the allocation methods used in those firms which do not use variable costing, together with some expressed needs for changes and the reasons for this.

(i) *The firms' revenue segmentation and price-determination methods*

The firms in the survey practiced revenue segmentation to a considerable extent. Roughly speaking, two-thirds of the firms surveyed divided revenues by products or order types in one form or another, and another two-thirds by customer type. The basis for segmentation in the two dimensions varied considerably from industry to industry and between firms of different size, however. This indicates a high correlation between theory and practice on this point, and is also a basic prerequisite for a price differentiation and profitability analysis of various sales segments.

As far as price determination is concerned, the firms surveyed—across the product range (from standard, though custom-made, to one-off custom-specific products)—were strongly market-oriented. Thus, 6 out of 10 firms answered that the market *alone* determines price, while 2 out of 10 replied that both the product cost calculation and the market affect pricing. By comparison, only 1 out of 10 said that product costs exclusively determine price.

These results are not dependent on the product range and/or the form of production. The tendency is the same for manufacturers of standard, custom-made, and unique products. Very few firms use a fixed rule for determining their sales prices. A fixed rule signifies a *mechanical mark-up percentage* on the calculated product cost (whether including solely variable costs or also involving elements of fixed/capacity costs), independent of the order type or customer type concerned. For both types of firms, or segments of firms, about 90% stated that the sales price of their products is determined according to 'what the market can bear', or indicated methods from the multiple-choice answers which are strongly market-oriented, and therefore non-mechanical. These results contrast sharply with the implicit and explicit prerequisites of which the *first* ABC model by Kaplan (in collaboration with Cooper) are based (Johnson and Kaplan 1987).

(ii) *The form of product cost calculations and their use in pricing and revenue/cost analyses of sales segments*

Somewhat surprisingly, about 4 out of 10 firms stated that they based their product cost calculations on one or other form of full-cost principle. Furthermore, the same proportions carried across all examined decision situations (i.e. price determination *vis-à-vis* the market, make or buy, non-routine 'differential' situations, investment decisions, and budgeting) and follow-up situations (i.e. profitability analyses of products and/or customers, cost control, and inventory valuation). It should be noted, however, that here, full cost covers all perspectives specified by respondents, including portions of costs 'which do not vary in relation to the decision/analysis situation'. This result corresponds closely to the results of a survey of the mid-1980s (Rohde 1987). The result is surprising given what current Danish management accounting theory exposes. For these firms the calculations encompass a hotchpotch of costs with different divisibility, variability, and reversibility (including even depreciation costs). This proportion, however, represents a sizeable reduction compared with the results of the first empirical (interview) survey in the area (covering the period 1951–5, Fog 1958), where practically all firms used full cost in the sense employed here. The reason was evidently the preceding long period of price controls. The results of the present study also represent a slight decrease compared with the situation at the end of the 1970s, when about half the firms surveyed used this method (Rasmussen *et al.* 1979).

The result should be interpreted in conjunction with the finding that firms also state (see point (i) above) that their price setting is controlled either exclusively by the market or by both the market and the product cost calculation.

The firms' cost structure also plays a role. Product-variable costs constituted more than half the total costs, and depreciation alone constituted about 10%, for nearly 9 out of 10 respondents. The fact that the survey population consisted of a lot of firms whose cost structures are predominantly made up of product-variable costs means that there was less risk that an arbitrary allocation of costs would have unfortunate consequences for (short-term) economic decision making.

The result contrasts with that of the Sørensen and Israelsen (1994) survey, in that 9 out of 10 firms carried out profitability analyses of products and/or customers in stepped contribution margin hierarchies on one (product-unit and/or single-customer level) or several levels. By several levels is meant, for example, the product-unit, batch, product, and product-line levels in the product dimension, and the individual customer order, individual customer, customer group, and market segment in the customer dimension. If this population reflects any general trend, it is one that is quite reassuring to the (Danish) academic world.

(iii) *Firms' calculation methods and their need for change*

The main conclusion regarding firms which allocated non-product-variable costs to products is that they currently use traditional allocation bases. The large majority of firms which included such costs as wages for cleaning, repairs, materials movement, and warehouse personnel in the calculations used direct labour hours or direct wages as an allocation mechanism. As regards parts of the costs of production scheduling, marketing, purchasing, product development and quality control, the most important allocation base for most firms was typically attribution by sales. Sales were also the most widely used allocation base for general administration, depreciation, and financial costs, though processing time and machine time were also important. It must therefore be concluded that firms which use allocation methods *mostly use them in the form of what the ABC method describes as 'volume-related' or 'unit-level drivers'.* In this regard, the survey of progressive firms showed no deviation from the norm.

In spite of these results, about half the firms, when directly asked, confirmed an awareness of ABC, though only 10% claimed to be using it. Of the 40% which had knowledge of ABC, it might be inferred from Bjørnenak (1994) that about half these remain 'non-adopters' while the other half 'have not evaluated it'.

About two-thirds of the enterprises surveyed expressed a need for changes in their product cost calculation. Among the many reasons for this, 'increased competition' and 'increased automation in the production process' were given twice as often as 'increase in the number of product variants' and 'increase in the capacity costs' relative share of the total costs'. Considering the large degree of market orientation in pricing, this result must be taken to suggest that changes in the calculation methods are triggered not by the need for methods for allocating rising capacity costs, but, to a much greater extent, by the need for greater insight into the firm's changing profitability patterns resulting from growing market competition.

The Diffusion of Modern Cost Management Techniques

The firms in Sørensen and Israelsen's survey were medium and large Danish manufacturers from all parts of the industrial spectrum, albeit with a certain over-representation of firms from the 'food, drink and tobacco' (FDT) industry. Where this survey covered the same areas as that of Andersen and Rohde (1994), the results will not be repeated here.

General Characteristics of the Survey Population

We begin by describing the cost structure, basic cost accounting systems, forms of production, and manufacturing control systems of the participating firms, together with their generic strategy.

The cost structure includes a wide variety of manufacturing, sales, and administrative costs. Expressed as a percentage of the manufacturing production costs, material costs average 57%, direct wages 22%, and manufacturing overhead (MOH) 21%, but vary widely (these results are similar to those of Joy and Blayney 1990, for Australian firms). In 1 out of 4 firms, however, MOH was more than twice as large as direct wages, something which is usually seen as being highly significant in modern cost management theory. Sales and administrative costs average 15% of turnover, again with big variations. Batch production is the most common of all production forms, making up over 50% of all cases, with small batches being just as common as large batches. Most firms use one of the newer manufacturing control systems, with about 20% using both material requirements/resource planning (MRP, I&II) and just-in-time (JIT), while flexible manufacturing systems (FMS) are used in 10% of cases. A further 10% indicated that they use combinations of these.

Just under 60% stated that their main strategy was differentiation, as opposed to cost leadership. This involves all firms in the iron, metal, machine, and graphics industry.

The most widely used traditional cost accounting system was responsibility accounting, which about half the firms used. The next most widespread system in use—subject to some reservation because of inconsistencies in the answers—was variability accounting (a rudimentary cost recording system as described above), used by about 1 in 4 firms. Job-order accounting (10%) was mainly used by one-off product manufacturers, while process-costing systems were used mainly in the FDT industry. Based on specific information on a number of system characteristics, the authors concluded that in 1994, when the survey was undertaken, none of the respondents used ABC.

Many reported changing their accounting systems, with 2 out of 3 firms carrying out significant changes over the past 5 years, though mostly in the form of more advanced computerization. Over half the firms were dissatisfied or only partly satisfied with their present system, and about 80% of these had either planned, or were considering, changes in these systems. Again, these changes mostly concerned computers, though 1 in 4 firms which were dissatisfied or only partly satisfied with their current system were considering changes in the calculation system—only 3 of these explicitly mentioned ABC, however. These results are summarized in Table 2.1.

Table 2.1. Planned or considered changes of accounting systems among companies which are dissatisfied or only partly satisfied with their present system (% of responding firms)

Satisfaction with system/changes	Total	Planned changes	Considering changes	No response
Dissatisfied/partly satisfied	55	32	15	8
Nature of change:	43	28	15	
1. New computer system (IT) or changes within current system	24	17	7	
2. New management accounting system (not further specified)	4	2	2	
3. New product costing system or similar	15	9	6	
3A. Activity-based costing specifically mentioned in item 3	6	2	4	

Results

Apart from the previously mentioned results, this section will address (i) whether the size of the MOH can be explained by the firm's strategy or by the complexity of its production or sales, (ii) the most important performance measures, as well as the use of (iii) target costing, and (iv) benchmarking and strategic cost analyses.

(i) *The relationship between strategy and the size of overhead costs*

It is usual to assume that differentiation leads to higher manufacturing overheads than production of standard products, and that firms with high product complexity will have higher overhead costs than focused producers (Cooper and Kaplan 1988; Fisher 1993). As mentioned above, MOH proportions vary considerably in the surveyed firms, but this variation is *not* due to the firms following a differentiation strategy or a cost-led strategy. Moreover, there is no relationship in the questionnaire results between production/product complexity and proportions of MOH. Thus a complexity measure based on number of product lines, production stages, product parts, suppliers, etc., shows *no* correlation with the size of the firms' overhead costs in production. Conversely, a relationship can be demonstrated between sales complexity—reflected in the number of distribution channels and market segments—and the spread (between 1% and 40%) in sales and administrative costs. The above lack of correlation is probably affected by the fact that the firms represent different industries, though not necessarily a population representative of Danish manufacturers. Furthermore, it must also be acknowledged that the assumed relationship noted above would be better approximated by a longitudinal study of evolving complexity versus manufacturing overheads.

(ii) *Performance measures*

The survey shows which of a number of preselected financial and non-financial performance measures the firms both use and regard as the most important from a strategic point of view. The most widely used traditional performance measures are material costs and labour costs per unit, which are used in 7 out of 10 firms. With regard to non-financial performance measures, 'inventory turnover', 'percent on-time-deliveries', and 'outgoing quality yield' are the most widely used (5 out of 10). In terms of strategic importance, firms named 'percent on-time-deliveries' (40%), 'outgoing quality yield made' (28%), 'labour costs per unit' (21%), 'material costs per unit' (19%), 'inventory turnover' (19%), and 'direct labour productivity' (17%) as the most important.[3]

An analysis of the relationships shows that, as expected (see e.g., Takikonda and Takikonda 1989), the most important performance measures for firms using MRP(I&II) are 'material and labor costs per unit', together with 'on-time-deliveries' (7–8 out of 10).

Firms with JIT production regard 'on-time-deliveries' as the most important, closely followed by 'set-up times', 'inventory turnover', 'machine utilization', plus 'material and labour costs per unit' (7–8 out of 10).

In sum, as far as the strategically most important performance measures are concerned, all firms with FMS and most of those with MRP and JIT regard on-time-delivery as the most important. From another point of view, nearly all firms which have an above-average direct labour percentage regard performance measures concerning labour productivity as among the most important. It is also worth noting that non-financial performance measures are widely used by firms with a cost leadership strategy. On the other hand, not all firms with a differentiation strategy attach primary importance to time and quality. Firms in the FDT industry in particular use (not surprisingly) performance measures in connection with materials—material costs per unit, materials yield, and material variances—and regard these as the most important.

(iii) *Target Costing*

The main results show that about half the firms systematically include target costs in the development of new products. Of these, 8 in 10 pass on these costs in negotiations with component suppliers. The target profit is expressed mainly by a measure for the contribution margin percentage. Over a quarter of these firms state that they use 'cost tables' (Yoshikawa *et al.* 1990) in connection with product design. There is no difference in industry frequency and company size, but a slight majority of firms have a differentiation strategy, and it is characteristic that all these firms use modern production forms and methods. Product development is to a large extent interdisciplinary. For example, sales and production departments are involved in this activity in 80% of firms, purchasing departments in 50%; but only 20% involve the accounting department in product development.

The relatively high use of target costing is undoubtedly related to the fact that, at least during the past 20 years, Danish technical degree courses have attached a high degree of importance to 'value analysis' (the modern term being 'value engineering').

(iv) *Benchmarking and strategic cost analysis*

There is a more modest use of benchmarking and strategic cost analysis. Benchmarking is used by 1 in 4 firms, of which half carry out systematic analyses of key processes, with only one-third of these having developed information-sharing agreements with partners.

From a value chain point of view, strategic cost analysis is carried out by 1 in 3 firms. The majority of these (two-thirds) include only their own costs in the analysis, while the rest also include subcontractor and/or customer costs.

Conclusion

The two studies indicate that Danish firms have a very market-oriented pricing policy, setting different prices in different market segments. This orientation is also reflected in a detailed specification of the overall financial result in relevant revenue/cost segments (products, markets, etc.), mainly using a hierarchical contribution margin approach with specifications in one or more steps. This principle is by far the most important in those firms described here as 'progressive'. There is thus a healthy interface between Danish theory and practice in this area.

Of the so-called new cost management techniques, the use of non-financial performance measures is widespread. Considering the size of Danish companies—and combined with a distinct flexibility and service-mindedness—it is hardly surprising that on-time delivery is considered by far the most strategically important. Target costing is, under another name, obviously well known to Danish industry, while benchmarking and strategic cost analysis are only in their infancy in terms of usage. At the moment, however, ABC appears to be common only among subsidiaries of foreign groups.

Whether ABC will be used more in the future can perhaps be discerned from statements by leading Danish consultants. In conversations with Danish company managers, these consultants have observed an increasing interest in activity-based cost management (ABC-M). In these consultants' opinion, a major reason for the late acceptance of the concept in Denmark has been a not inconsiderable academic scepticism, especially with regard to the first full-cost-oriented solutions, with the result that none of the major industrial companies has so far implemented the system; hence there has been no example for the much larger number of smaller firms which still characterize the industrial landscape. In light of the changes in ABC's theoretical basis, which better match the Danish views described here, there are good reasons to expect an increasing use of ABC-M in coming years.

APPENDIX A

An example of hierarchies of accounts in the department and the objectives for the use of resources dimensions.

Hierarchical accounts of departments

- Company as a whole
  - Production dept. en bloc
    - Production dept. A
      - Workplace A_1
      - Workplace A_2
      - Workplace A_3
    - Production dept. B
      - Workplace B_1
      - Workplace B_2
      - Workplace B_3
    - Production dept. C
      - Workplace C_1
      - Workplace C_2
      - Workplace C_3
  - Marketing dept. en bloc
    - Advertising dept.
    - Sales dept.
    - Distribution dept.

Hierarchical accounts of objectives

- Objective in general
  - Product-manufacturing objective in general
    - Category X products
      - Product X_1
        - Batch X_{11}
          - Component X_{111}
    - Maintenance objective
  - Marketing objective
    - Distribution objective
      - Regions
        - Types and customer per region
    - Sales objective
      - Regions
    - Advertising objective

Note: Translated from Madsen 1959 and, excluding depreciations, also in accordance with Madsen 1970.

Notes

1. To the international audience, Hansen is probably best known for his contribution to financial accounting theory (Hansen 1977).
2. In these areas, Worre's concepts are compatible with, and were partly developed at the same time as, those of Paul Riebel in Germany, though there is no mutual reference between the two authors.
3. Apart from the fact that 'on-time-deliveries' is ranked first by the Danish firms, the order is the same as that found for successful firms in Europe in 1988 (Maskell 1989). It is worth noting that 'incoming quality' is assigned practically no importance in the Danish firms, whereas US firms regard it as the most important.

References

Andersen, M., and Rohde, C. (in co-operation with KPMG C. Jespersen Ltd.) (1994), *Empirisk undersøgelse af kalkulationspraksis* (Copenhagen: KPMG C. Jespersen).

Berliner, C., and Brimson, J. A. (1988) (eds.), *Cost Management for Today's Advanced Manufacturing* (Boston: Harvard Business School Press).

Bjørnenak, T. (1994), *Aktivitetsbasert kalkulasjon* (Oslo: Fagbokforlaget).

Clark, J. M. (1923), *Studies in the Economics of Overhead Costs* (Chicago: University of Chicago Press).

Cooper, R., and Kaplan, R. S. (1988), 'Measure Cost Right: Make the Right Decisions', *Harvard Business Review*, 66 (Sept.–Oct.): 96–103.

—— —— (1991*a*), *The Design of Cost Management Systems: Text, Cases, and Readings* (Englewood-Cliffs, NJ: Prentice-Hall).

—— —— (1991*b*), 'Profit Priorities from Activity-Based Costing', *Harvard Business Review*, 69 (May–June): 130–7.

—— —— (1992), 'Activity-Based Systems: Measuring the Costs of Resource Usage', *Accounting Horizons*, 6 (Sept.): 1–13.

Cyert, R. M., and March, J. G. (1963), *A Behavioural Theory of the Firm* (Englewood Cliffs, NJ: Prentice-Hall).

Fisher, T. M. (1993), 'Variantenvielfalt und Komplexität als Betriebliche Kostenbestimmungsfaktoren', *Kostenrechnungspraxis (KRP)*, 36: 27–31.

Fog, B. (1958), *Priskalkulation og prispolitik* (Copenhagen: Harcks).

Goetz, B. E. (1949), *Management Planning and Control; A Managerial Approach to Industrial Accounting* (New York: McGraw-Hill).

Hansen, P. (1945), *Industriens interne Regnskabsvæsen* (Copenhagen: Harcks).

—— (1958), 'Kontrol med Forretningspolitikken', in P. Hansen (ed.), *Håndbog i Regnskabsvæsen*, 2nd edn. (Copenhagen: Harcks).

—— (1975) (ed.), *Håndbog i Budgettering* (Copenhagen: Lederskab og Lønsomhed).

—— (1977), 'The Accounting Theory of Profit; An Analysis Based on Material from Practice', in W. T. Baxter and S. Davidson (eds.), *Studies in Accounting* (London:

ICAEW). (Based on 'Alternative økonomiske overskudsbegreber', *Handelsvidenskabelig tidsskrift*, no. 4 (1953).)

—— (1980), *Profitcenter-organisation* (Copenhagen: Institut for Lederskab og Lønsomhed).

Israelsen, P. (1989), 'Lader Vagn Madsens og Zakken Worres tanker og ideer omkring virksomhedens omkostningsregnskab sig forene?', in L. Nørreklit and B. Warming-Rasmussen (eds.), 'Aktuelle forskningsprojekter i og omkring revision', *Faglige Artikler*, no. 23: 179–208.

—— (1993), *Activity versus Variability-Based Management Accounting* (Copenhagen: Jurist og Økonomforbundets Forlag/DJØF Publishing).

Jantzen, I. (1939), *Basic Principles of Business Economics and National Calculations* (Copenhagen: Gad). (Original in Danish, 1924.)

Johnson, H. T., and Kaplan, R. S. (1987), *Relevance Lost: The Rise and Fall of Management Accounting* (Boston: Harvard Business School Press).

Joy, M. P., and Blayney, P. J. (1990), *Cost and Management Accounting Practices in Australian Companies, Survey Results* (Sydney: University of Sydney, Monograph no. 7).

Larsen, A. (1990), 'Jagten på omkostningernes hemmelighed', *Civiløkonomen*, no. 4: 13–15.

Madsen, V. (1951), *Bidrag til Belysning af Rationaliseringsproblemerne i Industrivirksomheder* (Copenhagen: Munksgaard).

—— (1959), *Regnskabsvæsenets opgaver og problemer—i ny belysning* (Copenhagen: Gyldendal).

—— (1964), *Virksomhedsledelsens problemer i organisatorisk belysning* (Copenhagen: Teknisk Forlag).

—— (1970), *Budgettering* (Copenhagen: Teknisk Forlag).

—— (1976), *Strategi og budget* (Copenhagen: Nyt Nordisk Forlag/Arnold Busk).

—— and Polesie, T. (1981), *Human Factors in Budgeting; Judgement and Evaluation* (London: Pitman Press).

Maskell, B. (1989), 'Performance Measurement for World Class Manufacturing', *Management Accounting* (UK), 67: 32–3.

Polesie, T. (1976), *Ändamålsbudgettering—beskrivning och analys af tillämpninger* (Lund: Studentlitteratur).

Rasmussen, K., Sørensen, P. E., and Pedersen, J. (1979), *Rapport over undersøgelse of anvendelse af internt regnskabsvæsen som ledelsesinstrument i danske industrivirksomheder* (Aarhus: Aarhus Business School).

Riebel, P. (1959), 'Das Rechnen mit Einzelkosten und Deckungsbeiträge', *Zeitschrift für handelswissenschaftliche Forschung*, 11: 213–38.

—— (1967), 'Kurzfristige unternehmerische Entscheidungen im Erzeugnisbereich auf Grundlage des Rechnens mit relativen Einzelkosten und Deckungsbeiträgen', *Neue Betriebswirtschaft*, 8: 1–23.

Riis, H. C. (1932), *Omkostninger og deres Behandling ved Bogføring og Kalkulering i Handels-og Industrivirksomheder* (Copenhagen: Det Schønbergske Forlag).

Rohde, C. (1987), 'En analyse of udvalgte principielle og praktiske problemer forbundet med de i regnskabspraksis anvendte fremgangsmåder ved udarbejdelse af såvel totale som aktivitetsopdelte periodiske resultatopgørelser, der danner informationsgrundlag for den økonomiske styring i handels- og fremstillingsvirksomhed', Ph.D. diss., Copenhagen Business School.

Schneider, E. (1945), *Industriel Regnskabsvæsen* (Copenhagen: Harcks).

Simon, H. A. (1961), *Administrative Behavior* (New York: Macmillan).

Sørensen, P. E., and Israelsen, P. (1994), 'The Diffusion of Modern Cost Management Techniques in Danish Manufacturing Companies', working paper, Aarhus School of Business.

Takikonda, L. A., and Takikonda, R. J. (1989), 'Success in MRP', *Management Accounting*, 70 (May: 34).

Worre, Z. (1966), *Nøglefaktorer i virksomhedens økonomiske tilpasningsproces* (Copenhagen: Nyt Nordisk Forlag/Arnold Busk).

—— (1970*a*), 'Det styringsorienterede regnskabsvæsen i støbeskeen', unpublished book MS, Copenhagen Business School.

—— (1970*b*), 'Realiteter og skinproblemer omkring interne afregningspriser', *Faglige Artikler*, no. 9: 147–71.

—— (1971), 'Standardomkostningsregnskabet for materiale- og lønomkostninger', *Faglige Artikler*, no. 10: 7–62.

—— (1972), 'Regnskabsvæsenets opgaver i en virksomhed med produktion til ordre og lang produktionstid', *Faglige Artikler*, no. 11: 11–43.

—— (1991), *Omkostningsregnskab og omkostningsstyring*, vols. 1 and 2 (Copenhagen: FDC).

—— (1994/5), 'The Evolutionary Development from Pure Imitative Cost Accounting to a Danish Concept of Management Accounting', *Informatik & Økonomistyring*, no. 2: 71–101.

Yoshikawa, T., Innes, J., and Mitchell, F. (1990), 'Cost Tables: A Foundation of Japanese Cost Management', *Journal of Cost Management*, 4 (Fall): 30–6.

3

Drivers of Management Accounting in Finland

Kalervo Virtanen, Teemu Malmi, Juhani Vaivio, and Eero Kasanen

Introduction

Finland provides an interesting laboratory setting for studying the turmoil in management accounting which is supposedly sweeping the world. There has been, in the not too distant past, a remarkable shift in Finnish management accounting practices, from full costing to variable costing. The recording of costs in official financial statements has likewise been increasingly based on variable costing. If the call for greater use of refined full costing or resource consumption models in advanced technological environments has merit, it should be made in Finland.

In this chapter, we attempt to understand the managerial thinking underlying cost accounting in Finland and to discuss trends which appear most sustainable. We specifically address the question of what makes Finnish cost accounting what it is, and what might lie ahead. To begin with, we contrast cost accounting changes in the 1950s and 1960s with the shift that is perceived to be taking place now, in the mid-1990s. Calls for cost accounting changes from full costing to variable costing during the 1950s were triggered by changes in market conditions, and were backed by claims to sound economic logic not dissimilar to those made in relation to the current cost management movement. We explain why many Finnish companies changed their cost accounting methods from full costing to variable costing during the 1950s, and use these insights to analyse current changes in cost accounting.

In the second part of the chapter, we study current calls for change. We analyse the existing situation on the basis of interviews with senior executives in a number of major Finnish enterprises (see Appendix 1) about their cost management practices, recent changes in cost accounting systems in

We greatly appreciate Professor Jaakko Honko's insights on cost accounting development during our long discussions with him. Further, we would like to thank Professor Fedi Vaivio for his remarks. We are grateful for Professor Kari Lukka's helpful comments and for the use of his survey results. Our sincere thanks are also extended to the numerous managers and academics we interviewed for their time and contribution. Financial support from the Foundation of the Helsinki School of Economics is gratefully acknowledged.

their companies, as well as the pressures for change they are beginning to perceive. The views of some academics and cost management consultants involved with cost management on the same issues were also solicited. Statistics on the relative frequencies of applied cost accounting methods in Finnish companies based on a recent survey study are also discussed (Lukka and Granlund 1995; see also Appendix 2; Laitinen 1995; Malmi 1995; Rautajoki 1995).

In the concluding part we fuse together the above elements. We point out that although there have been isolated experiments with variants of resource consumption models such as ABC, companies do not feel a pressing need to switch over to systematic full costing. It is thought, however, that if movement towards harmonization of financial accounting within the European Union gains momentum, it is possible that Finnish financial accounting and subsequently management accounting practices will move towards full costing. It is also noted that managers seem to be primarily interested in effective cost management programmes, not simply in cost allocation techniques. They further stress the need for multi-dimensional real-time cost information.

The chapter is structured as follows. The shift from full costing to variable costing is first analysed. Current calls for moving from variable to full costing are assessed. In the final section, a discussion of the drivers of cost accounting in Finland is provided.

From Full Costing to Variable Costing

Prelude: Developments before the Second World War

Some insights into early developments in Finnish cost accounting are useful for understanding the widespread changes that were to follow during and after the Second World War. (For a thorough overview of the evolution of Finnish accounting research and practice during the last 100 years, see Näsi 1990 and 1994.)

Characteristically, the earliest writings on cost accounting were not academic, since business schools did not exist in the nineteenth century, but tended to take the form of practitioner-oriented manuals (Lilius 1862 was the first accounting textbook written in the Finnish language). The first specialist academic Finnish textbook on cost accounting appeared towards the end of the 1920s (Kaitila 1928). In this—now seen as a classic—a firm definition of accounting stemming from German *Rechnungswesen* and a scheme of systematization were introduced. Kaitila described a two-stage costing procedure, discussed main and auxiliary cost pools, as well as various allocation bases in the first, intermediate, and second stages, and included a 25-page discussion devoted to capacity questions. In brief, the book was a fairly comprehensive presentation on full costing, even by today's standards. Kaitila's book remained on the curricula of the Helsinki School of Economics until the late 1940s.

Cost accounting for product pricing decisions was a regular theme in more practically oriented writings in the 1930s (see Näsi 1990, 1994), in which knowledge of 'true product costs' was often sought. The many problems of full costing were acknowledged and discussed, but at a more general, broad level, without any thorough consideration of specific cost accounting techniques. In some leading Finnish companies, elementary, but nevertheless rigorous, cost accounting approaches were already taking shape, with full costing[1] being adopted as the country entered the war economy.

The 1940s: Embracing Full Costing

The breakthrough for cost accounting in Finland happened during the 1940s, under exceptional circumstances. Finland had to run a strictly regulated wartime economy. Business activity came under official scrutiny and control. Thus, quite paradoxically, the impetus for developing cost accounting was not born from within the enterprise or created by market pressures, but originated in government stipulations. As prices of rationed products were fixed by state officials, companies had to produce accurate information, especially on production costs.

As a consequence of the wartime measures adopted by the State, full costing became compulsory in all industrial firms from the beginning of the 1940s (see Ministry of Supply's regulation of 27 June 1942, in Appendix 3). Price restrictions had a fundamental and protracted effect on Finnish cost accounting, particularly since some of these extended far into the 1950s. Additionally, elaborate cost accounting records provided a basis for setting nominal prices for the massive production which, in accordance with the peace treaty, was to be handed over as war reparations to the Soviet Union.[2]

Other State initiatives also influenced Finnish cost accounting during the 1940s. When financial accounting legislation was rewritten in 1945, cost accounting became obligatory for industrial firms. This was related to another section in the law, which stated that inventories should be valued on the balance sheet such as not to exceed the lower of historical cost or net realizable value. The law defined the historical cost of inventories as direct purchasing and manufacturing costs plus the portion of indirect purchasing and manufacturing costs absorbed at normal annual volumes. Thus changes in legal requirements for financial reporting contributed to the move towards systematic full costing.

These forces, coupled with the intellectual impact that German and Scandinavian academics had on Finnish scholars, influenced and powerfully guided developments in cost accounting in Finland, resulting in a uniform emphasis in the calculations of *ex post* full unit costs. The allocation of overhead costs, even on the basis of methods that were not very sophisticated, was considered essential. The cost-based pricing scheme of the regulated economy of the 1940s seemed, nevertheless, to have enabled firms to profit from these somewhat cumbersome impositions. One manager in charge of cost accounting at that time remarked that a clever cost accountant always earned his salary.[3] Finnish cost accounting, to borrow Horngren's popular terminology, was living its own 'absolute truth' era.

The 1950s: From Cost Accounting to Management Accounting

Towards the end of the 1950s, Finnish cost accounting was subject to rapid, dramatic changes that substantially widened its confines. Cost accounting expanded from merely serving parochial, regulated price setting to become management accounting.

Market forces gave a wholly new role to accounting, which was now regarded as a crucial management tool, serving primarily *ex ante* purposes. Planning and decision making were key words driving this epoch. Following wider international currents, Finland also became sceptical of 'absolute truth' concepts, replacing the notion with 'conditional truth', which was characterized, for instance, by relevant cost thinking and the principle of 'different costs for different purposes'.

The Finnish accounting apparatus was now to include a variety of instruments, like standard costing, budgeting systems, methods of investment planning, appraisal and control, as well as elementary responsibility accounting. Within a relatively short period of time, by the beginning of the 1960s, retrospectively focused accounting gave way to a forward-looking, managerially oriented approach in both industry and academia.

This sharp turn was a consequence of several parallel developments. After the war, Finnish companies faced a new and turbulent environment. They now faced competitive market conditions, as regulatory restrictions were dismantled. They were experiencing rapid economic growth, deep structural changes in many industries, rationalization, and the introduction of modern production technology.

At the same time, within academia, an entire generation of teachers and researchers was making room for another. These younger accounting scholars, in contrast to their predecessors, who had relied on early German traditions, were shifting their attention toward Anglo-Saxon, especially American, approaches. Three young accounting professors at the Helsinki School of Economics, Martti Saario, Henrik Virkkunen, and Jaakko Honko played major roles in this transition. Saario was an original financial accounting thinker (Saario 1945, 1949, 1959; Lukka and Pihlanto 1994). Virkkunen and Honko combined Finnish tradition with Anglo-American influences. They elaborated on management accounting, Virkkunen especially on cost accounting (1951, 1954, 1960), Honko on capital investment decision making (1955, 1959, 1963). The new generation did not completely turn its back on the German connection, however, as evidenced, for example, by the lecture the lecture notes and textbooks they used.

It is noteworthy that Virkkunen's (1951) doctoral dissertation, which addressed cost accounting, was a path-breaking management accounting study in Finland. Intriguingly, the study focused, in Cooper and Kaplan's terminology, on unit and batch level costs. Later, Virkkunen published the first modern academic cost accounting textbook (1960). The textbook emphasized managerial decision making. Both contribution margin and full-costing approaches were described and discussed. Interestingly, from the point of view of contemporary ABC writings, Virkkunen considered batch and product levels, as well as customers, as possible cost objects. Furthermore, he suggested transaction-based second-stage allocation bases (p. 121).

The Variable Costing Agenda of the 1960s

It seems that the management accounting revolution of the 1950s, besides being concerned with the aforementioned issues, was strongly centred on the notion of 'right' product costs. A curious path of development can be traced, starting with a Danish professor of accounting, Palle Hansen, at the Copenhagen School of Economics. Assisted by his Finnish colleagues, Hansen arranged seminars for the top management and accounting staff of Finnish companies. In these successful gatherings, he propagated and popularized the United States-inspired, new accounting message: the principles of contribution approach and variable costing. Soon, contribution analysis and variable costing had gained a firm following among managers and accounting practitioners, inspiring a large number of often vociferous proponents.

The argument in favour of the contribution approach and variable costing was tempting—almost compelling in the post-war circumstances. Because the rules of an unrestricted market were different, companies had a lot to learn while setting their prices. A flexible, market-sensitive attitude was needed in pricing policy. Firms could no longer expect to automatically cover costs by simply engaging in accurate full-cost accounting. They had to earn their money in the market; considerations other than costs were to enter decision making. Of essence was the question of how competitors would react, given a set price. It was now increasingly uncertain whether firms could charge customers a full cost-based price.

Variable costing coupled with cost–volume–profit analysis, the argument continued, offered a convenient and correct way to minimum prices or to fix price ranges. It provided a practical overall instrument for realizing active pricing policy. Furthermore, full product costing was harshly criticized as rather burdensome and as resulting in arbitrary allocations of fixed overhead costs. Decision-theoretic, relevant cost thinking was seen to be rooted in sound economic theory.

Despite its powerful appeal, variable costing had its opponents (see e.g. Hautakangas 1966; Carlson 1964), many of whom were in senior management positions in enterprises. Certain companies continued to use full costing internally.[4] The possibly inherent fallacy in setting prices according to variable costs, and especially the risk of 'forgetting' fixed costs, were emphasized. Among accounting professions, heated discussions on the advantages and weaknesses of both variable and full costing took place, occasionally turning into rather heated debates (Ahola 1966; Hautakangas 1966).

Academics felt a need to change their lecture notes in the 1950s. Academia was receptive to variable costing, showing clear signs of sympathy, but refrained from active engagement or other support. For instance, Virkkunen (1960) gave equal weight to the principles and applications of both full and variable costing in his textbook, but underlined the applicability of variable costing especially in short-term decisions. Within academia, a slightly detached, independent attitude was cherished.

Variable costing became gradually accepted in Finnish practice during late 1950s and the 1960s, forming the nucleus of the management accounting reform. It could be asserted that because of the popularity of variable costing—which remains a characteristic feature of Finnish cost accounting—the emphasis in accounting shifted from pedantic calculation of costs towards management of profits. From the 1950s onwards, profit-conscious pricing and product-mix decisions, profit planning, as well as short-term CVP analysis and close monitoring of profitability, were all offshoots of the contribution approach and variable costing movement.

Financial Accounting's Impact on Variable Costing

A fuller explanation of the fairly rapid advance and extensive use of variable costing requires an examination of Finland's original financial accounting regulations (see Majala 1994). This brings us back to Martti Saario, whose theories of financial accounting affected the country's accounting philosophy and university teaching, as well as practical solutions in the field (Lukka and Pihlanto 1994). Moreover, they strongly influenced tax and accounting legislation from the 1960s, giving an indirect but considerable boost to variable costing. Cost accounting was again to be moulded by the evolution of financial accounting.

Saario's expenditure–income theory focuses on the income statement, maintaining that the prime task of financial accounting is to indicate the firm's distributable profit; the balance sheet is given a secondary role (Saario 1945, 1959). On the other hand, the theory of the priority order of costs

(Saario 1949) states that the firm's various costs should be covered from earned income in a certain logical order of priority. Examined more closely, both theories have some important parallels to the contribution approach and variable costing.

The impact of these ideas was to be felt through the 1968 Act on Business Taxation and the Accounting Act of 1973. The basic elements of Saario's conceptual framework were embedded in these Acts. Consequently, Finnish law requires that inventory valuation in financial statements be based on variable costing. Only variable manufacturing costs of work in process inventory and finished goods inventory are shown on the balance sheet as product costs, which therefore do not include fixed manufacturing costs. This contrasts with the approach applied in many other countries, where fixed manufacturing costs are allowed to enter balance sheet inventories.

Acceptable financial accounting practice in Finland appeals to variable costing ideals as follows: variable costs alone should be traced to individual products. Since fixed costs are principally capacity costs, they should be treated accordingly—i.e. as a necessary pre-condition of production. Consequently, fixed costs are not included in stock valuation. In Finnish income statements, variable manufacturing costs of goods sold and all fixed manufacturing, marketing, and administrative costs for that particular period are deducted as expenses from earnings. In contrast with the general Anglo-Saxon or Continental practice whereby manufacturing costs are lumped together as part of 'cost of goods sold', the Finnish income statement separates variable and fixed costs, which more or less steers companies toward the contribution approach and variable costing perspective (Majala 1994: 97).

Finnish accounting law states that companies should be able to show, calculatively, variable purchasing and manufacturing costs of inventories. The law does not, however, stipulate systematic requirements for enterprise cost accounting.

Given that the country's accounting regulations and institutions have not forced companies to practice full costing, variable costing increasingly became the norm, particularly during the 1970s, and is now extensively used by Finnish companies.

In sum, financial accounting in Finland is based on variable costing and the disclosure of variable versus fixed costs. Attacks on full-costing inventory valuation methods which form the basis of financial accounting in many countries and which are often criticized in the ABC literature have not altered the development of cost accounting systems in Finland. Market-driven competitive pricing, economics-oriented academic teaching on marginal relevant costing, and variable costing-based financial accounting have thus had a quite specific influence on enterprise cost accounting systems.

From Full to Variable Costing: The Driving Forces

Overall, our analysis of driving forces of the cost accounting shift in Finland, beginning in the 1950s, can be summarized in three main points. First, there was a market-based need for variable costing in the new competitive environment. In other words, cost accounting change in the 1950s was partly a result of the changing needs of the enterprises. Second, academic debate and large-scale consulting on the relative merits of alternative solutions played a major role in facilitating the change. Third, changes in financial accounting legislation reinforced management accounting change, making the shift from full costing to variable costing ultimately permanent.

Contemplating more broadly the state of management accounting in Finland, one might assert that the 1970s was a period marked by the following features. Academic teaching and research expanded from cost accounting to management control systems, especially responsibility accounting and performance measurement, as well as planning and control methods of capital investments. The crucial role of management accounting in management decisions was emphasized. Traditional cost accounting techniques moved backstage, to be treated as routine management accounting, as happened internationally.

Empirical surveys of large Finnish companies show that modern management accounting techniques in the areas of capital budgeting, management control, and responsibility accounting were widely accepted, and exhibited no notable divergences from wider international practices (Honko and Virtanen 1975; Honko *et al.* 1982; Virtanen 1986).

A specifically Finnish trait must here be emphasized: academic accounting knowledge effectively infiltrated the management accounting practice of Finnish companies. Because Finnish accounting professors had close contacts with major Finnish companies, novel ideas and techniques were quickly transmitted and experimented with in actual practice. In addition, academically educated accountants reached important positions in company hierarchies. Typically, the Finnish managing director works closely with the financial director, often forming the core of the top management team. Furthermore, in divisionalized companies especially, an influential controller function, at various organizational levels, has been firmly established.

Contemporary Cost Accounting Practice

Seeds of Change

Although Finnish cost accounting has remained relatively stable for well over a decade, with other management accounting concerns like responsibility accounting and performance evaluation attracting attention, some pressures on established practice have nevertheless appeared recently. First, in anticipation of entry into the European Union in 1995, Finland has started to harmonize its laws with EU directives. When the Accounting Act of 1973 was partially rewritten in 1992, its regulations on inventory valuation were also 'Europeanized': manufacturing companies with a high relative share of fixed costs are now allowed to allocate fixed purchasing and manufacturing costs to inventory values, providing that systematic cost accounting exists. Although the dominant principle of inventory valuation remains anchored to variable costs, this could have, among other consequences, considerable impact on cost accounting. Second, a number of arguments and calls have been raised in favour of activity-based costing, reflecting a variety of goals. This has clearly redrawn interest towards cost accounting problems, as seems to have happened internationally. The dilemma of allocating, allocating better, or ignoring fixed overhead costs has been making a re-entry into the Finnish accounting debate.

The basic arguments in favour of replacing old cost accounting with new cost accounting systems can be summarized as follows (see Kaplan 1983, 1984; Johnson and Kaplan 1987; Cooper 1988–9; Brimson 1991; Turney 1991). (1) Market conditions, especially global competition and the relatively high portion of fixed costs associated with the use of advanced manufacturing technologies, have created a need to analyse, allocate, and, in particular, manage fixed costs better. (2) Using several cost drivers allows better economic analysis than using single driver-based overheads. (3) Financial accounting systems, especially crude inventory valuation methods, have fostered inappropriate management accounting systems which provide inaccurate information. The list resembles the list of causes underlying the cost accounting shift in Finland in the 1950s; only now the direction of the change from full to variable costing is reversed.

In the following, we first describe what the actual cost accounting situation is in Finland. Here we rely on the results of a recent survey (data from late 1992) by Lukka and Granlund (1995). We contrast their findings with results of more recent surveys relating to emerging management accounting methods. We then summarize the main conclusions stemming from our field interviews with managers (see Appendix 1).

Survey Results on Finnish Management Accounting Practices

Finnish management accounting practices in the 1980s, in the face of the new challenges of resource consumption models like ABC, are relatively advanced and oriented towards managerial decision making. Academic teaching has emphasized the need for several cost drivers, including non-volume-based drivers (Virkkunen 1960: 121), and a division between batch- and product-level costs (Virkkunen 1951: 54–67) since the 1960s. Companies have adopted these ideas to varying degrees.

For inventory valuation purposes, variable costing has typically been used, as required by law until 1993. For managerial information needs, variable costing is widespread, although full costing has not been uprooted entirely. Companies do not typically have a plant-wide overhead rate. Classification of costs into fixed and variable is deeply entrenched in managerial discourse. A widely used cost accounting framework, embraced both in academia and in business practice, is the multi-layer contribution margin analysis (Honko 1959). For a description of contribution analysis, see Bromwich and Bhimani 1994: 116–22, which describes a more sophisticated contribution approach which subsumes capacity constraints and strategic analysis. The multi-layer contribution approach used by numerous Finnish companies is, in essence, similar to this approach.

Against this tradition, the prolific consulting industry has advocated novel cost accounting approaches. Activity-based costing (ABC) and its derivative, activity-based management (ABM) have been marketed to Finnish companies, with the same zeal as in other Western countries. Well-organized seminars and lectures have been arranged for managers and accounting professionals, repeating the argument that ABC/ABM better fits the modern industrial environment and is essential for long-term survival. Finnish accounting academics, by contrast, have for the most part chosen to retain a balanced position.

A survey study of 135 Finnish companies carried out by Lukka and Granlund (1994) investigated Finnish cost accounting practices in manufacturing companies (see Appendix 2 for details of the study). Below is a summary of their findings concerning current manufacturing technology. Batch production has a central role in Finnish manufacturing, as 67.4% of the companies in the study use this mode of production in one way or another. Life-cycles of products were often characterized as long, and were not considered to have been getting shorter in the last few years. The level of automation has increased in recent years, and this trend is expected to continue in the future. By contrast, only limited indications of changes in cost structures were observed. For example, direct labor constitutes, on average, about 20% of total costs. Just-in-time (JIT) and total quality management (TQM) philosophies are utilized by a surprisingly large number of companies, 31.9% and 15.6% respectively. Further, Lukka and Granlund report that with regard to monitoring manufacturing firms' production performance, various types of quality aspects scored highest. On cost accounting issues the survey study produced the results shown in Table 3.1.).

The survey by Lukka and Granlund also indicates that material and manufacturing overheads are usually allocated on a volume basis, but other overheads are assigned according to the total manufacturing costs of products. Also non-volume-related allocation bases, such as set-up quantity and value added, are used, although none of the companies reported having

Table 3.1. Principles, methods, calculations, and novel applications used in product costing in Finland

Product Costing Principles		Sample (%) (N=130)
Variable costing		41.5
Full costing		30.8
Variable and full costing		26.9
Other combination		0.8
Total		100
Product Costing Methods	**Frequency**	**Proportion (%)**
Process costing	41	51.4
Job-order costing	38	47.5
Both	1	1.3
Total	N=80	100
Product Cost Calculation	**Frequency**	**Proportion (%)**
Variable manufacturing cost	24	18.3
Total manufacturing cost at the average level of activity	13	9.9
Total manufacturing cost at normal level of activity	8	6.1
Total cost at the average level of activity	20	15.3
Total cost at normal level of activity	6	4.6
Variable manufacturing cost + other/others	37	28.2
Other combination	23	17.6
Total	N=131	100
Application of New Product Costing Methods		
Product costing method	**Is currently being implemented (%)**	**Is currently being considered (%)**
Activity-based costing	6.0	23.9
Value chain analysis	0	3.8
Target costing	1.5	5.2
Life-cycle costing	0.8	1.5
Other	0	0.8

Source: adapted from Lukka and Granlund 1995: 152–4, 171.

applied ABC. Standard costing, alone or with other methods, was deployed by 68.7% of the respondents.

Although new operating philosophies, especially JIT and TQM, and to a lesser extent others, including activity-based management (8.2% of the companies reported ABM applications), have been adopted by Finnish companies, so-called new accounting methods have not spread accordingly. Pure ABC, or other new cost accounting methods like target costing or life-cycle costing, had not been adopted so far. Only 5.9% of the companies reported that they were in the process of implementing ABC, while many others (23.7%) stated that they were considering the development of an ABC system.

As the data used by Lukka and Granlund dates back to 1992, we complement their results concerning modern cost accounting practices with the latest research findings. Laitinen (1995) found 11% of companies using ABC and 13% currently implementing ABC in his survey conducted in 1993. Rautajoki (1995) reported 24% of units of meal and engineering industries using, and 10% currently implementing, ABC in Finland. Malmi (1995) studied the adoption of ABC in metal and engineering industries in more detail. Based on his evidence, ABC is used in 14% of units, 8% of units are currently implementing it, and 15% are considering adopting it. Taken together, this more recent evidence clearly suggests that new cost accounting methods, and especially ABC, have raised the interest of Finnish firms (see Table 3.2). What is also intriguing is that in most units (76%) studied by Malmi the existing cost accounting system is still in use. ABC is complementing or extending it. Only 17% of units indicated that their old cost accounting system has been totally removed and replaced by an ABC system.

Table 3.2. Application of ABC in Finland.

	Lukka and Gran (N=135)	Laitinen (N=183)	Rautajoki (N=183)	Malmi (N=287)
Year of data collection	1992	1993	1994	1995
In operation (%)	0	11	24	14
Is currently being implemented (%)	6	13	10	8

Sources: Lukka and Granlund 1995; Laitinen 1995; Rautajoki 1995; Malmi 1995.

Lukka and Granlund also claim that other 'new' cost accounting methods, like target costing or life-cycle costing, have not been adopted so far. On this issue, confirming interview evidence also exists.

As regards the purposes and perceived value of cost information, companies indicated pricing decisions, product profitability analysis, tender accounting, cost reduction efforts, and budgeting as the most important. Other features characteristic of current Finnish cost accounting include the wide use of non-financial measures, the most important being delivery reliability, labour productivity, schedule attainment, and throughput times.

Interview Evidence on Finnish Cost Accounting Practices

We investigated in some detail the existing practices and future prospects of cost accounting in some leading Finnish large and medium-sized companies by way of interviews. These were conducted during autumn 1993 and spring 1994. Companies representing important industries in the Finnish economy, often facing tough international competition and together forming the country's industrial backbone, provided the present study's empirical evidence. In particular, the forest industry, metal and engineering, electronics, and the chemical industry were targeted. Further information regarding the sample is given in Appendix 2.

On the basis of the interview evidence, no substantial change towards new practices has yet occurred in Finnish cost accounting. Leading Finnish companies seem ready to explore new ideas and sometimes to try them, but it would be hasty to conclude that any permanent change has taken place.

By interviewing company controllers and accounting staff, we first gauged the actual uses of cost information. The product-mix decision was identified as providing the most significant motivation for calculating product costs. Other important uses included make-or-buy decisions and pricing. It was found that calculating costs per customer and per market segment, as well as often by specific product groups, was clearly an emerging practice. For cost reduction, cost accounting information was not found to be of critical importance.

Turning to the users of cost information, it appeared that top management in divisionalized companies was concerned mainly with divisional profits and the 'bottom line', and did not pay very much attention to product cost accounting. Attention was focused primarily upon financial accounting concerns and responsibility accounting for wider group control purposes; calculating product costs was seen as a task of specialists serving operative levels within company hierarchies. Although we should guard against drawing too definitive conclusions, it appeared also that ABC/ABM experiments, where they had been attempted, had extended the use of cost accounting information beyond the realm of accountants. Cost consciousness among, for instance, plant engineers may have increased.

In fact, many of the companies (8 out of 12) claimed to have experimented with ABC or ABM. Notably, no company-wide, comprehensive group level efforts had been launched, but smaller local initiatives had been taken within individual business units. In divisionalized companies where financial results are primarily their responsibility, managers may choose any internal cost accounting system they like.

Most of these projects, however, did not appear to us to have been successful as yet. The main problems which seemed to have inhibited a rapid, smooth implementation of ABC/ABM projects were tied to the non-availability of necessary data, the complex process of data collection, and the heavy workload involved in maintaining and updating these new systems of calculations. Also, as an interviewee pointed out, when complex systems are understood by only a handful of people, they tend to stand or fall with the fate of these key individuals. A related problem has to do with the difference between providers and users of information. As one ABC-system project leader indicated: 'We have been building an ABC system internally together with company ADP personnel for almost two years. However, it just seems to me that the prime users of product cost information, marketing personnel, are not interested in the system at all.'

But a few companies, we think, were happy with their new cost accounting odysseys. Most notably, when referring to these exercises, interviewees spoke of activity-based management rather than ABC. We interpreted this as ABM *de facto* denoting a larger managerial reorientation of the entire business. What is basically sought is a remodelling and redefinition of crucial business processes and critical activities, using the insights gained to manage the overall process of change.

Our findings further corroborated the results of Lukka and Granlund with respect to novel cost accounting techniques other than ABC/ABM in the Finnish context. No other practices, like target costing, life-cycle costing, or backflush accounting, had been tried in the companies visited.

Finally, we obtained interesting answers to the question of where interviewees thought management accounting development was heading. First, the need to produce more accurate information about product costs was recognized. Second, development projects like ABM were valued. Third, and perhaps most significant, is that the managerial need for a refocused, more flexible cost and profitability analysis along novel dimensions was often underlined: cost accounting should produce, in addition to product costs, information about customers and market segments in particular. Thus, although no dramatic changes in Finnish cost accounting are discernible, some pressures for change and development are becoming evident.

From Variable Costing to Full Costing?

From our historical analysis of the previous cost accounting shift in Finland in the 1950s, we conclude that three drivers were essential for major, permanent change: (1) a real, market-based need to change company operations; (2) an active academic debate and consultation on the relative merits of alternative solutions; (3) pressure induced by a change in the financial accounting legislation to move towards a new cost accounting system.

Currently, there is evidence of existing market-based pressures for change. Although our interviews did not provide conclusive indications, survey evidence points towards a stiffening competitive environment. Also, Finland has become a member of the European Community, and many industries, such as the food industry, now face entirely different competitive conditions (precondition 1). Extensive cost management consulting services are also available, and active academic debate takes place (precondition 2). And a harmonization of financial accounting is gaining ground in Europe (precondition 3).

Cost accounting in Finland is responsive to these forces. Managers exhibit a high degree of cost awareness, and are experimenting with new cost accounting methods. Nevertheless, it seems unlikely that these experiments will lead current practice from the marginal contribution analysis framework to systematic full costing. Instead, two trends are evident. Managers appreciate ABM and other cost management projects which lead to a better understanding of the business process and which help streamline operations. Also there seems to be a call for multidimensional, flexible cost information.

APPENDIX 1 Interview Data from Companies[a]

Group (turnover MFIM)	Unit (turnover MFIM)	Industry	Interviewee
Agfa-Gevaert Oy (182)		Distributor	Managing Director
Kone Oy (10,813)	Kone Group (10,813)	Machines & equipment	Finance Vice-President Aimo Rajahalme
	Instruments (174)		Controller Timo Helles
Kymmene Oy (16,297)	Nautor (116)	Yachts	Financial Manager Ole Sundkvist
Kyro Oy (886)	Board & Paper (546)	Paper	Financial Manager Seppo Heikkinen
Neste Oy (63,089)	Neste Chemicals (11,990)	Chemicals	Controller Marjut Virtanen
			Assistant Vice-President Päivi Pesola
Oy Nokia Ab (23,697)	Mobile Phones (6,314)	Electronics	Controller Maria Norrgran
	Telecommunications (4,578)	Telecommunications	Finance Vice-President Antti Wäre
Orion-yhtymä Oy (3,600)	Orion-Farmos & Orion Pharma International (1,854)	Pharmaceuticals	Group Vice-President Pauli Torkko
			Department Manager Harri Hagman
			Financial Planning Manager Rauni Tiainen
Rauma Oy (25,326)	Lokomo (324)	Machinery	Executive Vice-President Heikki Järvinen
			Controller Raimo Vehviläinen
Unitas Oy (14,141)	Suomen Yhdyspankki (11,609)	Banking	Manager Raimo Pesonen
Vaisala Oy (392)		Electronics	Group Controller Roger Homberg
Yhtyneet Paperitehtaat Oy[b] (16,367)	Jämsänkoski (1,500)	Paper	Finance Vice-President Jorma Mäkinen
			Controller Ari Karila

[a] Interviews were conducted during autumn 1993 and spring 1994, and all figures refer to the situation in 1993. In addition, the following individuals were interviewed: Professor Jaakko Honko; Researcher Jouko Karjalainen, Helsinki University of Technology; Partner Olli-Pekka Lumijärvi, KPMG Management Consulting; Researcher Pekka Pallasto, Helsinki University of Technology.

[b] Part of Rauma Oy.

APPENDIX 2

Survey Details

The survey was conducted by K. Lukka and M. Granlund, both from the Turku School of Economics and Business Administration. Its goal was to describe and analyse the present state and trends of development of cost accounting practices in large and middle-sized Finnish manufacturing units.

The population of the study was manufacturing firms or units with 50 or more employees. 1,082 such firms were identified, many having more than 1 such unit. A 28-page questionnaire was mailed to a random sample of 309 firms or units in December 1992. The response rate was 43.7%, and the number of units analysed was 135.

78.5% of units employed 50–249 persons, while 21.5% employed 250 or more persons. The following table illustrates the size of the units in the study:

	Mean	Median	Standard Deviation	Range
Number of employees	223	120	298	50–1977
Turnover (MFIM)	158	63	273	3–2020

The units came from the following industries (number of units in parentheses): metal products (20); food (17); electrical engineering (11); paper and pulp (10); machines and equipment (9); timber products (9); glass, pottery, and stone (9); clothes, leather products, and shoes (8); gum and plastic (8); and textiles (7). Other industries were represented by 5 or fewer units.

Most of the respondents (66.7%) represent the accounting function of the unit. The rest were unit managers (14.8%), persons from production function (9.6%), and administration managers (4.5%).

APPENDIX 3

Legislation and Regulations

Kansanhuoltoministeriön päätös teollisuustuotteiden kustannuslaskennan perusteista (Ministry of Supply's Regulation on the Cost Accounting Principles of Industrial Products), 27 June 1942.

Kansanhuoltoministeriön päätös kaupan hinnoitteluperusteista (Ministry of Supply's Regulation on the Pricing Principles of Commercial Enterprises), 12 October 1942.

Kansanuoltoministeriön päätös teollisuustuotteiden kustannuslaskennasta (Ministry of Supply's Regulation on the Cost Accounting of Industrial Products), 6 July 1943.

Kirjanpitolaki (The Accounting Act), 6 July 1945.

Kirjanpitoasetus (The Accounting Ordinance), 9 August 1945.

Kirjanpitolaki (The Accounting Act), 10 August 1973.

Kirjanpitoasetus (The Accounting Ordinance), 19 October 1973.

Kirjanpitoasetus (The Accounting Ordinance), 30 December 1992.

Laki elinkeinotulon verottamisesta (The Company Tax Act), 24 June 1968.

Notes

1. This is evident, e.g., in the cost accounts of Enso-Gutzeit Oy, a major paper and pulp producer, in its Pankakoski factory in 1932.
2. Archival documents showing product pricing calculations for this production can be found for companies like Lahti Oy's woodworks and A. Ahlström Osakeyhtiö, a leading engineering company.
3. We found more evidence supporting such claims in, e.g., Lahti Oy's archival data for 1949–51.
4. This uninterrupted practice can be traced, e.g., in Enso-Gutzeit Oy's Pankakoski plant.

References

Ahola, P. (1962), *Katetuottolaskennan perusteet* (Principles of Variable Costing) (Helsinki: Tammi).

—— (1966), 'Marginalistinen ajattelu teollisuuden laskentatoimen kehityspiirteenä maassamme' (Marginalism as a Development Feature of Finnish Accounting), in J. Honko and J. Lehtovuori (eds.), Suomalaista Liiketaloustiedettä *1966* (Finnish Business Economics 1966), (Helsinki: Wellin and Göös).

Brimson, J. A. (1991), *Activity Accounting: An Activity-Based Costing Approach* (New York: John Wiley & Sons).

Bromwich, M., and Bhimani, A. (1994), *Management Accounting: Pathways to Progress* (London: CIMA).

Carlson, C. E. (1964), 'Uuden tuotteen hinnoittelu' (Pricing New Products), *Tehostaja*, 9: 10–14.

Cooper, R. (1988*a*), 'The Rise of Activity Based Costing—Part One: What is an Activity-Based Costing System?', *Journal of Cost Management for the Manufacturing Industry*, 2 (Summer): 45–54.

—— (1988*b*), 'The Rise of Activity Based Costing—Part Two: When Do I Need Activity Based Costing System?', *Journal of Cost Management for the Manufacturing Industry*, 2 (Fall): 41–8.

—— (1988–9), 'The Rise of Activity-Based Costing—Parts One to Four', *Journal of Cost Management for the Manufacturing Industry*, 51 (Summer 1988–Spring 1989).

—— (1989*a*), 'The Rise of Activity Based Costing—Part Three: How Many Cost Drivers Do You Need, and How do You Select Them?', *Journal of Cost Management for the Manufacturing Industry*, 3 (Winter): 34–46.

—— (1989*b*), 'The Rise of Activity Based Costing—Part Four: What Do Activity-Based Cost Systems Look Like?', *Journal of Cost Management for the Manufacturing Industry*, 3 (Spring): 38–49.

Hautakangas, T. (1966), 'Realisointiperiaate käytännön laskentatyössä (The Realization Principle in Accounting Practice), in J. Honko and J. Lehtovuori (eds.), *Suomalaista Liiketaloustiedettä 1966* (Helsinki: Weilin and Göös).

Honko, J. (1955), *Koneen edullisin pitoaika ja investointilaskelmat, taloudellinen tutkimus* (The Economic Life of a Machine and Calculations Concerning the Economics of Capital Investments) (Helsinki: Helsinki Research Institute for Business Administration).

—— (1959), *Yrityksen vuositulos* (The Annual Income of an Enterprise and its Determination) (Helsinki: Helsinki Research Institute for Business Administration).

—— (1963), *Investointien suunnittelu ja tarkkailu* (The Planning and Control of Capital Investments) (Porvoo: WSOY).

—— and Virtanen, K. (1975), *The Investment Process in Finnish Industrial Enterprises. A Study of the Capital Investment Planning and Control Process in the Fifty Largest Finnish Industrial Enterprises* (Helsinki: Helsinki School of Economics).

—— Prihti, A., and Virtanen, K. (1982), *Critical Areas in the Capital Investment process of Enterprises. A Study of Success and Failure of Strategy and Capital Investments in the 30 Largest Finnish Industrial Enterprises* (Helsinki: Helsinki School of Economics).

Johnson, H. T., and Kaplan, R. S. (1987), *Relevance Lost: The Rise and Fall of Management Accounting* (Boston: Harvard Business School Press).

Kaitila, I. V. (1928), *Teollisuusliikkeen laskentatoimen perusteetosa I—omakustannuslaskenta* (Foundations of Industrial Accounting—Part I—Full Costing) (Jyväskylä: Gummerus).

Kaplan, R. S. (1983), 'Measuring Manufacturing Performance: A New Challenge for Managerial Accounting Research', *Accounting Review*, 58/4: 686–705.

Kaplan, R. S. (1984), 'The Evolution of Management Accounting', *Accounting Review*, 59/3: 390–418.

Laitinen, E. K. (1995), 'Toimintolaskennassa ongelmina', *Yritystalous*, 3: 66–9.

Lilius, A. (1862), *Käytännöllinen opastus yksinkertaisesta kirjanpidosta varsinkin tehdastelijoille ja ammattilaisille* (Practical Guide on Simple Bookkeeping for Manufacturers and Craftsmen) (Turku).

Lukka, K., and Granlund, M. (1994), 'Kustannuslaskenta Suomen teollisuudessa: nykyinen käytäntö ja kehitystrendit' (Cost Accounting of the Manufacturing

Industry in Finland: Current Practice and Trends of Development), *Finnish Journal of Business Economics*, 43/2: 142–79.

—— and Pihlanto, P. (1994), 'Martti Saario (1906–88) the Developer of Finnish Accounting Theory', in J. R. Edwards (ed.), *Twentieth-Century Accounting Thinkers* (London: Routledge).

—— Majala, R., Paasio, A., and Pihlanto, P. (1984), 'Accounting Research in Finland', in A. G. Hopwood and H. Schreuder (eds.), European Contributions to Accounting Research: The Achievements of the Last Decade, (Amsterdam: VU Vitgeverij/Free University Press).

Lumijärvi, O-P. (1993) (ed.), *Toimintojohtaminen* (Activity-Based Management) (Jyväskylä: Weilin and Göös).

Madsen, V. (1969), *Redovisningens roll i 70-talets styrsystem* (The Role of Accounting in the Control Systems of the 1970s) (Göteborg: Bonniers).

Majala, R. (1994), 'Chapter III—Finland', in J. Flowers (ed.), *The Regulation of Financial Reporting in the Nordic Countries* (Stockholm: Fritzes).

Malmi, T. (1995), 'Activity-Based Costing in Finnish Metal and Engineering Industries', unpublished working paper.

Näsi, S. (1990), *Laskenta-ajattelun kehitys viime vuosisadan puolivälistä nykypäiviin* (The Development of Accounting Thought from the Middle of the Last Century to the Present Day), Acta Universitatis Tamperensis, A291 (Vammala).

—— (1994), 'Development of Cost Accounting in Finland from the Last Century to the 1960s', *European Accounting Review*, 3: 489–514.

Rautajoki, P. (1995), 'Tuotta vuuden mittaus ja analysointi metalliteollisuudessa, Tampereen Teknillinen korkeakoulu', *Tutkimasraportteja*, 1.

Riistama, V., and Jyrkkio, E. (1971), *Operatiivinen Laskentatoimi* (Cost and Management Accounting) (Jyväskylä: Weilin and Göös).

Saario, M. (1945), *Realisointiperiaate ja käyttöomaisuuden poistot tuloslaskennassa* (Realization Principle and Depreciation in Profit Calculation (Helsinki: Helsinki Research Institute for Business Administration).

—— (1949), 'Kustannusten etuoikeusjärjestyksestä' (On the Priority Order of Costs), in *Hugo Raninen 50 vuotta* (Helsinki: Kanppatieteellinen Yhdistys (The Finnish Association of Management Research)).

—— (1959), *Kirjanpidon meno-tulo teoria* (Expenditure-Revenue Theory of Bookkeeping) (Kenruu: Otava).

Turney, P. B. B. (1991), *Common Cents: The ABC Performance Breakthrough* (Hillsboro, Ore.: Cost Technology).

Virkkunen, H. (1951), *Teollisuuden kertakustannukset, niiden degressio sekä käsittely kustannuslaskennassa* (Initial Costs for Product Types and Lots in Manufacturing as a Cause for Decreasing Unit Costs and their Treatment in Cost Accounting). (Helsinki: Helsinki Research Institute for Business Administration).

—— (1954), *Laskentatoimi johdon apuna* (*Das Rechnungswesen im Dienste der Leitung* (Accounting as a Management Tool) (Helsinki: Helsinki Research Institute for Business Administration).

—— (1960), *Teollisen kustannuslaskennan perusteet ja hyväksikäyttö I ja II* (Principles and Applications of Cost Accounting I and II) (Helsinki: Helsinki School of Economics).

Virtanen, K. (1986), 'Steuerung in finnischen divisional organisierten Unternehmen' (Management Control Practices in Finnish Divisionalized Firms), *Zeitschrift für betriebswirtschaftliche Forschung*, 6: 517–32.

4

Management Accounting Practice in France[1]

Michel Lebas

Management accounting in France is rooted in two contradictory, yet complementary, approaches: (1) a normative cost analysis approach focusing on product costing for valuation purposes and cost flow analysis and (2) an *ad hoc*, physically based, information-for-decision-making approach called the *Tableau de Bord*.

French management accounting practice is different from what is found in most national traditions in the field. France's originality lies in having an almost universally accepted single 'system' of cost analysis and product costing, applicable to all industrial and trade sectors, both for profit and not for profit.[2] The current version of this system is described[3] in a decree of the Ministry of Finance and Economy published as Title III of the 1982 *Plan Comptable Général*. Previous versions of the system have been developed by industry professionals into an official industry-specific chart of accounts and costing plans for over 20 industries. Other industries have developed unofficial plans. Each of these plans is a variant of the basic system 'customized' to fit the specific needs of each industry.

Unlike the situation in the United States or the United Kingdom, where only industries dealing with the government need to follow certain rules for product cost calculation, the French approach, in a spirit of facilitating 'fair' competition, applies to all industries, whether or not they have dealings with any state agency. The basic system of costing will be described in the second section of the chapter. The first section will review some of the historical background related to the separation of financial and management accounting in France.

Further to the costing system mentioned above, almost all French businesses use a *Tableau de Bord* approach for their management reporting and performance evaluation needs. As we will see in the third section, the *Tableau de Bord* is, in its very principle, unconnected to the costing system. It emphasizes physical information in so far as these are anticipatory measures of upcoming cost and accounting data. It uses graphic designs and presentations to inform management—in a very compact, condensed, dynamic format—about the key issues the firm faces and some diagnostic measures relating to the ability of the firm to achieve its objectives.

The fourth section will show that the two currents on which management accounting practice is grounded in France can be combined in a single approach which is not far removed from the concepts behind activity-based management.

Introduction: The Background

A Little History

The period between the two world wars was extremely fertile in France.[4] In terms of reflections pertinent to management accounting, the main issues were monism, full or partial costing, joint cost apportionment, inventory valuation (as opposed to costing for decision making), and choice of bases for asset depreciation.

Then, as now, there was no organization officially representing management accountants in France, unlike the highly organized management or cost accounting institutes found, e.g., in Australia, India, the United Kingdom, and the United States. The debates on accounting issues took place as much within industrial engineering associations as within the (mostly financial) accounting community. This phenomenon may explain in large part the existence of two different approaches to the concept of management accounting information. The industrial engineering associations were active in the scientific management movement. Their reflection took place essentially under the auspices of the CEGOS (Commission Générale d'Organisation Scientifique), organized by a federation of businesses. The notion of product cost became especially important during the world economic crisis of 1929–37 as many of the rules of trade changed. Protectionism, government price setting, exacerbated competition, etc., created the need for a common method of costing so that fair competition could help businesses grow or stay alive and thus help reduce unemployment.

At the time, the domain of management accounting was referred to by most in the industrial engineering community as 'Comptabilité de Rendement', i.e. yield accounting or productivity accounting. Its purpose was, explicitly, to provide the rationale for the creation of economic value by businesses and to assist in finding ways to save money and increase profitability. At the same time, it largely required that everyone use similar rules so as to avoid predatory costing[5] which ultimately proves detrimental to all.

Because of the emergency created by the 1929 Great Depression and the need to implement cost analysis systems rapidly, without having to rethink the whole accounting process, management accounting was created alongside the pre-existing financial accounting system. Thus, French management accounting and financial accounting were explicitly separated in the late

1930s. The principle of their ultimate connection has never been challenged, however. A single economic event may be treated differently in each accounting system, but it remains the same event, and the final results must be reconcilable. While financial accounting emphasized (and still does to a great extent) the impact on the patrimony or estate of the firm, management accounting focused on the identification of cost flows and the construction of product costs, rather than the wealth creation process (as it attempts to do now).

The Modern Period

Although the basic management accounting system in France has remained virtually unchallenged and unchanged since the publication in 1937 of the *Méthode des sections homogènes ou des tableaux de répartition* by CEGOS,[6] the relationship between financial and management accounting has been refined with the successive General Charts of Accounts and with the needs of the economy. The current recommendation is to use 'mirror' accounts to capture financial accounting events in the cost analysis system, thus officially creating a costing system which is seen by many as subordinated to the financial accounting system, although the intent was essentially that an economic event be captured once and only once. Cost information mainly explains *ex post* how wealth was created. However the current *Plan Comptable* authorizes—and provides a chart of accounts that supports—the use of anticipatory cost measures in budgeting and standard costing.

The Essential Role of Government in French Accounting

French management accounting operates in an environment where state interventionism is strong, where about one-third of the economy is state-owned or state-directed (since 1945), and where 'spending budgets' (as opposed to profit budgets) are often a way of life in a management culture that has long operated in a protectionist environment. The privatizations of 1986–8 and those that have taken place since late 1993, as well as the less regulated business environment created by the successful development of the European Union after the ratification of the Treaty of Maastricht, offer challenges to past traditions of costing and performance reporting. The French costing tradition should be able to weather these 'storms', since its descriptive representation of the firm is universal and does not depend on the political or economic context.

The seminal work on modern France accounting was performed by the Commission interministérielle de normalisation des comptabilités, a semi-governmental body created in 1945. Its work led to the 1947 first French General Chart of Accounts. This was later revised in 1957 and 1982. All modifications are studied and promulgated by the Conseil National de la

Comptabilité, which operates under the auspices of the French Ministry of Finance and Economy. The main emphasis of the *Plan Comptable* is financial accounting. A management accounting section appeared in the official document only in the 1982 revision, and remains 'optional and indicative'.[7]

The French economy emerged only about 20 years ago from an environment of regulated 'market' prices. The emphasis of management accounting had been, since the Second World War, on determining the full cost of products, on which to base the negotiation of a selling price with the supervisory governmental authority. This approach was logical until the early 1970s, since, until then, demand had exceeded supply, and production capacity was used in full. The second half of the 1970s saw the beginning of an era in which production capacity regularly exceeded demand. Full costing had been strongly challenged in the late 1960s by the introduction of direct or variable costing,[8] but the current management mentality still strongly favours full costing. The 'cultural revolution' represented by the simultaneous acceptance of both full and variable costing, depending on the nature of the decision to be assessed, has not run its full course yet. Activity-based costing is undoubtedly an opportunity to reopen the debate about causality of costs, and constitutes a real challenge to the mind-set of French managers.

In the 1960s a very large number of future senior managers or future academics were trained in business schools in the United States. They brought back with them the new concepts of the basic missions of the management accountant as defined by Gordon Shillinglaw[9] and Charles Horngren[10] in their first textbooks, which were popularizing William Vatter's concept of relevant costing.[11] In France, although André Cibert had been teaching these concepts since the late 1950s, largely in his course at the École des Hautes Études Commerciales, his ideas remained confidential, despite a first publication in 1964,[12] until his very influential *Comptabilité Analytique* was published in 1968.[13] Relevant costing meant a departure from product costing for price setting and valuation. It also meant that decision-making support was a central element of the mission of the management accountant. From then on, a schism appeared in the profession between those close to decision making who favoured management accounting for decision making, thus finding a high degree of convergence with the *Tableau de Bord* orientation, and those whose number is dwindling (due only to retirement), who hang on to the importance of costing as an end in itself. Thus, so far, any official document is a diplomatic compromise between the two orientations: e.g., the *Plan Comptable* in its Title III emphasizes costing as the purpose of *analytical accounting* (the equivalent of cost accounting) while simultaneously suggesting (see next main section below), albeit timidly, that the accounting data thus produced be used also for decision making and performance evaluation.

The Conceptual Foundations of French Management Accounting

French management accounting is rooted in two contradictory yet complementary traditions:

1. A tradition of government intervention leading to a compulsory chart of accounts, applicable to all businesses since 1947, which is a long-established, universally accepted method of cost calculation with a double emphasis (1) on costing for inventory valuation (historical full costing) and (2) on 'fuller' costing as a basis for pricing (including many 'supplemental costs' such as cost of capital, risk, R&D, warranty, contingency-allowances, etc.) in a cost-plus pricing approach. Resource allocation (or capital budgeting) and the effects of management accounting on financial markets are completely outside the sphere of interest of accountants.
2. A tradition of engineers occupying leadership positions in industry and management of businesses, not just in the manufacturing area but also in finance, banking, services, and general management. Today, around 50% of chief executive officers (*présidents-directeurs-généraux* and *directeurs généraux*) in France are engineers by training. Unlike many traditional accountants, industrial engineers view the firm as a dynamic system. Their priority is decision making. They need information that is as real-time as possible and that reports on the system's ability to produce positive results in the future. These managers tend to see accounting almost exclusively as an accessory, a price to pay to placate some stakeholders (tax authorities, lenders, investors protected by minimal legal disclosure obligations, labour unions), not as the main source of data on which to base decisions.

Two major components of French management accounting emerged from these two traditions:

1. The *méthode des sections homogènes*,[14] the standardized cost flow approach to process and product costing, was 'invented' and implemented by the CEGOS (as early as 1927, and officially published in 1937). Its purpose was to provide a standardized approach to costing in order to allow firms to compete better through the use of similar costing methods.
2. The *Tableau de Bord* emerged from the engineers' needs for information regarding *pilotage*, or steering of business. It focused on monitoring physical and financial indicators to assess and anticipate performance. The *Tableau de Bord* constitutes a coherent set of selective ascending and descending (and lateral) information that feeds the three levels of management (strategy, management, operations).

The *Méthode des sections homogènes*: A Structured Cost Analysis Framework

Purposes

'Comptabilité analytique d'exploitation' has been the traditional French term for cost accounting since 1945; it literally means 'analytical business accounting'. Definitions of the concepts is uses are provided in the 1982 *Plan Comptable*. The purposes of the system mainly concern costing, but as the list below shows, there are many openings for management accounting, i.e. decision-oriented accounting.

The purposes of the *comptabilité analytique* are

on the one hand,
—to identify the cost of the various functions performed by the enterprise;
—to provide a basis for the valuation of certain elements on the balance sheet;
—to explain the economic result (income) by calculating costs of products (goods and services) and comparing them to corresponding selling prices;
on the other hand,
—to forecast the various costs and incomes (standard cost and budgets, e.g.);
—to identify and explain variances between forecasts and actuals (cost control and budget control, e.g.);
and,
—in a general fashion, to provide all the information which could facilitate decision making.
In order to achieve these purposes, the analytical business accounting system must be strictly adapted to the organizational structure of the firm and to the specific business it is involved in.

Characteristics of Costs

According to the *Plan Comptable*, all costs can be described by a position along three axes: domain of application, content, and time at which the cost is calculated. Thus the costs can be historical or forecasted (time axis), relevant to a product, an activity or process or function (field of application axis), and full or partial costs (content axis).

Figure 4.1, translated from the *Plan Comptable*, illustrates the conceptual description of costs, which is very open and can accommodate, theoretically if not culturally, modern visions of the firm as a constellation (or a chain) of value-creating processes or a network of activities, as well as the traditional standard or historical costing.

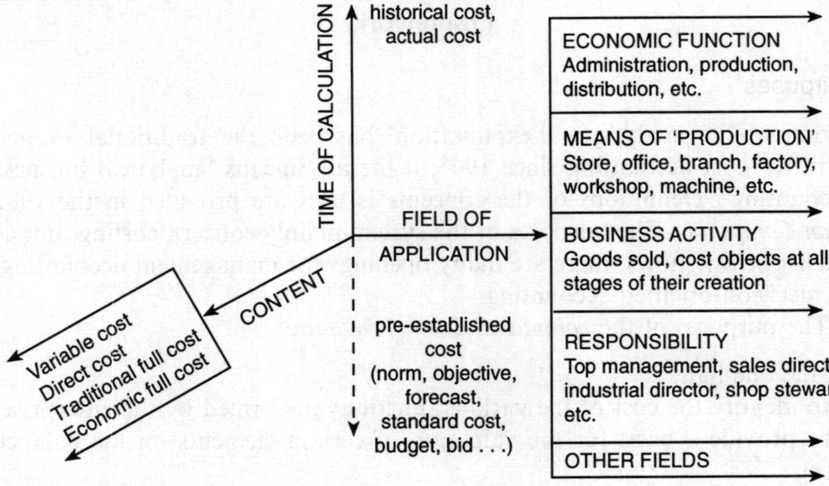

Fig. 4.1. The cost characteristics as described in the 1982 Plan Comptable Général

Framework for (Cost) Analysis (*réseau d'analyse*)

This method is a direct adaptation of the *méthode des sections homogènes* developed and promoted by the CEGOS as early as 1927. Its name is still commonly used to describe the framework of cost analysis. The method is structured around *centres d'analyse*, or 'centres for analysis' (the French traditional term is *section*, and the term 'responsibility centre' is also frequently used). Such a centre is *de facto* a cost pool. It generally maps on to a responsibility centre; however, it is defined not on the basis of the responsibility itself but on the basis of the output (*œuvre*) of the centre. Such an identity between cost pools and responsibility centres makes the French cost-analysis procedure totally consistent with the needs of budgetary control. Nevertheless, such a link is often under-utilized.

By construction, the *méthode* requires that a centre for analysis be described by one and only one unit of measurement of its service or output (*unité d'œuvre*). The 'activity' of the centre is 'homogeneous' in terms of that unit of measurement. If a centre for analysis provides several outputs, it should either be broken down into finer *sections*, or the most relevant service unit should be retained as the descriptor, or 'output driver'. Commonsense limits to the fineness of the breakdown are imposed by information processing costs (and by relevance to decision making—essentially in a responsibility accounting logic). The *Plan Comptable Général* does not impose any constraint on the fineness or coarseness of the division into sections beyond the simple separation of the basic activities or functions such as purchasing, manufacturing, selling, and administering. However, most firms use a division which matches their budget responsibility structure quite closely, so as to be able to use the cost analysis information in the budget control process.

A major difference between this approach and the ABC approach is that the primary division of the firm is vertical, i.e. functional or organizational, not horizontal or transfunctional. Centres which may be described by the same unit of output will not be regrouped or consolidated (their responsibilities are different). Although the centres are not cross-functional in the description provided by the *Plan Comptable*, nothing therein prevents the system designer from defining the centres as *sections* of a value chain. The sum of all the centres actually describes the process of providing value to the customer, simply reflecting in the traditional French approach a mental representation of the firm that differs from the one currently used in the ABC/ABM approaches. However, there is no emphasis on the concept of value creation for the customer (the concept of value that dominates is that of value for the owners), and there is no built-in challenge to the existing process of value creation.

The centres form a network[15] within which costs flow and are attached to cost objects (organizational or product-based, intermediate or final) as they consume the service provided by each centre. The cost network is a description of consumption patterns, not of causality patterns, as would be the case in an ABC approach.

The Cost Flow within the 'Network for Analysis'

While French financial accounting looks at *charges* (i.e. cost) by nature of expenses, French management accounting looks at them by *destination*, i.e. by the purpose for which they are incurred. The destinations are either products and services (in the case of direct costs) or *sections* or responsibility centres (in the case of all indirect costs). The network for analysis is the process of cost attachment which will, in a two-stage process, lead to all cost being traced to the income statement at some point, either through the valuation of products or services manufactured and then sold, or through direct attachment to the periodic income statement.

In the first stage, all *charges* have been attached either to a cost object or to a centre for analysis, the latter being analysed in terms of their physical output (*œuvre*). The resources a centre consumes are presumed to be consumed in order to produce that output. The users of the output should therefore be 'billed' for the quantity of *œuvre* they consume. The output is measured by a (unique to this centre) 'unit of service', or *unité d'œuvre*. The latter is almost always expressed in physical units, such as machine hours, man hours, mass of materials handled, number of manipulations, etc. The cost of that unit of service is the amount that will be 'billed' to the 'user' each time it consumes (or enjoys the benefits of) a unit of service. The system, in its second stage, emphasizes cost reduction through reduction of consumption of physical units of service, which each manager has control over.

All centres for analysis (or *sections*) are classified in terms of who the beneficiaries of their *œuvre* are: If the users of the output are other centres for analysis, the centre is called a *section auxiliaire*, or secondary cost pool, or secondary centre for analysis. The term 'secondary' refers mainly to the fact that the service rendered by such a responsibility centre is related to the end-product or customer in the second degree only, and that a second stage of attachment will be required before the costs can be finally attached to the end-product. The costs of such a secondary cost pool will therefore be first allocated to the 'principal' centres[16] (the consumers) before being eventually attached to cost objects by way of the *unité d''œuvre* of the *sections principales* in which they were 'poured' (*déversées*). If the users of the output are cost objects that will eventually be sold, the centre is called a *section principale*, or primary cost pool. The cost accumulated in the primary cost pool will be attached to the cost objects proportionately to their usage of the *œuvre*.

The two major characteristics of this French cost flow method are:

1. It strongly recommends the use of physical units for the allocation of overhead, i.e. costs accumulated in a primary or secondary cost pool. Burden rates based on percentages of other costs are allowed when no other alternative exists and when they represent an 'acceptable' solution.
2. It is completely compatible with both variable and full costing, as well as with budgeting by responsibility centre and with standard costing. The costs that 'flow' through the network for analysis (i.e. from centre to centre, mirroring physical flows) can either be all the costs (full costing) or only the variable costs (variable costing, while the fixed or period costs go directly to the income statement) or standard costs (standard costing). Illustrations in Boxes 2 and 3 show that current practice does not always follow the official recommendations exactly.

Given that the framework of analysis must be adapted for each type of business, the CNC (Conseil National de la Comptabilité, the official accounting standard-setting body, part of the Ministry of Finance and Economy) has asked that each industrial sector define a 'basic', or minimum, cost analysis framework tailored to its activities or process. This cost analysis framework is to be incorporated in the industry-specific standard financial accounting chart of accounts. Between 1957 and the mid-1970s, some 22 industry-specific analytical charts of accounts have been developed by representative professions of these sectors. They represent 'ready-made' management accounting charts of accounts for each major French industry. The management accounting part of these charts of accounts is not compulsory, but is generally followed, as it represents minimal sound practices which facilitate competitiveness. The charts of accounts for those industries whose main line of business requires government contracts, such as telecommunications, aviation and aerospace, electronics and defence, are used by government agencies as the reference for cost audits. They are *de facto* compulsory.

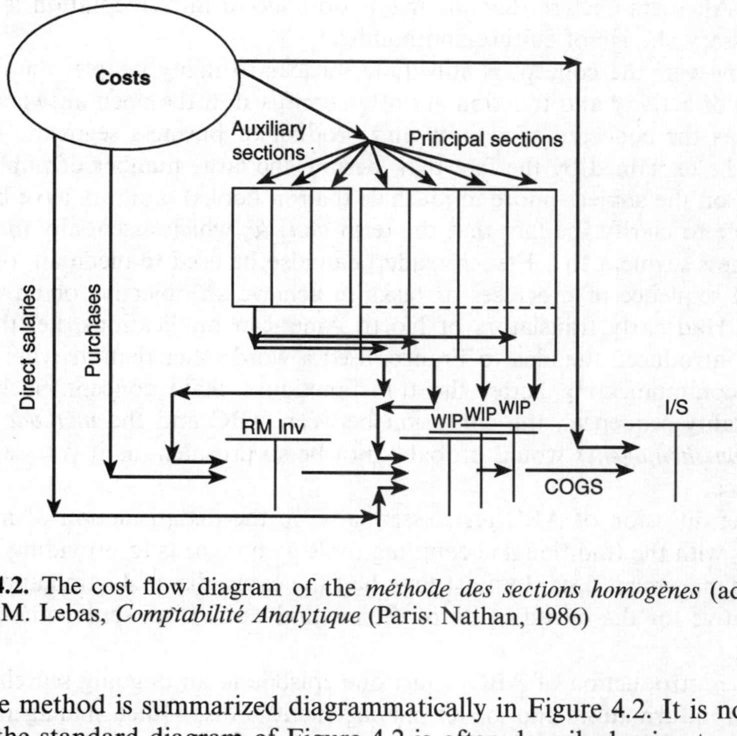

Fig. 4.2. The cost flow diagram of the *méthode des sections homogènes* (adapted from M. Lebas, *Comptabilité Analytique* (Paris: Nathan, 1986)

The method is summarized diagrammatically in Figure 4.2. It is notable that the standard diagram of Figure 4.2 is often described using terminology borrowed from hydraulic engineering: costs 'flow' and are 'poured' (*déversés*) from one cost pool to another, in a 'network' (*réseau d'analyse*) until they are matched with sales proceeds. The system is essentially dynamic and descriptive. It can be adapted to the needs and the strategy of the firm without any conceptual problem, since there are no constraints on which cost pools are created or which units of service are used to transfer costs between cost pools.

The system implied by the method can accommodate ABC approaches without any problem, since the cost pools can be redefined as transverse to the responsibility centres. The problem of the introduction of ABC in France is mainly one of changing the state of mind and the expectations of managers, not one of having the technical tools to handle the cost flows.

Box 1 presents the results of a survey on the introduction of ABC in French firms.

Box 1. Perception and diffusion of ABC in France

The survey shows that the term 'ABC' is rather well known by firms in the sample, 82% of respondents acknowledging knowledge about ABC, and 33% declaring use of some form of ABC in their accounting, of which 38% consider their ABC accounting as their main accounting system. All users declare that the major obstacle to implementation is the necessary change of culture and mind-set.

However, the concept is still quite unclear to many people: the concepts of activity and function are often confused in the open answers, as well as the concepts of activity and product or business segment. This may be explained by the fact that, despite the large number of publications on the subject (more in journals than in books), authors have been unable to clarify the fact that the term *activité*, which essentially means business segment to a French reader, can also be used to mean an 'organized sequence of processes or tasks to achieve an objective or an output'. Had early translators of North American publications, i.e. those who introduced the idea to France, used a word other than *activité*, e.g. one communicating better the transfunctional chain concept, such as 'causality sequence', the confusion between ABC and the *méthode des sections homogènes* would probably not be so prevalent as it is today in France.

The diffusion of ABC rests essentially on the dissatisfaction of managers with the traditional accounting tools with regards to providing useful management data. In most than half the cases, dissatisfaction and the initiative for the introduction of the method came from senior management.

The introduction of ABC is just one episode in an ongoing search for better information and better management tools. Other management innovations that have preceded ABC are, in decreasing order of frequency, according to the respondents: process management, business process re-engineering, life-cycle management, integrated logistics, target costing, total quality, and value analysis.

ABC is not diffused evenly throughout all industrial sectors: 100% of the respondents in the computer and information technology field had introduced ABC, and 80% of the responding firms in the health field had also done so; but only 15% of respondents in the automotive component or the construction industries had introduced ABC, and only 8% of service businesses claimed to have introduced an ABC-type approach.

ABC remains mainly the prerogative of medium to large organizations: 93% of the responding firms which have introduced ABC have sales of over 2 billion French francs.

Responding firms do not see ABC so much as a way of getting better costs (a goal for only 46% of the firms) as a way to understand and design better process through a strategically carried activity analysis (the goal for 77% of respondents).

ABC, as it is used today in France, remains essentially a strategic, motivational tool, not so much a costing tool. A similar conclusion was found by P.-L. Bescos and C. Mendoza in their book *Management de la performance* (Paris: Éditions Comptables Malesherbes, 1994), which relates in-depth case analyses of the introduction and use of ABC in 4 French firms.

Adapted from the unpublished results of a questionnaire survey of a sample of 70 French firms (70 respondents out of a target sample of 400) carried out by Eurogroup Consultants in the first half of 1994.

Current practice tends to follow quite accurately the canons of the *méthode des sections homogènes* for all strictly industrial and commercial activities, but application of the method to the handling of headquarters overhead and to the costing of interdepartmental transfers knows many variations on the theme, as can be seen in Boxes 2 and 3.

Box 2. Allocation of Headquarters Overhead to the Various Units and Management: Accounting Practices in 7 Large French Industrial Groups in 1992

The seven industrial groups participating in the study are representative of the diversity and communality of current accounting practice in large groups. Following the *Méthode des sections homogènes* approach, they consider they have essentially adopted a causality approach for the allocation of all operational costs: cost are attached to the cost object (product, service, or department) that gives rise to the existence of the cost, thus merging, as is traditional in French accounting practice, causality and output of a *section*. They all display a pro-active cost management approach, with a clear objective of cost reduction, especially of headquarters costs (one representative industrial group has the stated objective of reducing headquarters costs by more than 50% over 3 years without losing profitability, i.e. without passing on the 'eliminated' costs to captive subsidiaries whose profitability would thus be impaired).

(1) *Allocation of overhead practice*

The joint management costs (i.e. headquarters overhead costs) are difficult to trace to any specific unit or cause, however. The amount considered to be impossible to trace varies between 2 and 3% of total costs, with a third to a half of these overheads being basic or strategic R&D costs. The firms in the sample use a diversity of methods, which can be described as belonging to three possible families of ways of handling the problem of 'allocation'. These three possibilities are:

(a) No allocation to the units, with headquarters overhead then being covered by the 'dividends' paid by the various responsibility centres (real dividends in the case of subsidiaries, notional in the case of other responsibility centres) or absorbed by the operating profit of the parent if the parent is not a holding company.
(b) Allocation of the headquarters cost on the basis of a flat fee, or 'business tax'. The basis for this tax can be a function of sales, of added value, or strictly *ad hoc* as a function of strategic decisions. In the latter case, e.g., one of the firms charges R&D overhead costs (i.e. the costs remaining after the contractual research costs have been billed to the various buyers) inversely proportionally to the amount of contracted research ordered by the various units, as a way to encourage each unit to initiate research projects.
(c) 'Allocation' of overhead on the basis of some service (or combination of services) rendered by headquarters to the units. This means billing the various units for services at an arbitrary cost per unit (the amount of the unit arbitrary cost has, in all cases, been determined in the budget preparation period).

Figure 4.3 shows how the seven firms are positioned on the continuum of possibilities. Firm A did not treat all subsidiaries in the same way. Foreign subsidiaries were treated as shown by A2 while all domestic subsidiaries were treated as shown by A1. Firm C used a 'tax' approach for some subsidiaries and an allocation approach for others. This is recorded on Figure 2.1 as C1 and C2. The data show that 2.5 out of the 7 firms do not allocate their untraceable headquarters costs. Of the others, the equivalent of 2 use an internal 'tax' approach, while the remaining 2.5 use an allocation approach.

(2) *Accounting policies*

All 7 firms use a full-cost approach, but only 2 out of the 7 calculate a full cost per product sold including all costs of the firm. One of these two firms does not use this full cost for valuation purposes, but calculates it only once a year for strategic decision-making regarding pricing and product launch/abandonment decisions. All others limit their full costing to a product family in a given market, and use the full cost essentially for strategic and motivational purposes.

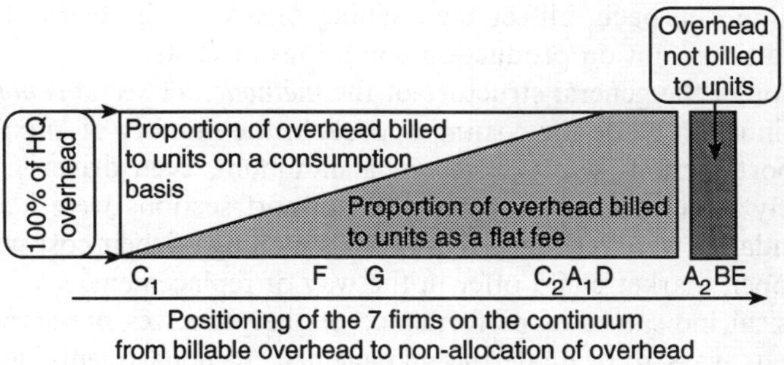

Fig. 4.3. The diversity of methods used for the attachment of headquarters overhead to the various units in a group

In their calculations, 6 out of the 7 firms fully absorb supplemental costs such as cost of capital, and do not consider that the absorbed costs and the financial accounting costs should necessarily be equal, since they do not answer to the same needs. The persons interviewed declared that motivational relevance is more important than economic or accounting accuracy. All declared that full costing is a way to direct the attention of the managers to the fact that they induce costs outside their own domain of responsibility, and that, in a cost management approach, every one must contribute to cost reduction, wherever it takes place.

Excerpted and adapted from Michel Lebas, 'Répartition des frais généraux dans sept groupes industriels français', *Revue Française de Comptabilité*, 252 (Jan. 1994): 51–8.

Box 3. Practices of 9 French Industrial Groups with regard to Interdepartmental Cost Transfers

The 9 industrial groups are 6 of those interviewed in the survey reported in Box 2 plus 3 more. They are representative of current practice and current interrogations in high tech and capital-intensive industrial groups. This survey, carried out in spring 1994, focused on the costing of interdepartmental transfers, within and between plants.

All groups interviewed were involved in intense cost management with the intention of cutting costs by significant amounts. Costing of flows between departments was found to be changing rapidly:

1. Costs tend to be traced as much as possible to the responsibility centre which gave rise to them. Extreme pressure was brought to bear on managers to treat costs as direct, variable, and controllable.
2. Product costs were no longer used to help determine selling price. Although only 3 of the firms interviewed explicitly used a target

costing approach, all set their selling prices on the basis of market conditions, not on production conditions or costs.

3. Although the general structure of the *méthode des sections homogènes* continues to guide the costing approach, the number of 'auxiliary' or support sections was reduced to a minimum, even driven out completely in certain cases. Where the support sections were kept, their boundaries were redefined to allow a matching of their cost with what the open market could offer in the way of replacement.
4. Physical indicators of performance of the processes pre-empted cost data as ways to evaluate the management of departments. Managers were held responsible not so much for total costs or unit costs but for creating continuing improvement in physical indicators which can be seen as drivers of costs and drivers of customer satisfaction.
5. Although physical indicators of output per service were available, overhead tended to be allocated on the basis of the economic added value at each stage, i.e. there was a regression towards an allocation of indirect costs as a proportion of other costs, which means a divergence from the recommended practice. Arguments for this practice run along the lines of simplicity and redundancy: 'physical indicators have already been used to manage the processes; there is no need to use the same information for costing since costing is not used for management.'
6. Costing has been so devalued that more than half the firms used market-based cost estimations to value the transfers, so as not to penalize the end-product cost. The rationale behind this view is that if department costs are higher than the market would allow, there is no need to penalize other, downstream departments. The task of management then becomes that of making sure that all departments, even though they may be mere cost centres, are market-competitive. Benchmarking is used extensively.
7. Costs transferred between departments are seen mainly as a way to exercise pressure on management to increase productivity and efficiency.
8. Two of the 9 firms have introduced, or are introducing, a separation between costs of capacity, which are transferred as a flat fee, and the cost of operating the capacity, which is transferred as a cost proportional to usage, based on a pre-agreed, very tight rate.
9. Each department used to have a budget and a summary account against the budget. The evolution is clearly, in all groups interviewed, towards keeping the cost budgets and the summary accounts at a more aggregate level.

The cost management approach was well developed in all the firms studied, and management accounting tended to be an integral component of the management process, not just a provider of (sometimes useful) data.

The *Tableau de Bord*: An Information System for Monitoring and Managing Performance

Unlike the cost analysis system described above, which was developed by 'official' discussion groups with clear objectives in mind,[17] the *Tableau de Bord* has only been theorized *ex post*.[18] Its practice emerged and evolved over time to meet the operational needs of managers. The *Tableau de Bord* is now established as a coherent concept which firms implement effectively, although few have completely succeeded in developing all aspects of the theoretical 'pure' model of *Tableau de Bord* found in the literature.[19]

The term *Tableau de Bord* literally means 'dashboard' of a car or 'instrument panel' of a machine or a vehicle. It represents the set of selected indicators that allow the manager or the engineer (or the pilot or the 'driver' of the machine or business) to successfully 'operate' the physical and human assets that are his or her responsibility, in order to fulfill the mission of the responsibility centre on an ongoing basis.

The *Tableau de Bord* is based on a representation or model of the organization as a system and of the relations of that system with its surrounding environment (some elements of that environment can be managed by the firm, while for others the firm can only be reactive) such as that illustrated in Figure 4.4. The basic hypothesis on which this information system is built is that managers need to monitor only variables about the status of the key parts of the system, including the outside of the system, such as competition, evolution of demand and tastes, technological innovations, etc.

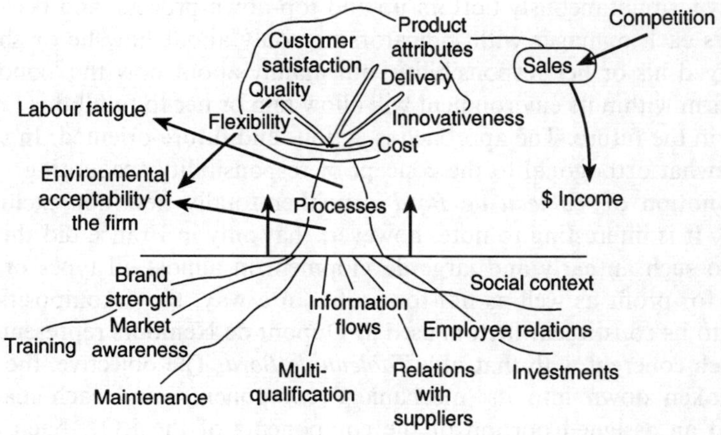

Fig. 4.4. The performance causal model (adapted from an idea of Douglas McBeth, UK Management Accounting Research Group Annual Meeting, London School of Economics, London, April 1993)

(since there may be different key—pro-active as well as reactive—variables for different managers and different time horizons, there will generally be several *Tableaux de Bord* reports for a business). These variables that need to be measured relate to action variables (or *leviers d'action*, i.e. action 'levers'), and facilitate or guide decision making in piloting the business or the responsibility centre.

The *Tableau de Bord* approach is not limited to the set of reports that are completed and transmitted to and between managers; it also encompasses the process through which the causal model is agreed upon (and committed to) and the action variables selected, and the indicators[20] identified to describe their status. It also includes the process of continuously challenging the relevance of the choices made, so as to be as much in line with the current situation of the firm as possible. The description of the firm and its representation by a set of key variables and the associated measures make the *Tableau de Bord* a device for the deployment and implementation of strategy.

The variables are allocated between managers in a systemic and co-ordinated way (allowing for co-responsibility on as many variables as is felt necessary by top management). The decisions and actions taken by each manager will allow the whole organization to reach (or not reach) its assigned or chosen objective. The indicators used to represent concretely the variable(s) must make visible the impact of the action selected on the objective. In the process of developing a *Tableau de Bord*, it is always the managers who define, in co-operation with senior management and with the management controller, the actual indicators (and their associated frequency and method of documentation) that will be used to describe the state of each key variable.

Thus, the *Tableau de Bord* approach is important both because it is a co-operative, simultaneously bottom-up and top-down process, and because it provides each manager with indicators not only about how he or she has discharged his or her responsibility, but mainly about how the 'condition' of the firm within its environment will allow him or her to fulfill this responsibility in the future. The approach is action- and future-oriented. In this, it is somewhat orthogonal to the concept of responsibility accounting.

The notion of *Tableau de Bord* is neither totally new nor exclusively French. It is interesting to note, however, that only in France did this tool undergo such an early and large development in almost all types of businesses, for-profit as well as not-for-profit. In a way, the decomposition of ROI into its constituent factors used at Dupont de Nemours represented an approach coherent with that of a *Tableau de Bord*. The objective, the ROI, was broken down into its 'mechanical' components, and each manager received an assigned portion of the components of the ROI. Each could determine easily whether the action considered would improve the ROI. The overall objective was achieved through the co-ordination that derived from the decision-tree-like approach.

In the same vein, but outside the financial model of performance, Ishikawa-type diagrams of causality ('herring-bone' diagram) are also totally coherent with the notion of *Tableau de Bord*, in that such diagrams offer models of causality, and indicate areas where action is most likely to effect positive results. For example, the diagram shown in Figure 4.5 indicates the various action variables which the manager has identified as having an impact on customer satisfaction. He or she will then need to choose those variables that are critical and define indicators of the status of these variables, so as to decide what to do to create overall success for the business.

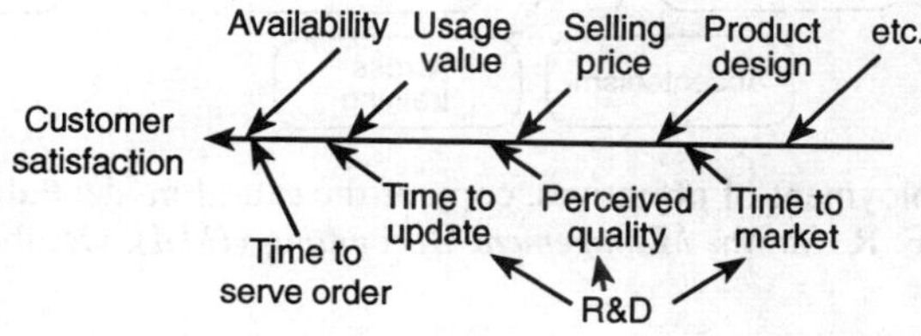

Fig. 4.5. An illustration of the components of customer satisfaction that need to be managed to guarantee performance of the organization (if customer satisfaction has been identified as one important component of performance)

Another version of a causal diagram and the associated indicators can be seen in Figure 4.6, which shows how one firm has deployed its strategy and the responsibilities for its successful implementation. Clearly each box will need to be documented with appropriate indicators to create a system of *Tableau de Bord*, but the basis is already present for the approach described here.

The most important element in this system of information for 'piloting' the organization is that the critical variables of success (or key success factors) be identified and that they be measured as soon as possible by physical indicators or measures. The report(s) constituting the *Tableau de Bord* can have short-, medium- or long-term components, since the business critical action areas (and therefore the critical variables) may require that decisions be made for several different time horizons. Essentially, one can say that there is a *Tableau de Bord* only if the data in the reports are relevant for future-oriented actions and if the report content is flexible in its approach and listed indicators: it must provide the minimum set of information needed by managers at any point in time.

Because it is destined to facilitate the work of managers, the *Tableau de Bord* is essentially visual and limited in its complexity. It does not give a major place to accounting-based information (which tends to be mostly

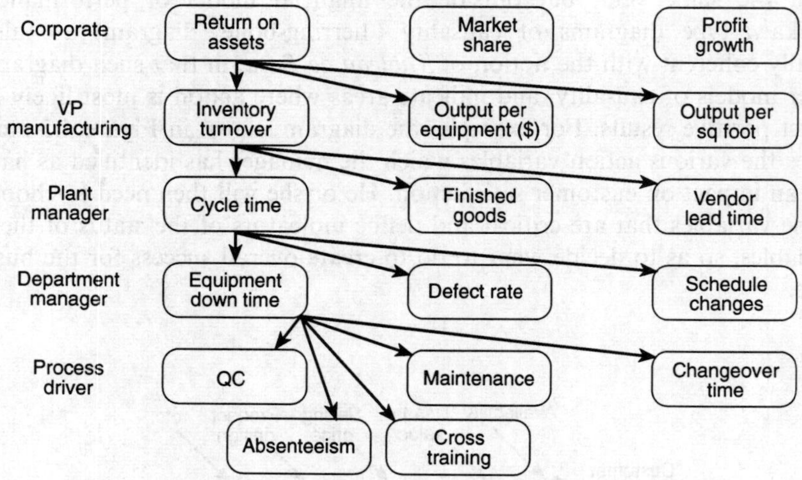

Fig. 4.6. The deployment of objectives, copy of the causal model (adapted from M. E. Beischel and F. R. Smith, *Management Accounting* (*IMA*), October 1991)

responsibility accounting-based). Physical information is considered to be anticipatory and a better base for decision making. The *Tableau de Bord* thus largely relies on physical indicators, as, for example, in Figure 4.7. However, all decisions have economic consequences, and the *Tableau de Bord* will also include—generally for information purposes, but also for decision purposes at higher levels in the hierarchy—synthetic accounting-type data in order to validate the decisions made previously and evaluate their consequences.

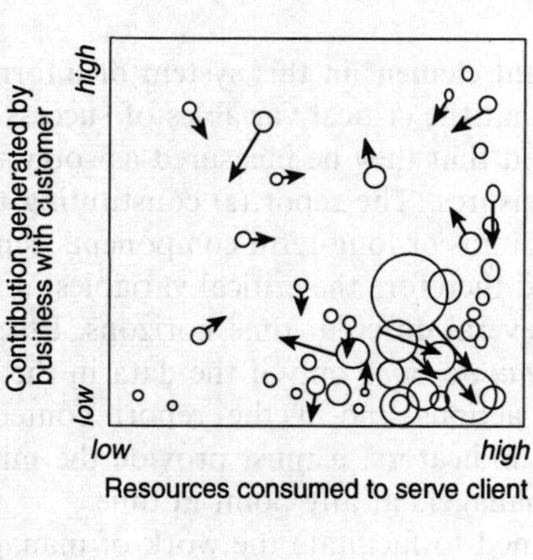

Fig. 4.7. An illustration of an indicator of the status of the customer portfolio in terms of real profitability

In Figure 4.7 each customer is mapped according to two axes, amount of resources consumed and amount of contribution generated. Each customer's relative volume is represented by the diameter of the circle used to describe its position. The arrows point at the evolution of the position of each customer since the last time the firm checked. The diagram could even be used to show whether the size of the customer's business with the firm is growing or shrinking. Such a diagram, without any burdensome column of numbers, indicates to the manager clearly that the situation is deteriorating, since there are few customers in the upper left-hand corner (the most desirable position from the firm's viewpoint), and most of the customers are located in the lower right-hand corner and are moving farther down and to the right. Such a diagram serves as a *clignotant*, or warning light. Immediate action is needed! It indicates which customers should be handled first, so as to see how the firm could serve them better with fewer resources consumed.

The *Tableau de Bord*: Three Targets for its Informational Content

The purpose of the *Tableau de Bord* is to inform. It serves simultaneously three groups:

1. Managers, by providing information on how well they are doing in terms of assigned performance and a report on the 'status' of the assets for which they are responsible with regard to the requirements of the situation. It is aimed much more at giving a vision of the future through analysis of the 'potential' of the responsibility centre (the ability to create results in the future) than at measuring past performance.
2. Peers, by providing information about how well the responsibility centre is likely to be performing in the future—and has been performing—in order for them to take anticipatory corrective actions to any originally agreed-upon plan.
3. The superior, through information about the future (and current) performance of the subordinate(s), since the superior's performance is largely the result of the performance of those to whom he or she has delegated a share of his or her mission.

The *Tableau de Bord* is different from the information documents that arise from a responsibility accounting system. Its purpose is not to account for what has been done, but to provide information about the status, future, present, and recent past of each of the key success factors for each responsibility centre and for the firm as a whole. It is totally defined by the organizational structure of delegation and linked to the deployment of objectives. Each indicator, or group of indicators together, is about an action variable, and must show how the action has affected and will affect the future achievement of the overall objective. It is not linked to a specific accounting cycle. The frequency of its production corresponds to that of decision making. A single responsibility centre may have several *Tableaux de Bord* if it has several time horizons of decision making.

The schema shown in Figure 4.8 synthesizes the functions of the *Tableau de Bord*. The system is used for consolidating performance-related information (future, present, and past) both upwards and laterally as exemplified in the figure. It is also used, however, for the deployment of strategic information downward. The choice of the key indicators by each level of responsibility has to be negotiated with the various partners, and that negotiation creates a unique opportunity for alignment of the components of the organization regarding objectives, strategy, and tactical choices. It also offers the possibility of defining the domain of responsibility of each participant. Because the *Tableaux de Bord* are so interactive between levels of responsibility, they are often described in French as being *gigogne*, or 'nested'.

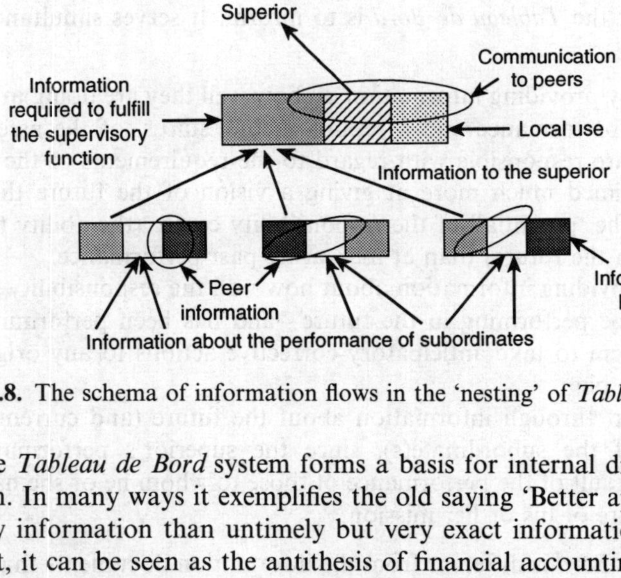

Fig. 4.8. The schema of information flows in the 'nesting' of *Tableaux de Bord*

The *Tableau de Bord* system forms a basis for internal dialogue and for action. In many ways it exemplifies the old saying 'Better approximate but timely information than untimely but very exact information'. To a great extent, it can be seen as the antithesis of financial accounting information, as this tool arose from the inability of the financial accounting system—and the slowness of the cost accounting system—to provide relevant, timely information for management decision making.

The two systems of management information, costing via the *méthode des sections homogènes* and the *Tableau de Bord*, must be reconciled in daily life, however, because, even if decisions can be made sooner and in a more systemic way on the basis of the *Tableau de Bord*, the ability to meet the expectations of shareholders and some of the other stakeholders is often measured by the 'bottom line', which is provided by accounting rules and cost calculations. It is thus important to see how the two approaches used simultaneously contribute to good management.

The Current State of the Art: Integration of the Two Approaches

As shown in Figure 4.9, Activity Based Management (ABM) can be seen as the integration of five 'logics' (or lines of reasoning) around a representation of the firm as a network of 'activities'.[21] The five logics are:

The logic of causality (explaining why resources are consumed).
The logic of valuation (attaching cost of resources to cost object).
The logic of co-ordination (co-ordinating the activities, e.g. through budgets).
The logic of organizational engineering (choosing the activities needed for the mission).
The logic of piloting (guiding the activities towards performance).

They feed into the management information system which we have called the *Tableau de Bord.*

The *méthode des sections homogènes* is one way of handling the logic of valuation. Dividing the firm into *sections* can be redefined as dividing it into 'activities', thus making the cost flow system evolve from a functional, responsibility-oriented, budget-based system towards a partial ABC approach. The physical units of service are too often considered by French management accountants to be cost drivers, without any understanding of the distinction between a driver of causality and an *ad hoc* basis of allocation. Firms that have introduced ABC have found that it is not technically difficult to work backward through the *réseau d'analyse* to get the logic of causality, since the French method calls for as few primary arbitrary allocations as possible. The real challenge is changing the mind-set of managers who are still dominated by a costing (valuation) approach as opposed to a causality (cost management) approach. A major obstacle to the implementation of 'real' ABC is the fact that budgeting in France is carried out using the same structure as the one used for cost analysis; i.e. the *sections* are most often also the budget responsibility centres. Although the logic of co-ordination is an explicit part of current French management accounting practice, it does not completely support the evolution of management towards transfunctional developments and co-responsibility of managers. The *Tableau de Bord*, however, with its emphasis on physical measures, co-ordination, and decision making, is totally coherent with the logic of piloting, and can be adapted very rapidly to a transfunctional approach. The French tradition of management accounting and ABM are therefore quite compatible conceptually, and it will take little evolution to reap all the benefits of ABM from an adapted French management accounting system.

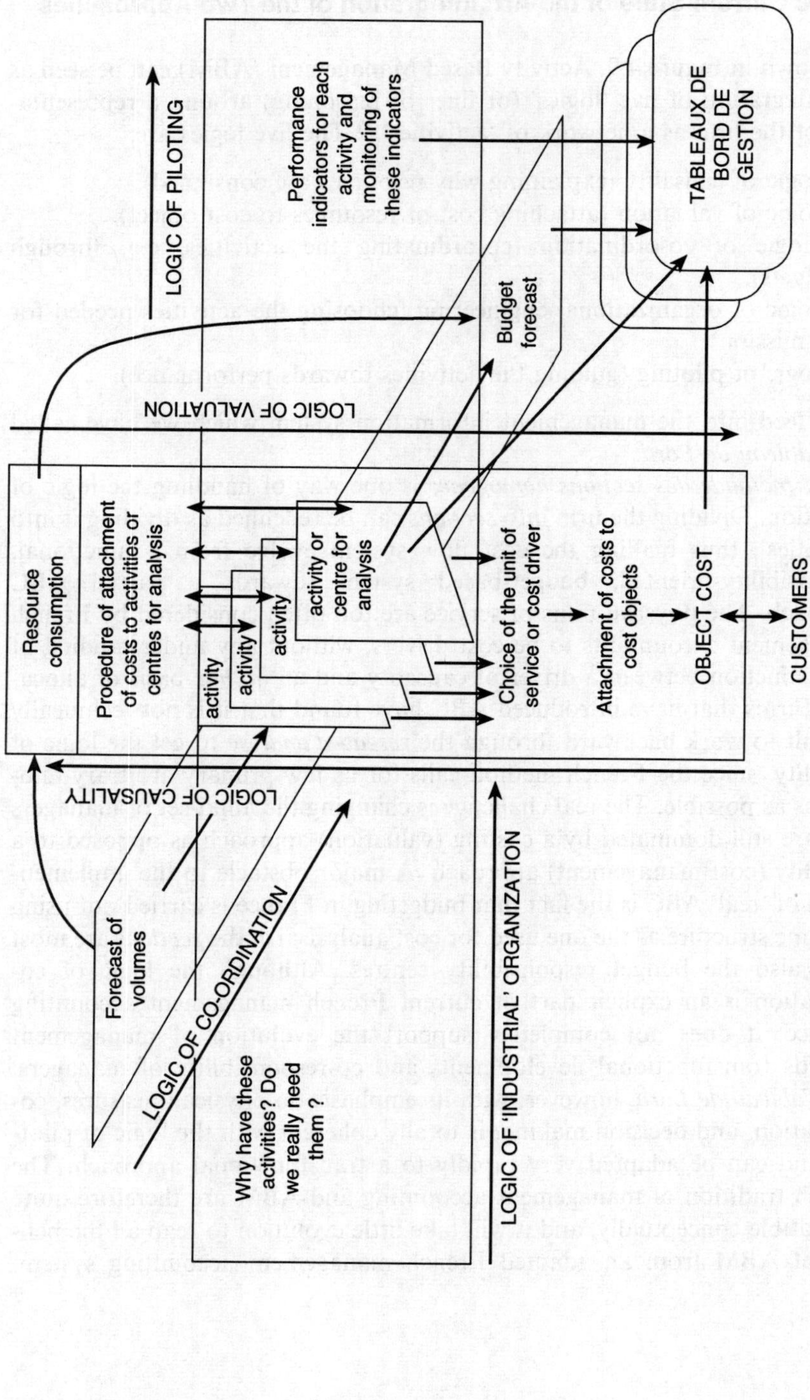

Fig. 4.9. An integrated view of the five logics of information management

There remain, however, some differences which may explain why ABC and ABM have not been considered as revolutionary in France as they have been deemed to be in the United Kingdom or the United States.

At first sight, a real difference between the *section homogène* plus *Tableau de Bord* approach and the integrated ABC or ABM approach of Figure 4.9 is that in the former, all units of service (which play the same role as the cost per unit of 'cost driver' if it is considered as an allocation basis) are volume-based (but volume defined in terms of output of the cost pool or centre for analysis). It should not be difficult for any firm to modify its traditional approach to fit the ABC/ABM approach in terms of causality, since all these units of service or units of output are physical, and the notion of causality is implicitly present.

One other significant, and more serious, difference between ABM and the French tradition is that in ABM there is a systematic challenge to the current way of doing things. ABM encourages business process re-engineering (BPR), while the French practice has not resolved the contradiction between the continuously evolutionary processes of the *Tableau de Bord* (focused on value creation) and the rigidity of the *méthode des sections homogènes* cost-flow approach. The network for analysis is almost 'cast in concrete', and is seldom reconstructed. The development of business process re-engineering in France will probably require an evolution of the management mind-set. It will also require a reduction in the cost of the information technologies supporting BPR. If these conditions are met, there will be a development in French practice of the logic of what we have called 'organizational engineering'.

Conclusion

In conclusion, one can say that the French tradition of management accounting, whether for costing or for management information, has evolved outside the financial accounting spheres. It was born almost 70 years ago, and it has continuously been adapted to the demands of management. It forms a coherent approach, even though its two sets of roots grew out of different needs at different times. Both approaches focus on the needs of managers, and rely heavily on modelling the firm's process. The management accounting practice uses physical (both in the *Tableau de Bord* and in costing), future-oriented information rather than financial, expired information. It is selective, and prefers timeliness over accuracy, tailor-made over standardized methods.

The actual solutions reached in the implementation of French management accounting can be considered as precursors of—or at least coherent with—the early stages of ABM. Minor modifications in current systems and practices should allow the next stage of the evolutionary process, and bring practice smoothly in line with the 'new' ideas of ABM. In France ABM is not a revolution; it is just the next stage of the continuous evolution of the management accounting field to meet the needs of managers (essentially driven by the adaptability and effectiveness of the *Tableau de Bord*). The impetus for that evolution comes from businesses, academia, and consulting firms. It is also fully supported and encouraged by official bodies such as the Conseil National de la Comptabilité (which is intending to publish, no later than early 1996, a revised *Plan Comptable* that will not be cast in bronze like its three predecessors, but will be designed to be continuously updated whenever the need arises) and the Ordre des Experts Comptables. Both have created working parties to help them assess the new concepts in management accounting and develop recommendations for the adaptation of practice.

Notes

1. This chapter draws heavily on an earlier version published by the *European Accounting Review*, 3 (1994), and on a presentation made at the Conference on Mediterranean Accounting and Culture held at the University of Siena, Italy, in October 1994.
2. For an extension of the *Plan Comptable* to the not-for-profit area, see Oct. 1994, *Revue Française de Comptabilité*, 260 (Oct. 1994): 18–28, about the new M14 accounting regulation for municipal agencies.
3. CNC, *Plan Comptable Général* (Paris: Imprimerie Nationale, 1982).
4. See, e.g., Romain Durand, 'La Séparation des comptabilités: origine et conséquences', *Revue Française de Comptabilité*, 240 (Dec. 1992): 72–81.
5. In the spirit of the time, price was determined on a 'cost plus' basis; therefore, knowledge of cost was critical to any economic activity. The choice of an agreed-upon basis for allocation of joint costs and fixed costs was obviously essential to creating a common ground for competition in which only the service, technical, or efficiency abilities of each firm would be the selective factors.
6. CEGOS, *Méthode uniforme de calcul des prix de revient* (Paris: CEGOS, 1937).
7. A revision of the *Plan Comptable* is under way under the auspices of the Conseil National de la Comptabilité. Publication is expected no later than early 1996. The years 1994 and 1995 are years during which a broad process of consultation with the profession was under way to identify new ideas and new needs that should be incorporated in the next National General Chart of Accounts.
8. G. de Bodt, *Direct costing et programmation économique de l'entreprise à produits multiples* (Paris: Dunod, 1964).
9. Gordon Shillinglaw, *Cost Accounting: Analysis and Control* (Homewood, Ill.: R. D. Irwin, 1961).
10. Charles T. Horngren, *Cost Accounting: A Managerial Emphasis* (Englewood Cliffs, NJ: Prentice-Hall).
11. William Vatter, *Managerial Accounting* (Englewood Cliffs, NJ: Prentice-Hall, 1950).

12. André Cibert, *Le Plan Comptable Commenté*: *de la comptabilité analytique à la gestion budgétaire*, *une monographie d'entreprise* (Paris: Foucher, 1964).
13. André Cibert, *Comptabilité Analytique* (Paris: Dunod, 1968).
14. The term *section homogène* has been replaced by the more neutral term *centre d'analyse* in the 1982 *Plan Comptable*, but, since the method remains exactly the same under a new name, we will continue to call it the *méthode des sections homogènes*.
15. The French term *réseau d'analyse* can literally be translated 'network for analysis'.
16. Like principal centres, secondary centres can also receive costs if they are also consumers of the output of another secondary centre for analysis. For elaboration of the mechanics of these *déversements* or 'pouring' of costs from centre to centre until they reach the products and the income statement, see M. Lebas, *Comptabilité Analytique de Gestion* (Paris: Éditions Nathan, 1986), ch. 5.
17. Since each participating body probably had different objectives, the final objectives as reported in the *Plan Comptable* are only compromises. While the representatives of the Ministry of Finance on the Committee might very well try to promote a system that would lead to as early tax payments as possible, or that would allow for the speedy consolidation of data into the national economic statistics, representatives from industry, on the other hand, might very well be more interested in designing a system of cost analysis that would help them in their decision making and in creating value for their stockholders.
18. For a review of the concept and of the literature see Jack Gray and Yvon Pesqueux, 'Evolutions actuelles des systèmes de tableaux de bord', *Revue Française de Comptabilité*, 242 (Feb. 1993): 61–70.
19. See e.g. J. L. Ardoin, D. Michel, and J. Schmidt, *Le Contrôle de gestion* (Paris: Publi-Union, 1986); E. Chiapello and M. H. Delmond, 'Tableau de bord: quand le rêve se confronte à la réalité?', *Actes du 1er Congrès AIM* (Jouy en Josas: Groupe HEC, 1992); or E. Chiapello and M. H. Delmond, 'Les tableaux de bord de gestion, outils d'introduction du changement, *Revue Française de Gestion*, 97 (Jan.–Feb. 1994): 49–58.
20. The term 'indicator' is preferred to 'measure', because it does not imply that the data should be exact. It merely suggests that most of the time the indication of directionality is enough or that timely approximations are, most of the time, more useful than exact but late data.
21. For further discussion, see M. Lebas, 'Current Issues in Management Accounting: from Costing to Management', in *ICWAI Seminar on Total Quality* (New Delhi: ICWAI, Feb. 1993) and 'Du coût de revient au management par les activités'. *Revue Française de Comptabilité*, 258 (July–Aug. 1994): 45–51.

5

Management Accounting
A German Perspective

Gerhard Scherrer

Introduction

The development of management accounting in Germany has resulted primarily from the efforts of academics rather than practitioners. This may be tied to the absence of an independent professional body. There is no professional body of management accountants in Germany such as the Chartered Institute of Management Accountants in the United Kingdom or the Institute of Management Accountants in the United States. There are *Wirtschaftsprüfer* (chartered accountants) and *Steuerberater* (tax advisers) in Germany, but no professional management accountants with their own authoritative body.

Management accounting in Germany has been influenced by different forces of change embedded in history (Coenenberg and Schoenfeld 1990: 95; Dorn 1992: 97 ff.). In broad terms, four phases of development can be identified (Schneider 1992: 87, 93 f.). The first relates to the calculation of net profit. The problem was the treatment of the implicit interest rate, imputed depreciation, and entrepreneurial income. The second phase addressed efficiency control, in the first instance by monitoring input quantities using only fixed transfer prices. The third phase entailed the calculation of product prices. These were first accounted for by using full costs. The issue was which costs should be covered by a current transaction. The costing rate, it was thought, should include the overhead cost and the profit (Schmalenbach 1928: 23). Thinking in full-cost terms was stimulated by the statutory instrument *Leitsätze für die Preisermittlung aufgrund von Selbstkosten* (Regulation of pricing based on cost prices) introduced in 1938. The fourth phase can be described as thinking in terms of relevant costs (Schneider 1992: 88), whereby principles of cost allocation were initially developed (Schmalenbach 1934; Henzel 1931; Lehmann 1951). The most important principle of cost allocation was the causation principle which underlined that cost should be apportioned to those units where a change in the unit directly causes a change in cost (Rummel 1949). According to this principle, only proportional costs are applied to products. Applying this concept to standard costs, Plaut imported the standard costing rationale into Germany (1953, 1955). Standard costing in Germany has subsequently evolved by adopting production theory concepts identified by Kilger (1993, 1961). His approach allows differentiated analysis of cost variances, and in particular of input quantity variances. This theoretical framework influenced the theory of production and sales planning (Kilger 1973).

This chapter is organized as follows: first an assessment of empirical research in German cost accounting; then discussions of actual costing, standard costing, and the use of short-term performance reporting and contribution margin accounting in German enterprises; followed by some concluding remarks on the outlook for future cost management developments in Germany.

Empirical Research in Cost Accounting in Germany

Cost Accounting Systems in Use

Empirical research in cost accounting has not been as fully developed as theoretical research in Germany. There is a similar lack of studies in Anglo-American research. There are only a few studies of the organization, use, and the outcomes of cost accounting practices in Germany. Hopwood's remark about the state of accounting research that 'It has to be recognized how little is known of the accounting endeavour' (Hopwood 1983: 302; Kaplan 1986: 429 f.) fully applies to the situation in Germany.

A survey of articles on cost accounting in the most influential business studies journals published between 1980 and 1990 (Küpper 1993: 605, reprinted in Table 5.1) indicates that conceptual problems comprise the main topic of interest in cost accounting research. Seventy-five per cent of all articles are concerned with the theoretical framework; 12 per cent present case-studies; and only 5 per cent report on cost accounting practice and provide empirical evidence. Empirical studies in Germany are primarily concerned with investigating the structure of cost accounting. Enterprises are studied in terms of cost accounting systems and practices.

Table 5.2 summarizes the types of cost accounting systems used by German enterprises. The figures in the table give the percentage of enterprises using a particular cost accounting system. Multiple choice was permitted in the survey on which the table is based. The studies varied in the information available. Those by Küpper (1983: 169) and Küpper and Hoffman (1988: 587) provide information only on the sample sizes (137 and 184 companies, respectively), not the industries researched. The study by Becker (1985: 603) classifies the companies researched, as belonging to four sectors of industry (see Table 5.3.). Hauer (1994: 21) uses a different classification of industries (see Table 5.4).

Table 5.1. Published articles on cost accounting in the German journals Betriebswirtschaftliche Forschung und Praxis, Controlling, Die Betriebswirtschaft, Der Betrieb, Kostenrechnungspraxis, Zeitschrift für Betriebswirtschaft, Zeitschrift für betriebswirtschaftliche Forschung

	Theoretical framework	Literature survey	Case-studies/ examples	Reports	Empirical research	Total
1 Fundamentals						
1.1 General	30	3	3	4	6	46
1.2 Theory of management accounting	25					25
1.3 Management accounting systems	22		2			24
2 Components						
2.1 Cost classification	23					23
2.2 Cost centre accounting	3		1	4		8
2.3 Cost application	5		10			15
2.4 Performance reporting	2					2
2.5 Gross margin and contribution margin accounting	6		2	1		9
3 Cost management						
3.1 Cost–volume–profit planning	2		1			3
3.2 Cost–volume–profit management	7				1	8
3.3 Pricing	2					2
3.4 Controlling instruments	8			1		9
4 Sector management accounting						
4.1 Sectors	15	2	1	1		19
4.2 Functions	4			2	2	8
5 Data processing and management accounting	20		7		2	29
Total	174	5	27	13	11	230

Several factors underlie the different results presented in Table 5.2. Empirical studies use various databases and different sampling sizes. Also, the industries studied vary considerably. Moreover, there were differences in the questionnaires used. It is likely too that the terms and system definitions used in the questionnaires were not always fully understood by the enterprises. Nevertheless, the findings give some empirical data regarding the cost accounting systems in use in Germany. The most common cost

Table 5.2. The use of cost accounting systems in Germany

Cost accounting systems	Frost and Meyer 1981	Küpper 1983	Becker 1985	Küpper and Hoffmann 1988	Hauer 1994	Average
Actual costing system using full costs	54.9	52.6	63.5	43.7	53.2	53.6
Standard costing						
using full costs only	34.4	—	47.5	—	34.2	38.7
using marginal standard costs only	10.7	17.8	5.0	18.6	10.5	12.5
combined full- and marginal standard costing	51.3	38.5	23.9	55.2	27.4	39.3
Contribution margin accounting	34.8	40.0	28.0	45.4	35.3	36.7
Activity based costing	—	—	—	—	3.2	3.2

Table 5.3. Classification of industries in Becker 1985

Sector	Sample
Primary and general producer	68
Capital goods	192
Consumer goods	192
Food, beverages, and tobacco	23
Total	480

Table 5.4. Classification of industries in Hauer 1994

Sector	Sample
Chemicals	23
Glass, rock, stone, and related mine products	16
Timber, paper	30
Metal, mechanical engineering	50
Electrical engineering	36
Food, beverages, and tobacco	9
Textile, apparel, garment, and leather	12
Others	35
Total	199[a]

[a] 12 due to multiple choice.

accounting systems, according to the averages in Table 5.2 are:

actual cost systems using full costs,
standard costing using full costs,
standard costing using full and marginal costs,
contribution margin accounting.

Activity-based costing deployed by 3 per cent of all enterprises, is, obviously, of little relevance to German enterprises at the time of the survey. There is no empirical evidence of the use of target costing in Germany. The limited use of activity-based costing and target costing in practice contrasts with the widespread, controversial coverage which these topics attract in the business studies literature. Authors emphasize the increasing importance of activity-based costing due to the rise of indirect manufacturing cost. The usefulness of target costing is based on the premiss that it is essential to monitor the costs not only in the period of production but also during the design process.

Marginal standard costing, favoured in the literature as better enabling decision making, is the sole cost accounting system in only 12.5 per cent of German enterprises. Thus, whereas theoretical research in cost accounting stresses mainly marginal costing (Adam 1970; Bohr and Schwab 1984; Riebel 1994: 409 ff.), the practice of German enterprises is dominated by thinking in terms of full costing. The contrast between theoretical research and the actual use of cost accounting systems becomes even more glaring in that the theoretically most developed cost accounting system of direct cost and contribution margin accounting by Riebel (1994) is rarely used. The plant-standard-costing system (Laßmann 1968; Franke 1972) based on mathematical models is almost unknown in practice.

The use of cost accounting systems has changed little in German enterprises in recent years, according to empirical findings. Full costing is the most important system. It is supplemented by indirect costing and contribution margin accounting. The widespread use of full costing using actual costs is surprising. Many German enterprises use this despite its failure to provide information for operational decisions and cost control, both of which are among the most important purpose of management accounting (Acherrer 1991: 68 f.).

Components of Cost Accounting in Use

Cost accounting is generally differentiated into cost classification, cost centre accounting, cost application (unit-of-output costing), and short-term performance reporting. The use of these components of cost accounting is widespread in Germany. Under cost classification, the cost accounting data are systematically gathered and classified into cost categories. The criterion of classification is the resource. The cost categories depend on the industry.

They are often defined, however, by a uniform classification of accounts, e.g. the German Uniform Classification of Accounts for Industrial Industries.

There are differences in the treatment of inputing costs. Over the past 10 years, the application of imputed costs has increased from 75 per cent (Becker 1984: 104) to 88 per cent (Hauer 1994, 33). The different categories of imputed costs in use and the relative number of enterprises applying them were identified by the empirical research as shown in Table 5.5. German enterprises mostly use imputed depreciation and implicit interest rates in the cost classification. Imputed depreciation is, in general, calculated on the basis of current cost of fixed assets (buildings, plants, machinery, fixtures, fittings, tools, and equipment). The implicit rate of interest is computed either on equity or total capital or on operating capital. The calculation of an entrepreneurial income is less important, because it needs to be calculated only for sole traders and partnerships. The earnings of the management are the entrepreneurial income in a company (stock corporation in the United States).

Table 5.5. Use of imputed costs in German enterprises

Categories of imputed costs	Becker 1985	Hauer 1994
Imputed depreciation	57.5	83.3
Implicit lease rate	—	30.0
Implicit interest rate	40.8 (equity)	75.6 (total capital)
Imputed entrepreneurial income	36.1	19.4
Imputed risk bonus	26.0	39.4

Cost centre accounting allows the allocation of costs to cost drivers (products), and helps the enterprise to control costs in defined reporting units. The literature gives the following guide-lines for forming cost centres (Kilger 1993: 304 ff.):

It must be possible to transfer costs as direct costs per cost centre to each cost centre.
Cost drivers must be measured in the cost centre.
Responsible reporting units must be clearly defined to monitor costs.

In practice, German enterprises follow these principles only with respect to the clear definition of reporting units. Empirical research indicates that most cost centres are organized as geographic reporting units in 24 per cent of all cases, as organizational reporting units in 81 per cent, and as profit centres in 71 per cent (Hauer 1994: 34).

Analysis of deviations of standard costs from actual costs can indicate the need for corrective action within an enterprise. Identification of the causes of deviation gives a basis for avoiding excessive costs in the future. Depending on the organization of an enterprise, global cost variances (production volume variance, input price variance, input quantity variance) and several specific cost variances can be identified (Kilger 1993: 627 ff.; Scherrer 1991: 434 ff.). The production volume variance is defined as the difference between the standard costs on the basis of budgeted activity and the standard costs on the basis of actual activity charged to the units. The input price variance is the cost difference between the actual and budgeted prices of internal and external goods and services. The input quantity variance is the difference between the costs of internal and external goods and services resulting from deviations in actual and budgeted input quantities (Laßmann 1990, cols. 1785 f.).

Empirical research on accounting for cost variances is concerned only with global cost variances. Many enterprises account for production volume variance, input price variance, and input quantity variance. Table 5.6 shows the relative number of enterprises accounting for global cost variances. In the cost application (unit-of-output costing), costs are accounted for per cost object. Cost object is, in most cases, a unit of output. A product line (a number of equal or comparable products) is also feasible as a cost object, especially if the enterprise calculates per order. Basic pricing practices are job-order product costing and process-product costing. In the empirical research, job-order product costing has been found to be the most frequently used product-costing system (88 per cent) among German enterprises. Only a few use process costing. The main objective of product costing is preliminary costing for bids. Many enterprises use it for reasons of efficiency control, calculating the profit earned by a product or by an order.

Table 5.6. Use of cost variance analysis in German enterprises

Cost variance analysis	Küpper 1983	Küpper *et al.* 1990	Hauer 1994
Production volume variance	60.9	50.7	47.5
Input price variance	68.4	59.0	—
Input quality variance	69.9	57.3	45.4

Empirical research provides little information about the frequency and organization of short-term performance reporting in Germany. It can be concluded from the answers to questions about contribution margin accounting and new research that short-term performance reporting is quite popular. Information about performance reporting as operating income or expenditure accounting on a full costing or direct costing basis is not available.

The Use and Functions of Actual Costing in German Enterprises

The above-mentioned empirical research in different cost accounting systems showed that more than half the German enterprises used only actual costing or actual costing as a supplement to standard costing. In particular, accounting for actual costs as a requirement for cost control is also used for the purpose of transferring costs to cost drivers (products, orders). The objective of transfer pricing to cost drivers can be the use of statistical accounting as a control of the preliminary costing, cost application in short-term performance reporting, accounting for inventoriable costs, and accounting for cost prices at orders of public authorities. Specific problems arise for German enterprises with regard to the two latter objectives.

Accounting for Inventoriable Costs

German company and tax legislation requires current and fixed assets to be valued in financial reporting at their purchase price or production cost less depreciation. Under *Handelsgesetzbuch* (*HCB*) (German Commercial Code) section 255, subsection 2, paragraph 2, obligatory inventoriable production costs are direct material cost, prime cost, and special production cost. The following expenses may be accounted for as inventoriable production costs in so far as they relate to the period of production: appropriate portions of the necessary indirect material cost, appropriate portions of the necessary manufacturing overhead, and depreciation in value of the fixed assets to the extent brought about through the manufacturing. The following costs accrued during the production period need not be taken into account for the production costs under *HGB*, section 255, subsection 2, paragraph 4: costs of general administration, expenditures for the business's social welfare arrangements, expenditures for voluntary social benefits, and expenditures for the business's pension scheme. Interest on capital borrowed to finance the production of finished goods and work in progress may be included in inventoriable costs to the extent that it accrues in respect of the period of production.

Bases for inventoriable costs are the actual costs provided by the cost accounting. Imputed costs must be eliminated for financial reporting purposes. Inventoriable costs of finished goods and work in progress are the only expenses relating to cash flows. Therefore, imputed costs can never be treated as production costs of finished goods and work in progress. Those imputed costs are the implicit lease rate, the implicit interest rate, the imputed risk bonus, and the imputed entrepreneurial income. Cost accounting data must be corrected for the balance-sheet value of assets if they are based on current (replacement) cost, e.g. depreciation of buildings, machinery, and equipment calculated not on the basis of their historical costs, but on the basis of replacement costs.

Cost-Reimbursement Contracts

The accounting of allowable costs in the case of contracts with public authorities is necessary for the calculation of cost prices of the contracted output. In Germany, statutory instruments have been enacted to achieve uniformity and consistency in accounting for contracts with public authorities and to avoid calculation of the cost price at excessive rates. These instruments determine the allowable resources and their prices plus the valuation of used quantities of resources. On this determination, accounting for unallowable costs is excluded.

The following statutory instruments of accounting for government contracts are in force in Germany:

Die Verordnung PR 30/53 des Bundesministers für Wirtschaft über Preise bei öffentlichen Aufträgen (Statutory instrument for prices of contracts with public authorities by the Department of Industry);

Die Leitsätze für die Preisermittlung aufgrund von Selbstkosten, LSP (Regulation of pricing based on cost prices);

Die Verordnung PR 1/72 über die Preise für Bauleistungen bei öffentlichen oder mit öffentlichen Mitteln finanzierten Aufträgen (Statutory instrument for prices of public construction work or contracts financed by government investment);

Die Leitsätze für die Ermittlung von Preisen bei Bauleistungen aufgrund von Selbstkosten (*LSP-Bau*) (Regulation for the calculation of prices of construction works on the basis of cost prices).

In contracting with public authorities, the market price should take precedence over the calculation of cost prices; i.e. public works should be based on prices formed by markets. Cost prices should be agreed on only under exceptional circumstances, which are (1) when there is no market price to be fixed, and (2) when there is a shortage or a lack of competition between suppliers, and the market price, therefore, is not objective. Only under those exceptional circumstances can cost prices be contracted. These cost prices are fixed cost prices, recommended cost prices, and reimbursed cost prices.

Fixed cost prices are cost prices based on preliminary costing. They must be negotiated before starting production, e.g. the manufacturing of a good, and must not be changed unilaterally. An adequate forecast of the costs for public works is essential to calculate the cost price. Recommended cost prices are estimated prices for public works. They are agreed on if the components of the preliminary costing are vague and an agreement on the preliminary costing is not reasonable in the view of both parties. A reason for recommended cost prices is insufficient information on all probable costs where the data are expected to be available during the process of performance, e.g. the production of a good. Reimbursed cost prices are cost prices calculated on actual costs. Under reimbursed cost prices, the contractor is reimbursed for the expenditure plus an incentive fee by the public authority.

Cost pricing systems are allowed under the following rules:

1. Cost prices should be fixed prices as far as possible.
2. If a fixed cost price is not available, a recommended cost price must be contracted in the first instance. This recommended price must be changed to a fixed cost price before the end of performance.
3. A reimbursed cost price is allowable only if another price (market price, fixed cost price, recommended cost price) is not possible.

The statutory instrument regulating the calculation of prices of buildings on the basis of cost prices (*LSP*) provides a minimum layout of the calculation. *LSP* no. 10, section 3, describes it as follows:

	Material costs
	Manufacturing costs
	Development and designing costs
	Administrative costs
	Distribution costs
=	Cost of sales
	Markup/incentive fee
=	Cost price

The Use of Standard Costing in German Enterprises

The most important stand costing systems in German enterprises are the modified standard costing and marginal standard costing supplemented by direct labour costing. The planning period is normally the year. On the basis of such cost accounting data, a budget is predetermined for each month as the interval of the planning horizon. Cost management is also often in terms of a period of one month.

Cost Budgeting

Optimum budgeting versus standard budgeting

Theoretically, the objective of cost budgeting is provision of an optimum budget. An optimum is achieved if, subject to the constraints, the parameters of the actions are planned in such a way that the targeted profit is maximized. Subject to the parameters of the external sales market (fixed sales volume, fixed product prices), an optimum budget is planned if the alternative parameters of production (factor costs, input, production method) are set in types and quantity of produced units of output so that the costs are minimized (Kilger 1973: 16).

In practice, budgeting in German enterprises is done not as optimal cost budgeting but as standard cost budgeting. Under standard budgeting, targets are set by the executives for the planning period (e.g. the reduction of throughput time by *x* per cent or the limitation of scrap). Standard budgeting sets target costs of an entity for the managers in charge of cost centres such that they may be met with some effort. Target costs derived from optimum budgets are found to be demotivating, because those budgets are out of reach, and the actual costs are constantly out of step with the budget.

Based on standard budgeting, a master budget is compiled by summarizing the cost centres of the enterprise. As this is done using past data, expected cost variance for the period in question has to be taken into account. Such cost variance can be caused by planned activities such as changes in the line of products (changes in the type and/or quantity of products) and changes in the production method (in machinery and tools, in degree of utilization, in batch size).

In budgeting, direct product costs and indirect product costs can be identified.

Budgeting direct product costs

Direct product costs are costs that can be traced to one unit of output in an economically feasible way. German enterprises budget especially direct material cost, direct labour cost, and special production cost. Budgeting uses technical data for the necessary material and labour costs. Typically, budgeting of direct labour costs takes place as follows in a German enterprise. The first step involves measuring the production lead time. This is based on the targeted expected level of performance (planned performance). The planned production time is determined in two steps: (1) determination of the standard operation time based on normal output, and (2) estimation of the variance between normal output and targeted performance.

The standard operation time of individual time studies is estimated according to the *REFA-System* (*Verband für Arbeitsstudien und Betriebsorganisationen e.V.*). Standard operation time is defined as the time which an employee needs to do a task properly under standard conditions. The standard operation time according to *REFA*, as a standard measure of work flows, is analysed in terms of a basic time, compensating rest, and delay time. For a custom-made order there are standard set-up times and standard execution times. Set-up time as a standard preparatory time for the execution of an order by the employee is the time it takes to organize the operating resources for the execution of an order and to set up the operating resources. The execution time is the standard time for the employee to produce (process) one unit of output.

The standard time of an order can be subdivided as shown in Figure 5.1. As can be seen, set-up time and execution time are each subdivided into

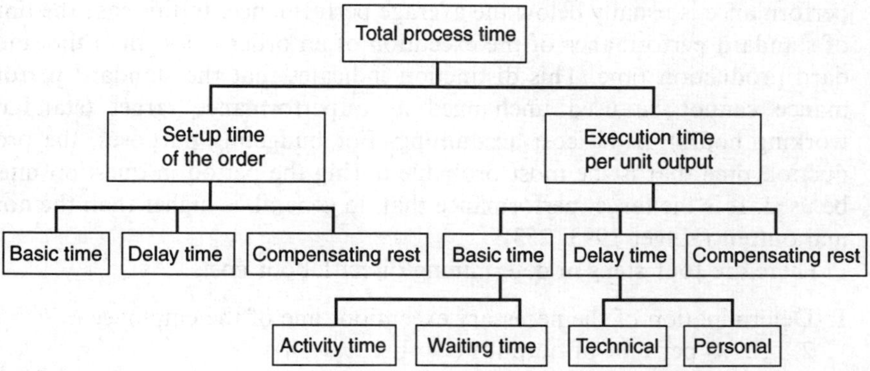

Fig. 5.1. The subdivision of the total process time

basic time, delay time and compensating rest. These terms are defined as follows (REFA 1978: 46 ff.):

The basic time is the total of all standard times of the operations per unit of output that are necessary for a systematic execution of an order by the employee. Activity time and waiting time together are the basic time.

The delay time is defined as the total of all standard times per unit of output of the order that is additionally required by the employee in order to systematically execute the order. It is, furthermore, divided into technical delay time (additional activity and interruptions caused by technical failures) and personal delay time (personal breaks).

The compensation rest is the total of all standard times per unit of output of the order necessary for the relaxation of the employee.

The levelled time (normal output) is especially important for the planning of the standard time of set-up and execution (planned performance). Planned performance can be defined only if the employee is suitable, experienced, fully trained for the job, and may fully develop his or her abilities without any constraints.

The normal output (standard production time) is the basis of the planning of the production time in the planning period. Standard performance of an employee is defined by level and rate of performance (factors of production). Both measure the ratio between the normal output and the reference output. If the normal output is used as a reference, then the performance level is equal to 100 per cent and the performance rate is equal to 1. There are two relevant situations in the production planning process. First, when the rate of standard performance of the average output of the employee equals the normal rate of output. The time of standard performance of the execution of an order is then equal to the standard production time. Second, when the planned performance rate is greater than the normal rate of output. This situation is the rule, because the standard performance is usually below the average performance. In this case the time of standard performance of the execution of an order is less than the standard production time. This distinction indicates that the standard performance cannot be used unchanged as a performance target (standard working hours) in the cost accounting. For budgeting purposes, the production time that is the most probable during the period in question must be used. It is the target performance that, in general, is higher than the normal output (Kilger 1993: 253).

There are four steps in determining direct labour costs:

1. Determination of the necessary execution time of the employee h ($h = 1, 2, \ldots, \lambda$) per unit of output i (i = 1, 2, . . ., n).
2. Determination of the necessary normal set-up time of employee h per unit of output i.
3. Determination of the generally necessary total time of employee h per unit of output in a batch production.
4. Valuation of the process time of employee h using standard direct labour costs per unit.

Budgeting indirect product costs

Costs that cannot be traced as direct costs per unit of output are determined in two steps. First, all relevant cost categories are determined. Secondly, activity-proportional costs are allocated using reference figures, and stand-by costs are allocated by using the allocation base method. Cost budgeting in cost centres necessitates a subdivision of those centres in an enterprise under feasible criteria as per the principles mentioned above.

Most German enterprises use reference figures to allocate indirect costs to units of output. Reference figures are cost-driver measures. These measures relate to the consumption of resources. A reference figure must be defined for each centre, because there is no general reference figure appropriate to all cost centres (Agthe 1963: 39 ff.). A comprehensive system of reference figures to allocate indirect costs to the units underlies the modified marginal costing approach (Kilger 1993: 312 ff.). Its schema is presented in Figure 5.2. The system distinguishes, in the first instance, between direct and indirect reference figures. Direct reference figures are measures of the cost driver that can be derived from the output (production, quantity of output) of the production departments: e.g. the quantity of output, time (operating hours, machine hours), or physical units (weight, height, liquid measures). Indirect reference figures are measures of the cost driver calculated on the basis not of the output of the producing cost centre but of the input into another cost centre. Indirect reference figures are applicable to all indirect cost centres, i.e. cost centres that do not provide direct output of cost objects (units) but produce output to other cost centres (e.g. utilities, vehicles pool).

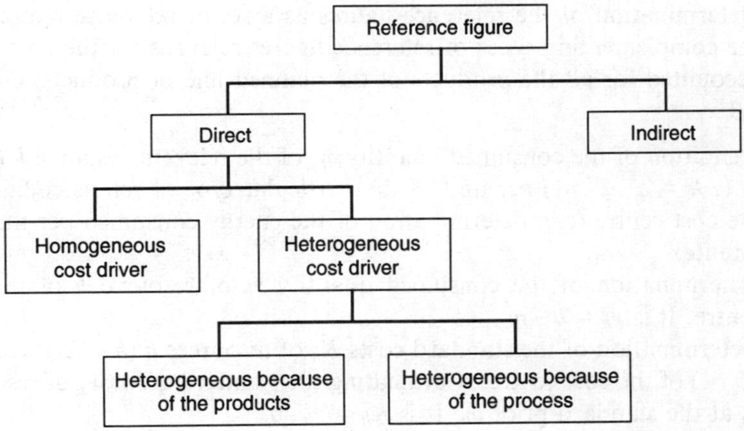

Fig. 5.2. The system of reference figures

Lower in the hierarchy, direct reference figures are further subdivided into homogeneous and heterogeneous cost drivers. The characteristic of the homogeneous cost drivers is that the input of resources is proportional to a single base. These are the cost centres where only one type of output is produced. Homogeneous cost drivers are also found in cost centres where several types of output are produced but all the costs are proportional to a single measure (reference figure). Heterogeneous cost drivers are characterized by the fact that not all the resource inputs are proportional to the reference figure. Under heterogeneous cost drivers, costs in one cost centre are transferred on the basis of various reference figures, e.g. operating hours, machine hours, time of the order, and set-up time. Heterogeneous cost drivers are caused by different factors, mainly the type of output (products) and the type of production process.

The most important indirect costs per unit that are unrelated to the level of performance and that are budgeted per cost centre are the expenditure on energy, on consumables, and auxiliary material, indirect (auxiliary) labour costs, and depreciation expenses calculated using the unit of production method. Labour costs, too, are frequently determined using reference figures, and are transferred to units (products).

Cost budgeting using reference figures that are proportional to the activity in a cost centre includes the following steps (Scherrer 1991: 232 f.):

1. Definition of the relevant reference figure (e.g. operating hours, machine hours). The relevance depends on the type of activity in a cost centre.
2. Definition of the reference figure. A reference figure may be understood as a set of reference figures β, of the relevant complementing types of reference figures per unit of output i (i = 1, 2, . . ., n) of the planned line of products (e.g. machine minutes per unit of product 1).

3. Determination of the reference figures as a set of reference figures b of the complementing types of reference figures relevant for the cost centre accounted for all the products of the planned line of products, i. e. $b = \sum_i \beta_i x_i$.
4. Definition of the consumed quantity η_h of the relevant resource h (h = $\lambda + 1$, $\lambda = 2, \ldots, 1$) per unit of the particular type of reference figure of the cost centre (e.g. determination of the energy consumed per machine minute).
5. Determination of the consumed quantity v_h of resource h of the cost centre. It is $v_h = b \cdot \eta_h$.
6. Determination of the standard costs K_h of resources h ($h = \lambda + 1, \lambda + 2, \ldots, 1$) of the cost centre by evaluating the standard quantity of resources v_h at the standard price q_h. It is $K_h = v_h \cdot q_h$.
7. Determination of the costs proportional to activity K of the cost centre by addition of the standard costs of each cost category. It is $K = \sum_h K_h$.
8. Determination of the rate of standard cost k of the cost centre per unit of the standard reference figure of the relevant type of reference figure (e.g. standard costs of the cost centre per machine minute). It is $k = K/b$.

German enterprises generally budget indirect stand-by product costs in cost categories. If a cost category consists of stand-by costs and performance-related costs, then there is a cost dissolution (cost splitting) using the systematic cost-splitting method; i.e. all those standard costs of the cost category are traced as stand-by costs that are necessary for the working order required by the entity even if the activity is reduced to nil (Plaut 1984: 25; Kilger 1993: 351 f.; Schweitzer and Küpper 1986: 319 ff.). Some enterprises use factors of expense variability (variation coefficients) to split the costs. Factors of expense variability are percentages that indicate the variable (proportional) fraction of the cost of a cost category (Agthe 1963: 104 ff.). They are set by the central controlling department of an enterprise according to past experience. The value of the factors of expense variability depends on the type of cost centre. In the manufacturing department, a direct production cost centre and indirect production cost centres (e.g. utility department, service department) are distinguished.

In planning indirect stand-by costs, German enterprises concentrate on the cost categories' operating costs (depreciation expenses plus maintenance and repair costs), labour costs (salaries plus benefits), and cost of capital (interest cost). Depreciation expenses are budgeted according to the relevant cost centre based on current prices of the operational resources in the cost centre. Operational resources are depreciated over their useful economic life. The existence of deterioration because of use and time is taken into account by enterprises by splitting cost into depreciation resulting from stand-by on the one hand and activity on the other. Other enterprises trace depreciation expenses entirely as indirect stand-by product costs.

Maintenance and repair costs are also budgeted per cost centre using maintenance schedules and estimates of the repair expenditure in the planning period.

Salary costs are budgeted in the cost centres for all the salaried employees of the cost centre. Fringe benefits paid only once a year (vacation bonus, Christmas allowances, and end-of-the-year allowances) are split into a monthly amount for budgeting purposes. Statutory incidental payments to wages and salaries (employer's contribution to social security), voluntary benefits (allowances for marriage, birth of children, and long service award), the costs of pension schemes, and other general social costs (costs of a canteen, factory-owned flats, rest homes, and sports centres) are added to social security costs in Germany. Social security costs are often budgeted by a general mark-up on salaries and wages.

There are several opinions as regards the treatment of capital cost (interest cost) in cost accounting in Germany (Lücke 1965: 4 f.). Some authors choose to exclude interest charges from cost accounting. They focus on the short-term character of cost accounting. Others include interest in cost accounting to the extent that it is necessary to finance operating resources; only interest payments as cost of capital (interest paid to creditors) are taken into account. Others prefer interest costs to be included in cost accounting whether or not they are related to cash flows. Most German enterprises follow the latter option. The implicit rate of interest is determined on the basis of the necessary operating capital or necessary operating assets. It is budgeted for those cost centres where the necessary operating assets are bound as necessary fixed or current assets.

Cost Control

Method and components of cost control

Most German enterprises use a performance report to control costs (Kilger 1993: 590 ff.). It compares actual cost accounting data with the targeted performance budgeted by using analytical measuring and forecasting methods. Targeted performance is a general yardstick for cost comparison, and is basic to the appraisal of existing variances between actual and targeted costs. The preferred approach to performance reports is the analysis of cost variances. It is practised as closed or partial performance reporting. The closed-performance report analyses the consumption of all resources whether or not they can be influenced by employees. The partial performance report concentrates on consumed resources that can be influenced by employees.

A further development of the partial performance report is operational control. It is applied in some companies in the steel industry (Wartmann 1963–5). Under operational control the performance report is related to a technical process or a period, e.g. a shift, an operation, a batch, an order, or a bigger manufacturing lot. Components of control are the determination and analysis of variances between budgeted and actual input prices (input price variance) and variances between scheduled and actual input quantities (input quantity variance) (Scherrer 1993, cols. 1168 ff.). The determination and analysis of quantity variances is essential to control within German enterprises.

Controlling the cost proportional to activity

Controlling direct product costs is necessary because cost variances (input quantity variances) have to be transferred to the producing cost centre on the basis of each cost category. Input price variance needs to be eliminated before controlling the direct product costs in three steps.

1. Determination of actual direct costs using the actual input of a direct cost category.
2. Determination of targeted direct costs using the budgeted input of a direct cost category.
3. Determination of the direct cost variance of a direct cost category by performance reporting and analysis of the identified cost variances (input quantity variances).

The identified cost variances constitute a global multifarious input variance. The causes are exogenous (not influenced by the cost centre) as well as endogenous (influenced by the cost centre). Typical influences on variances in direct material costs are:

Exogenous influences of the material, caused by a change of physical attributes of a material. Changed physical attributes can cause the use of a different input of material per unit.

Exogenous influences on production, especially differences in the efficiency between budgeted and actual production facilities, in extraordinary product design, and in changes of the mixture of substitutable resources.

Endogenous influences, relating to inappropriate use of materials, carelessness in production, leakage, theft, but also bad working conditions in a cost centre with material input (Scherrer 1991: 449 f.).

Indirect product costs are controlled for each cost centre in two steps. In the first instance, the total variance of costs of a cost centre is determined as a global cost variance. Those parts of cost variances for which the cost centre is not responsible because they result from exogenous influences are separated. The total variance is determined in three steps:

1. Determination of the actual direct product cost of the cost centre proportional to activity from the actual input of resources.
2. Determination of the targeted indirect product cost of the cost centre proportional to activity from the budgeted input of resources.

3. Determination of variances of indirect cost of a cost centre by performance reporting.

The analysis of the total variance (global input variance) of a cost centre attempts to identify the main reasons for the cost variance. The objective of the analysis is to eliminate the influence of external factors on the value of indirect product costs proportional to activity of the cost centre. Those cost variances that relate to the production are thereby determined. Factors relating to production are typically the following: changes of the production method from the scheduled method, changes in the actual batch sizes from the planned batch size, changes in the actual processing of the production facilities from the planned production facilities, changes in the actual yield of resources from that budgeted, and variances in the actual efficiency of the operating resources from that budgeted.

Particular deviations resulting from the above-mentioned factors are subtracted from the total variance of the cost centre. The residual deviation is an endogenous cost variance of the cost centre for which the manager of the cost centre is responsible. The residual deviation is examined for its causes. Endogenous cost factors that cause costs exceeding those budgeted are often inappropriate use of the operating resources, overrun of planned production times, the unnecessary use of energy, auxiliary materials, and expendables, increased maintenance and repair costs of operating resources, production interruptions, and scratch production.

Stand-by indirect product costs do not depend on the type, quantity, and value of the produced or sold products. They cannot, therefore, feasibly be traced to units or cost centres in the sense of a theoretical cause–effect principle or as a final principle (Riebel 1994: 67 ff.; Seicht 1990: 618 f.). A cost accounting system, e.g. activity based costing, disregards the principle of strict cost causation if it traces indirect stand-by product costs according to activities of production and sales. Intervals are the most important allocation base for indirect stand-by costs. A hierarchy of time allocation bases can be formed by ordering different time intervals (Riebel 1994: 94). Stand-by costs can be traced as direct costs to each interval on different levels of that hierarchy (e.g. year, half year, quarter, month).

Under standard costing as used by German enterprises, the controlling of indirect stand-by product costs is mainly a capacity utilization control of each cost centre of the entity (Kilger 1993: 654 ff.). Efficiency variances of the cost centres are determined from the planned or maximum activity by the capacity control. The determination of activity variances is traditionally combined with the determination of idle capacity and uses capacity analysis. Idle capacities have a twofold meaning to the German accountant. They indicate that fraction of the indirect stand-by product costs that cannot be traced to the produced units because the volume is too low. Additionally, they indicate the fraction of indirect stand-by product costs that are not inventoriable production costs of work in progress and finished goods (*HGB*, section 255, subsection 2).

The Use of Short-Term Performance Reporting and Contribution Margin Accounting in German Enterprises

Components of Short-term Performance Reporting and Contribution Margin Accounting

Short-term performance reporting and contribution margin accounting is used by many German enterprises. The units normally report on a monthly basis. Shorter periods are possible too. The short-term performance reporting and contribution margin accounting indicates the factors of performance of the entity. The reporting units are organized according to product lines, geographically (e.g. domestic, countries of the EU, North America, Japan, South-East Asia, and rest of the world), in terms of customers (e.g. bulk buyers, low-volume buyers), or profit centres.

Methods of Short-term Performance Reporting and Contribution Margin Accounting

All variations of the cost-of-sales method using full or direct costing are in use in German enterprises. Short-term contribution margin accounting, however, is generally based on the cost-of-sales method using direct cost. In the use of short-term performance reporting and contribution margin accounting, there are differences in the time horizon, since short-term performance reporting and contribution margin accounting use actual costs or standard costs. There are different treatments of the variations in stock to calculate the contribution margins. Using standard costing, open and closed methods of short-term performance reporting and contribution margin accounting are distinguished (Kilger 1993: 759 ff.).

Open methods

Open methods of short-term performance reporting and contribution margin accounting (operating results per unit) determine the revenue per unit or per product line, the marginal cost of sales, and the contribution margin of units sold accounted for targeted and actual values in the planning period/time horizon. Variances between targeted and actual profits of the relevant period can thereby be split into effects of revenue or of sales of each product or product line of the enterprise.

Table 5.7 shows a possible version of the method of short-term performance reporting and contribution margin accounting. Δ measures the variances between targeted and actual revenues, targeted and actual marginal

Table 5.7. Operating profit per unit

Product i/ product line j	Revenues			Marginal cost of sales			Contribution margins		
	targeted	actual	Δ	targeted	actual	Δ	targeted	actual	Δ
$i = 1.1$									
$i = 1.2$									
⋮									
$i = 1.m$									
$j = 1$									
$i = 2.1$									
$i = 2.2$									
⋮									
$i = 2.m$									
$j = 2$									
⋮									
$i = n.1$									
$i = n.2$									
⋮									
$i = n.m$									
$j = n$									
Σj – Stand-by costs = Operating profit									

costs of sales, and targeted and actual contribution margins. The deviations determined allow the analysis of differences between targeted profit and actual profit.

The open methods of the short-term performance reporting and contribution margin accounting are a simplification in so far as they do not separately account for variations in stock.

Closed Methods

The closed methods of short-term performance reporting and contribution margin accounting determine the revenues, the marginal costs of sales, and the contribution margin of units sold in the planning period/time horizon as targeted and actual values per product or product line, as does the open method. The difference is the separate accounting for stocks and variations in stocks. The method of closed short-term performance reporting and contribution margin accounting is subdivided in three components:

1. Operating performance accounting: accounts for the cost of production at targeted and actual cost of the units produced in the reporting period.
2. Inventory accounting: accounts for the stocktaking and inventory changes by the registration of the opening stock and the changes due to production in the period. There are different values of the stocks in the inventory accounting, viz. the targeted cost of the stocks, the actual cost of the stocks, and the cost variances of the production department.
3. Profit and loss accounting: accounts for the targeted contribution margins and the actual contribution margins of the products sold.

Outlook

Cost accounting in Germany is expected to change gradually as a result of a growing awareness and discussions about the extension of traditionally used actual costing and standard costings with modern cost accounting systems, e.g. zero-based budgeting, activity based costing, benchmarking, or target costing, due to changes in theoretical costing frameworks and increased competition. It appears that enterprises are ceasing to use general allocation bases to allocate indirect costs to the costs per unit of output. Time allocation bases are becoming increasingly important for the allocation of administrative costs and costs of other indirect departments to customers or products. The slump in sales experienced during the last recession in many industries, e.g. the car industry and the mechanical engineering industry, has simultaneously directed many companies' attention toward target costing (Dellmann and Franz 1994: 19). The car industry in particular is looking for cost management strategies based on customer-required design and associated prices. There are indications that such trends will continue in the foreseeable future.

References

Adam, D. (1970), *Entscheidungsorientierte Kostenbewertung* (Wiesbaden: Gabler).

Agthe, K. (1963), *Kostenplanung und Kostenkontrolle im Industriebetrieb* (Baden-Baden: Verlag für Unternehmensführung).

Becker, H. P. (1984), *Verwendung und Gestaltung der Kosten- und Leistungsrechnung in mittelgroßen Industrieunternehmen* (Darmstadt: S. Toeche-Mittler).

—— (1985), 'Einsatz der Kostenrechnung in mittelgroßen Industrieunternehmen—Eine empirische Untersuchung', *Zeitschrift für betriebswirtschaftliche Forschung*, 37: 601–17.

Bohr, K., and Schwab, H. (1984), 'Überlegungen zu einer Theorie der Kostenrechnung', *Zeitschrift für Betriebswirtschaft*, 54: 139–59.

Coenenberg, A. G., and Schoenfeld, H. M. W. (1990), 'The Development of Managerial Accounting in Germany: A Historical Analysis', *Accounting Historians' Journal*, 17: 95–112.

Dellmann, K., and Franz, K. P. (1994), 'Von der Kostenrechnung zum Kostenmanagement', in K. Dellman and K. P. Franz (eds.), *Neuere Entwicklungen im Kostenmanagement* (Bern, Stuttgart, and Vienna: Haupt), 15–30.

Dorn, G. (1992), 'Geschichtliche Entwicklung der Kostenrechnung', in W. Männel (ed.), *Handbuch der Kostenrechnung* (Wiesbaden: Gabler), 97–104.

Franke, R. (1972), *Betriebsmodelle, Rechensysteme für Zwecke der kurzfristigen Planung, Kontrolle und Kalkulation* (Düsseldorf: Bertelsmann Universitätsverlag).

Frost, A., and Meyer, P. (1981), *Ausgestaltungsformen der Kostenrechnungssysteme in deutschen Großunternehmen—Eine empirische Untersuchung* (Kiel).

Hauer, G. (1994), 'Hierarchische kennzahlenorientierte Entscheidungsrechnung—Ein Beitrag zum Investitions- und Kostenmanagement', D.Phil. thesis, Regensburg.

Henzel, F. (1931), *Erfassung und Verrechnung der Gemienkosten in der Unternehmung* (Berlin and Vienna: Spaeth und Linde).

Hopwood, A. (1983), 'On Trying to Study Accounting in the Contexts in which it Operates', *Accounting, Organizations and Society*, 8: 287–305.

Kaplan, R. S. (1986), 'The Role for Empirical Research in Management Accounting', *Accounting, Organizations and Society*, 11: 429–52.

Kilger, W. (1961), *Flexible Plankostenrechnung*, 1st edn. (Cologne and Opladen: Westdeutscher Verlag).

—— (1973), *Optimale Produktions- und Absatzplanung, Entscheidungsmodelle für den Produktions- und Absatzbereich industrieller Betriebe* (Opladen: Westdeutscher Verlag).

—— (1987), *Einführung in die Kostenrechnung*, 3rd edn. (Wiesbaden: Gabler).

—— (1993), *Flexible Plankostenrechnung und Deckungsbeitragsrechnung*, 10th edn., rev. K. Vikas (Wiesbaden: Gabler).

Küpper, H.-U. (1983), 'Der Bedarf an Kosten- und Leistungsinformationen in Industrieunternehmungen—Ergebnisse einer empirischen Erhebung', *Kostenrechnungspraxis*, 169–81.

—— (1993), 'Internes Rechnungswesen', in J. Hauschildt and O. Grün (eds.), *Ergebnisse empirischer betriebswirtschaftlicher Forschung: Zu einer Realtheorie der Unternehmung, Festschrift für E. Witte* (Stuttgart: Sohäffer-Poeschel), 601–31.

Küpper, H.-U. and Hoffmann, H. (1988), 'Ansätze und Entwicklungstendenzen des Logistik-Controlling in Unternehmen der Bundesrepublik Deutschland—Ergebnisse einer empirischen Erhebung', *Die Betriebswirtschaft*, 48: 587–601.

Laßmann, G. (1968), *Die Kosten- und Erlösrechnung als Instrument der Planung und Kontrolle in Industriebetrieben* (Düsseldorf: Stahleisen).

—— 1990), 'Plant Models', in E. Groohla *et al.* (eds.), *Handbook of German Business Management*, vol. 2 (Stuttgart, Berlin, etc.: C. E. Poeschel and Springer), cols. 1777–87.

Lehmann, M. R. (1981), *Industriekalkulation*, 4th edn. (Stuttgart: C. E. Poeschel).

Lücke, W. (1965), 'Die kalkulatorischen Zinsen im betrieblichen Rechnungswesen', *Zeitschrift für Betriebswirtschaft*, 35, supplement, 3–28.

Plaut, H.-G. (1953), 'Die Grenz-Plankostenrechnung', *Zeitschrift für Betriebswirtschaft*, 23: 347–63.

—— (1955), 'Grenzplankostenrechnung', *Zeitschrift für Betriebswirtschaft*, 25: 25–39.

—— (1984), 'Grenzplankosten- und Deckungsbeitragsrechnung als modernes Kostenrechnungssystem', *Kostenrechnungspraxis*, 20–6 and 67–72.

REFA, Verband für Arbeitsstudien e.V. (1958), *Das REFA-Buch*, vol. 2, Zeitvorgabe, 8th edn. (Munich: Carl Hauser).

REFA, Verband für Arbeitsstudien e.V. (1978), *Methodenlehre des Arbeitsstudiums, Part* 2, *Datenermittlung*, 6th edn. (Munich: Carl Hauser).

Riebel, P. (1994), *Einzelkosten- und Deckungsbeitragsrechnung, Grundfragen einer markt- und entscheidungsorientierten Unternehmensrechnung*, 7th edn. (Wiesbaden: Gabler).

Rummel, K. (1949), *Einheitliche Kostenrechnung auf der Grundlage einer vorausgesetzten Proportionalität der Kosten zu betrieblichen Größen*, 3rd edn. (Düsseldorf: Stahlheisen) (1st edn.: *Grundlagen der Selbstkostenrechnung* (1934)).

Scherrer, G. (1991), *Kostenrechnung*, 2nd edn. (Stuttgart and New York: Gustav Fischer).

—— (1993), 'Kostenabweichungen', in K. Chmielewicz and M. Schweitzer (eds.), *Handwörterbuch des Rechnungswesens*, 3rd end. (Stuttgart: C. E. Poeschel), cols. 1168–79.

—— and Wimmer, K. (1992), 'Kostenabweichungsanalye', *Regensburger Diskussionsbeiträge zur Wirtschaftswissenschaft*, 246 (Regensburg).

Schmalenbach, E. (1908–9), 'Über Verrechnungspreise', *Zeitschrift für handelswirtschaftliche Forschung*, 3: 165–85.

—— (1934), *Selbstkostenrechnung und Preispolitik*, 6th edn. (Leipzig: Gloeckner).

Schneider, D. (1992), 'Entwicklungsschwerpunkte zur heutigen Kostenrechnung', in W. Männel (ed.), *Handbuch der Kostenrechnung* (Wiesbaden: Gabler), 87–96.

Schweitzer, M., and Küpper, H.-U. (1986), *Systeme der Kostenrechnung*, 4th edn. (Landsberg: Verlag moderne Industrie).

Seicht, G. (1990), 'Cost Accounting', in E. Grochla *et al.* (eds.), *Handbook of German Business Management*, vol. 1 (Stuttgart, Berlin, etc.: C. E. Poeschel and Springer), cols. 611–22.

Wartmann, R. (1962–5), Entwicklung, Aufbau und Rechengänge eines mathematischen Hochofenmodells, Teil I–VII, *Archiv für das Eisenhüttenwesen*, 34: 879–85; 35: 15–20, 159–67, 173–81, 373–80, 911–54; 36: 609–10.

6

A Survey of Management Accounting Practice in Greek Firms

Apostolos Ballas and George Venieris

Introduction

During the past decade there has been increased interest in the literature (mainly the Anglo-Saxon literature) about management accounting and costing in particular. This was attributed mainly to changes in the production techniques employed by many firms, which, according to the proponents of the new costing techniques, made traditional costing methods irrelevant. These criticisms struck a chord with many firms, and the proposed changes in costing technology were rapidly adopted by a number of companies, mainly in North America.

The development of accounting in Greece differs considerably from that in other European countries. This can be traced to both specific cultural factors and institutional factors. A major determinant of the state of accounting in Greece has been fiscal policy. In the special case of cost accounting, for many years, rules for the determination of the production cost of goods in many industries were influenced by the government's decision that the prices of some goods be kept at an artificially low level. Another factor influencing the development of accounting, management accounting in particular, is the size of Greek companies. The vast majority (99%) employ fewer than fifty persons. Even those that are big (by Greek standards) are usually family-owned and managed. Thus information, especially information about the company's finances, is available only to a limited number of people.

The purpose of this chapter is to describe the state of the art of management accounting practice in Greek firms. Our investigation was undertaken through a series of interviews with selected large firms. It is mainly a study of how things are, rather than a discussion of how things ought to be. Management accounting practice in Greece has not been investigated before, although in 1991 Venieris looked at cost accounting practices. Questions relevant to our study were included in the two studies of management in Greece (1972, 1986) and the survey on the Hellenic General Accounting Plan (1993) conducted by the Hellenic Management Association.

The structure of this chapter is as follows. The first section deals with accounting education and the status of the accounting profession. We then describe the provisions of the Hellenic General Accounting Plan and tax law regarding cost accounting, which represent standard practice for a significant number of Greek firms. Subsequently, we discuss the methodology used in our study, and in the final section the results of our interviews are presented.

The Accounting Profession in Greece

The Greek general public's opinion of accountants is self-contradictory. The most frequently held view is that you go to an accountant in order to minimize your tax liability. The logical consequence of this view is that for many companies, especially small ones, the only function that they expect their accountants to fulfil is to make certain that the requirements of the Eforia (tax authorities) are satisfied. At the same time, for many other people, accounting has an air of scientific exactness, and cost data in particular, as our results show, of indisputability.[1]

It is potentially for this reason that in the early 1980s cost accounting had its heyday. The incoming, socialist, PASOK government was convinced that companies were colluding to artificially raise their prices. The Department of Trade hired scores of personnel (of whom many had only a very vague idea of accounting) as cost accountants in order to compute the 'definitive' production cost for many goods, ranging from bread to medicines and including livestock feed. In addition, it issued successive circulars which attempted to regulate trivial details of cost measurement. The result of this activity was that price ceilings were imposed on many goods. A direct consequence of this policy was substantial losses for many firms, while others ceased production altogether and started importing the goods they produced before. Eventually, this policy was abandoned. Its effects on the attitudes of Greek managers are best summarized by a comment of one of the managers interviewed: 'I refuse to divulge cost data to *anyone* unless they clearly state what they plan to use them for.'

The professional status of accountants (with the exception of auditors)[2] in Greece is not defined explicitly in any law. This contrasts with standard practice for other professions in Greece, whose (professional) rights and responsibilities are expressly codified in law. There are many people who describe themselves as accountants who have no formal education in accounting. Usually they perform subsidiary accounting tasks (i.e. bookkeeping), but in many small companies they are also responsible for interacting with the tax authorities. Company law requires companies that meet certain size requirements to employ accountants who are graduates either of the Athens University of Economics and Business or equivalent institutions or of the polytechnics' (which in Greece are called TEI) accounting departments.

Up to 10 years ago, there were no university-level, stand-alone accounting departments. Thus students who wanted to follow an accounting-related career usually opted for the business administration departments of either the Athens School of Economics and Commerce or the Graduate Industrial School of Piraeus or Thessaloniki (as they were called at the time). The curriculum of these departments, in response to market pressure, put considerable stress on accounting and related subjects. Out of a total of 30 to 35 courses, students would take two financial accounting courses, one on taxation accounting and one on management (mainly cost) accounting. In addition, and depending on the school, there would be either a financial statements analysis course or an auditing course. This emphasis on accounting shaped the career paths of many graduates.

Recently, the University of Macedonia (as the Graduate Industrial School of Thessaloniki is now called) has launched a department of accounting and finance, and the Athens University of Economics and Business (formerly the Athens School of Economics and Commerce) is contemplating a similar move. However, it is too early to say what effects these departments will have on accounting education and research.

There are no professional accounting organizations in Greece (with the exception of the Soma Orkoton Elegkton (Body of Sworn-in Auditors), whose members are *practising* auditors). There are a number of 'trade unions' for accountants, but, as we have already said, these do not have any specific membership requirements. Prominent among them is the Panhellenic Accountants' Association, whose membership includes mainly tax but also financial accountants. There is also a Panhellenic Association of Cost Accountants, but its members are in no way comparable to those of the Chartered Institute of Management Accountants in the United Kingdom. To compensate for this absence of professional accounting associations, the Hellenic Management Association, which is the professional forum of Greek managers and has as its goal the advancement of scientific management, has established the Institute of Financial Management. This institute, by the very nature of its membership, has served as a forum for the promotion of modern accounting techniques, mainly through educational activities. Prominent among them is preparation for the United Kingdom's CIMA examinations.

The Hellenic General Accounting Plan (HGAP)

In 1981, following many years of effort, the Hellenic General Accounting Plan (HGAP) was adopted. In many ways it was a revolutionary concept for Greek accounting, and since 1987, when it was made compulsory, it has been the cause of significant improvement in the reporting practices of Greek firms.

The plan covers both the format of financial reports (though the rules are simply the requirements of the fourth directive of the EU) and financial record keeping. There are ten groups of accounts, clustered in three categories: financial accounting accounts (groups 1–8), management accounting accounts (group 9), and memorandum accounts (group 10). Of particular interest here is group 9, which covers cost accounting and is used by some firms for internal use financial statements. A fundamental principle of the Accounting Plan is that this group of accounts should be independent of financial accounting. The main accounts that are part of this group are presented in Table 6.1.

Table 6.1. Management accounting accounts in HGAP

Account number	Account title
90	Reciprocal Accounts
91	Cost re-classifications
92	Cost centres
93	Manufacturing costs
94	Stocks
95	Standard cost variances
96	Income—cost of goods sold
97	Differences in accounting treatment
98	Manufacturing income statement
99	Internal transfers

Since 1 January 1991 companies that meet certain size requirements must use the accounts of group 9 (and the related rules) in the computation of the cost of goods sold and inventories. Obviously, these numbers are for financial reporting purposes.

The Accounting Plan mandates the use of full costing[3] (though rules can be interpreted liberally, and firms may even use modern costing methods such as Activity Based Costing), and includes some rules for the determination of the production cost. These can be briefly stated as follows:

1. Cost elements must be grouped, for bookkeeping purposes, by type, not by purpose. This is done in the financial accounting accounts (group 6).
2. Periodically, cost elements are aggregated in group 9 accounts by purpose, in order to determine the cost of the basic functions of the firm. These functions, in accordance with the provisions of the HGAP, are production, administration, research and development, distribution, and finance. According to the plan, these functions should be subdivided in cost centres, but this is left to the discretion of each firm.

3. The cost of the administration, research and development,[4] distribution, and financial functions is, generally speaking, charged directly to the profit and loss account. In particular, it is stated more than once that financing costs should not be charged either to production cost or allocated to the cost of other functions in the firm.
4. Finally, costs should be differentiated into direct and indirect costs (overhead). Manufacturing overhead should be allocated to products on the basis of 'rational criteria'. Though the Accounting Plan does not specify what these should be, it has frequently been argued in Greek accounting periodicals and books that these may be direct labour, machine hours, etc.

Among the companies interviewed for this study, opinion about the usefulness of HGAP costing rules and group 9 is divided. Some companies find that they fully meet their needs, whereas others find them cumbersome and an unnecessary duplication of work that is already being done.[5] However, our sample was composed mainly of firms that were using cost accounting systems long before HGAP was made compulsory and which they did not abandon, since they felt that they were more suited to their needs. Thus, it is interesting to examine the reaction of the 'average' company on which HGAP was forced. The Institute of Financial Management of the Hellenic Management Association conducted a study of reactions in 1993 in order to petition the government for improvements to the plan. Answers to the question 'which are the main problems that your company faces from the application of HGAP' are particularly illuminating. Thirty per cent of the responses (respondents could give multiple answers) were dismissive of group 9 without providing any reason why they felt it was not useful; if we add those who gave more complete answers, close to 40 per cent of the responses[6] were against the cost accounting rules. Arguments against were frequently conflicting; for example, some thought that the rules were too detailed and should have been simpler, whereas others thought that they were not detailed enough.

In addition to the requirements of the Hellenic General Accounting Plan, companies in the past also had to cope with a series of frequently conflicting tax rules. Fortunately, with the adoption of Presidential Decree 186/92, the Code of Book and Records, the use of the Accounting Plan (though use of cost accounting rules is obligatory for very big firms only) has been made compulsory for tax reporting as well.

Methodology

The traditional textbook description of the aim of management accounting is that it should provide information within an organization to facilitate planning, managerial decision making, and control of the company's activities and functional units. This definition derives from a specific cultural context, namely the Anglo-Saxon one. The goal of this study is twofold: first to examine for what (internal) purposes Greek firms use accounting information, then to see how this information is produced.

In designing this study, we were faced with a number of methodological problems. The first, and perhaps the most difficult one, was how to choose the population of firms to study. Small companies (which are usually simple organizations) do not need management accounting systems, because financial accounting information, or even informal information exchange, is usually sufficient. Furthermore, centralized, hierarchical organizations will have limited use for management accounting, since most decision-making power resides at the top of the pyramid, where most information is collected too. Indeed, in such organizations, the development of management accounting systems may be actively discouraged, in order to better control the flow of information.

Greek companies tend to be small, with decision making centralized at the very top, usually in the hands of the owner of the company or a member of his family. For these reasons, any investigation of the state of the art in management accounting in Greek companies is a study of management accounting practice in a very small population of large firms. Smaller firms limit themselves to cost accounting as mandated by the Tax Code and a 'back of the envelope' cash budget (at best). Some slightly dated evidence on the extent of the use of management accounting information can be found in the 1986 survey of management in Greece conducted by the Hellenic Management Association. In a sample of firms with more than 30 employees, the survey revealed that only 77% of the firms had a written, formal budget, and less than 40% had a budget covering all the activities of the firm.[7] For the purposes of this study, we also interviewed Mr J. Kokinos, member of the steering committee of the Body of Sworn-in Auditors, of the working party for the Accounting Plan, and of the National Accounting Council. His view was that the management of fewer than 500 firms—though the real number is much smaller, since a lot of them are members of groups of companies—understand the cost data provided by the Accounting Plan. Furthermore, fewer than 200, with the afore-mentioned proviso, compute production cost figures at regular intervals during the accounting year. His opinion was that most firms are 'afraid of the discipline' that the use of cost data would impose on management. This point is reinforced by some of the answers we received in our other interviews. One manager admitted that his firm implements HGAP's cost-accounting provisions only superficially, and does not make frequent enough cost computations using its costing system because it cannot keep track of the inventory!

For these reasons, we selected a sample of 23 large firms representing various sectors of the economy which are considered to be professionally managed, with staffing policy based on objective criteria rather than family connections. In addition, firms considered for inclusion in the sample had to satisfy the criterion of 'good management' as evidenced by profitability (though a loss-making firm, Aluminum de Gréce, was included in the sample by virtue of its size and influence in the economy and accounting practice) and market leadership. Where possible, we opted for firms quoted in the Athens Stock Exchange, since this reduces the influence of large shareholders and increases the need for professional management. Of these, 14 agreed to participate,[8] though the sample is actually bigger, since in many cases they are groups of companies. Summary information about the firms included is given in Table 6.2. (The Appendix provides a brief description of the companies' activities.)

Table 6.2. Aggregates of companies interviewed

Total sales (billions of drachmas)	80.1
Net profits (billions of drachmas)	16.4
Number of employees	2925

The second methodological problem was that of data collection. This chapter represents the first attempt to document management accounting practice in Greek firms. While seemingly a straightforward project, it has entailed a serious research design problem, in light of problems of terminology and definition encountered by both the researchers and the managers who were asked to describe management accounting practice in their firms. Many terms were found to convey a different meaning to the researchers and the managers. This was evident from the beginning of the study, but was also anticipated from prior consulting projects and teaching in management development programmes. For example, when one of the authors referred to budget revision, he meant corrections to the budget after comparison with what actually happened. The manager, however, thought of revision simply as the process of comparing budgeted figures with actual ones. Likewise, the meaning of 'standard cost' varied from budgeted cost to *ex post* computed cost using standard cost for materials (the issue of standard costing was one of the most interesting, and is extensively discussed in the next section).

The usual approach to data collection in studies of this kind is through questionnaires mailed to companies. However, given the communication problems outlined above, for this study, we opted for 'directed interviews' with managers. We initially contacted the chief finance officer (CFO) of these firms, who then directed us to the heads of the budgeting and cost accounting departments (in one company all three responsibilities were undertaken by one person, whereas in five others the CFO was contacted only to negotiate access). In some cases, the department heads were all interviewed at the same time. Managers were asked to speak extensively about what their companies were doing and were asked to clarify ambiguities.[9] This method has the advantage that the actual decision-making process is documented. However, it also has the disadvantage, in comparison to the traditional survey-questionnaire methodology, that no statistical tests can be carried out.[10]

Our interviews with managers started with some general questions about the company and its management. We then proceeded to discuss costing, budgeting, and planning procedures. We finally asked our interviewees to comment on the use of management accounting information for financial control and performance measurement.

Interview Results

In this section we present the findings from the interviews with the managers. The structure of the section follows the interview outline presented in the previous section. We first present what is usual practice in the firms interviewed, before considering exceptions to the rule.

Management of the Company

The main items discussed under this heading were the firm's management style, the position of management accountants in the firm's hierarchy, and what drives management accounting development in the company.

Our sample included 6 companies with substantial ties to a multinational firm. This was not seen as a problem, since it has been argued that, in general, the influence of local management culture is likely to be stronger than the influence of foreign shareholders (Hofstede 1980).

All the companies surveyed, with two exceptions, had separate (from financial accounting) management accounting groups dealing with budgeting, cost accounting, and internal reporting. In three cases, the financial reporting group was not even part of the same directorate. This differs from Venieris's (1991) results, according to which, in 48% of the companies in his sample, cost calculations were carried out by the same employees who dealt with financial accounting. The exceptions were due either to size (a company with few employees cannot justify too many accountants, even though it was felt that there is a need for personnel dedicated to the task) or to managerial philosophy. More specifically, the finance manager in one company told us that his company did not use management accounting information except as a guide to setting prices, relying instead on non-financial operational information, because there is 'too much uncertainty' in their business environment.

These groups enjoy a high profile in their companies, reporting directly to the managing director or the management committee. With the exception of one company, the personnel of these groups consisted of people with an economics background, whereas in the past, engineers and production managers had considerable influence. In one case the directorate which included management accounting was headed by the person next in line to become chief executive officer (CEO), while another case exemplifies a characteristic of Greek management, namely that lines of communication can bypass the official organizational chart. According to the chart, the head of accounting reports to the assistant managing director, and he to the managing director. However, the head of accounting is the most senior (in terms of years with the company) among the managers and long past retirement age, but remains in his job because of the absolute trust that he enjoys with the managing director. Thus, practice is more like in the Army, where the colonel trusts the sergeant major more than the junior officers. It is thus not surprising that this company enjoys a reputation for its financial reporting and management accounting innovations by comparison with other firms in the same industry.

A different picture emerged in our discussions with one company, where the budgeting group did indeed enjoy a high profile, though not the costing group. Indeed, cost accountants told us that with the exception of specific projects where management could see a tangible, monetary benefit in the cost figures, they could not be sure what use senior managers made of the cost reports. Furthermore, in the company's revised organizational chart,[11] cost accounting was grouped with bookkeeping.

Many companies chose to comment on the relationship between the MIS group and the accounting group(s). The computer systems personnel, whose job is to support management rather than develop software for others or support production, were always grouped together with finance. This contrasts with the argument (by MIS theorists) that the MIS group should be independent, reporting directly to the CEO, in order to assist in strategy formulation. Some senior managers justified this practice by questioning 'how it could be otherwise', whereas others were emphatic that this made certain that the MIS people knew 'what a fixed asset is'. Thus, with one exception, managers felt that computerization of management accounting procedures was satisfactory. Indeed, one company no longer issues printed reports, but relies on managers to access information on-line.

No clear picture emerged as to what guides management accounting development in the Greek firms surveyed. Management consultants, 'technology transfer' from parent companies where appropriate, attending seminars, or even reading in their free time were all mentioned by managers as methods used to keep up with developments in the field. All but two of the companies surveyed stated that they would not rely solely on management consultants to change either their costing or their budgeting procedures (and at least one, not at all).

Costing

All the firms interviewed employed some variant of traditional costing techniques, if only for financial reporting purposes. Managers were asked to describe how these techniques were applied and whether they were satisfied with the costing provisions of the Accounting Plan. Furthermore, we asked whether any modern costing techniques (such as ABC) were being applied or considered for application.

Cost data are used by Greek firms primarily as a guide to pricing and also for production planning and product/client profitability assessments. In contrast to what accounting academics claim, managers of 13 firms (93%) in our sample listed as one of the most important uses of cost data the periodic computation of profit. This allows these companies to judge how well they are doing and to take corrective action.

Since the companies in our sample followed the provisions of the HGAP, they all computed product costs on a full-cost basis, even if only for financial reporting purposes. With the exception of one firm, direct costs were computed only as an intermediate stage in the computation of full costs. The one firm which used direct costs for decision-making purposes defined as a direct cost the rights it has on a product. In their long-term plans regarding the accounting system, they wanted to differentiate revenue that is attributable to a specific product and revenue that is derived from their corporate image and from distribution channels.[12]

The definition of overheads varied considerably among the companies in our sample, and in many cases it appeared to be based on past practice. Overhead allocation was based on simple rules such as direct labour or machine hours or production volume. However, we were told that this was not a 'blanket' rate for the whole plant, but rather, varied by department.

Four firms were using, or phasing in, Activity Based Costing.[13] In the introduction of ABC the influence of multinational parent companies is evident; two of the companies who introduced ABC did so at the suggestion of their parent companies. However, only the finance manager (and not even her deputies) of one of these companies appeared sensitive to the managerial implications of changing the costing system. She actually said that the biggest problem in implementing ABC was educating senior managers and trying to gain their support, and that in fact ABC was more about management than accounting.

Other firms which persisted in using traditional costing techniques did so because they were satisfied with the traditional methods, since they 'ensure comparability among plants' and are 'useful for production planning'. In two cases, the managers being interviewed appeared unaware of ABC.

Budgeting and Planning Procedures

Under this heading come both technical issues, such as the budget period, whether there is a special group in charge of the preparation of the budget, and frequency of revision, and management issues, such as reporting procedures and whether the budget is a result of a participative procedure or handed down from above.

When managers were asked how the budget was used, the most frequent reply was as a framework to the firm's planning process and a guide to expenditure during the year. One firm explicitly used the budget as a motivational device; the budgeted profit was a very conservative estimate, and represented an absolute minimum that the company's management was willing to accept. If profits were higher than the budgeted figure, then employees received as a bonus a percentage of the difference.

In the companies surveyed the budgeting process typically started from 6 months before the beginning of the fiscal year to 1 month after. All respondents emphasized that the budgeting process was fully participative, with lower-level managers allowed to set their own goals and the profit goal for the firm an aggregation of these mini-budgets. Guidelines were very rarely issued,[14] though in one firm it was stressed that 'these [goals] should be better than last year'. Other respondents stated that budget information had to emphasize forecasts compatible with market realities. Departmental budget forecasts were aggregated (and checked for compatibility) by the budgeting group, and the draft budget was submitted to top management. All managers interviewed confirmed that normally the budget was approved at that point. However, two of the companies, both of which are associated to multinational groups, had to get budget approval from international headquarters as well. After the budget was approved, it was distributed to all the managers. The emphasis on participation in the budget process seems to suggest that there is a hidden agenda: namely, that every member of the company should be familiar with the plans for the year. This attitude among the managers of the firms in our sample is in sharp contrast to the answers of an (unspecified) number of managers in the HMA (1986) study, who suggested that the budget is one of the most commercially sensitive documents of the firm, which should therefore be for the eyes of the owner-manager only.

As has already been said of the 14 companies surveyed, only 13 computed a budget covering all activities of the firm. In one of these firms, there were separate expenditure and revenue budgets, prepared by different people. The management philosophy of this company is that the sales people will sell every product produced, because they are of superior quality, and that therefore production people should not have to worry about revenues.

Of the 8 industrial firms in our sample, 7 included in their budgets both units of materials, labour hours, etc. and unit price, and computed a budgeted cost per product unit. In one company (among the non-industrial ones) regional managers were asked to prepare their budget forecasts as percentage changes from the previous year.

Twelve companies in the survey prepared long-term (3–5-year) budgets. In one company these were project / product-specific, whereas in the rest they covered all activities of the firm. In two companies, there was considerable input in the preparation from people with an engineering background, and this created antagonism and ill will with the accountants / finance managers involved in the process. No company indicated that they used discounted cash-flow techniques in evaluating long-term projects, but this may be attributable to investment evaluation being done by different departments.

Budgets were very detailed in their revenue and expenditure forecasts, though only 3 firms prepared cash-flow budgets. In one of these firms, during the preparation of the cash budget, the payment process of their customers was modelled. However, most of the companies in our sample were unusual in that they were either cash-rich or knew with a high degree of probability the timing of their inflows.

Financial Control and Performance Measurement

The final part of the interviews was about the use of management accounting data for financial control and performance evaluation. Two principal issues were discussed with the companies surveyed: (1) whether standard costs were computed and what each company understood by standard cost, and (2) how deviations from the budget were dealt with and whether they had any impact in the remuneration and career development of the managers responsible.

When managers were questioned on whether their firms computed standard costs both for labour and materials[15] and for overheads, all replied in the negative (though one firm plans to do this). In one firm, it was commented that standard cost 'does not suit our firm', but it was not clarified whether this referred to the firm's management style or the production process / product of the firm. Another firm (which operated partly in a regulated environment) did not compute standard costs because this would invite the regulators to question some of the expenditures and, consequently, the prices they were allowed to charge.

This overwhelming rejection of standard cost accounting led us to investigate the issue further. In the modern accounting literature there are two definitions of standard cost, the 'attainable' and the 'ideal'. The former are cost objectives, whereas the latter are 'scientifically' predetermined costs of materials, labour (through time and motion studies), and overheads. On the basis of their responses, we found that to Greek managers, standard costs meant ideal costs (which is what is taught in Greek universities). However,

7 companies prepared budgets which included both units of resources to be produced and unit costs, which were the lower-level managers' goals. This suggests that these Greek companies do in fact compute standard costs based on attainable standards.

Performance measurement was undertaken by assessing deviations from the budget rather than analysing variances (which were normally not computed) from standard costs. Managers were then asked to explain both negative and positive deviations from the budget. However, it is unclear whether these deviations had any impact on the remuneration of the managers responsible (with the exception of one company which, as stated above, awarded bonuses for actual profits exceeding those budgeted). Although in all companies, managers were evaluated on whether they had achieved their budget targets, all senior managers when asked about the performance–remuneration relationship in their company hedged their answers, refusing to mention exactly what circumstances would have a negative effect on middle-level managers' careers. Indeed, the same manager quoted earlier on ABC impressed us again by saying that 'deviations should have an impact on remuneration', placing a very strong emphasis on 'should'.

In concluding this section, it is only fitting that we refer more directly to the issue of cost management. Only two companies in our sample mentioned that they measured costs in order to improve the efficiency of their operations or control expenditure. In fact, one company mentioned that they had decided against using ABC because 'it might suggest inefficiencies in our operations and then what will we do?' In another company we were told that 'we are a young company', and therefore 'management allows us some slack in implementing the budget'. Cost control and, even more so, continuous improvements (*kaizen*) in attempting to increase the efficiency of operations is a concept foreign to Greek management culture, which, because of the traditional family structure of business, places considerable emphasis on largess in employer–labour relations.[16] To the best of our knowledge, no Greek industrial firm uses JIT, either for its supplies or in delivering to its customers.

Summary and Conclusions

For the average Greek company, accounting is driven mainly by fiscal considerations. It is perhaps for this reason that the accounting profession has not received the recognition and social status accorded other professions.

Most Greek firms are small by international standards, and are family-owned and managed. Thus, when the Hellenic General Accounting Plan introduced a systematic way for firms to compute their costs, most firms focused on the problems of applying the plan, rather than viewing it as an opportunity to improve their management.

This study is a first attempt to examine the status of management accounting in Greece. The interviews carried out with managers in selected Greek firms suggest that management accounting has a very high profile, that modern cost-measurement approaches are not unknown to these firms, and indeed that many are in the process of adopting some of the emerging techniques. In preparing budgets, the managers of Greek firms said that they consulted widely, and that top management did not try to impose goals from above. Management accounting information is used by Greek firms for production planning, in formulating their pricing policy, and for general planning purposes. However, with the exception of 2 firms, the Greek enterprises investigated did not use management accounting information for cost-reduction purposes, and indeed, at least some positively eschewed such a use of cost information.

The accounting literature assumes in the main that the way a company accounts for its activities and the resources that they consume is intrinsically linked to the way it is managed. By comparison with previous studies, we found that management accounting practice in Greek firms has developed considerably during the past few years. This is evidenced by both an improvement in the status and qualifications of people involved in management accounting and the adoption of techniques such as ABC. No doubt, differences remain in the application of these techniques in Greek companies versus other European companies, which maybe understood in terms of cultural elements in Greek management.

APPENDIX

A Brief Introduction to the Firms Surveyed

Aluminum de Grèce S.A.I.C. produces alumina, aluminum, and aluminum alloys. The French group Pechinéy is one of its biggest shareholders, and its facilities represent the biggest private sector investment in Greece, ever.

Alpha Credit Bank S.A. is the biggest privately owned commercial bank in Greece.

Antena S.A. is the biggest electronic mass media group in Greece, with interests in US and Australian radio stations, and its TV channel has the highest ratings.

Athenian Brewery S.A. is a subsidiary of Heineken SA, and produces and imports beer and mineral water. It is the most profitable industrial firm in Greece.

Chemical Industries of Northern Greece S.A. is a producer of fertilizers, cooling liquids, livestock feeds, etc.

Delta Dairy S.A. produces dairy products, fruit juices, frozen vegetables, and animal food. Its 'Life' juices were a major innovation creating a new market.

Elais's main activities include the production of margarine, cooking fats, olive oil, etc. and the import, export, and trade of all types of industrial products. Its main shareholder is, indirectly, Unilever BV.

Hellenic Bottling Company S.A. is a franchisee of Coca-Cola in Greece. It has the highest market capitalization among the firms quoted in the Athens Stock Exchange, and it fully owns subsidiaries in Cyprus, the United Kingdom, and many Eastern European countries.

Hellenic Telecommunication Organization S.A. is the monopoly supplier of trunk telecommunication services. It is state-owned, but recently a new law was passed allowing for its partial privatization.

Intracom S.A.'s main lines of business are the construction of telecommunications equipment and software development.

Mechanica S.A. is the biggest public works contractor in Greece.

Neoset S.A. produces furniture structures for both domestic use and work-places.

Spot Thompson Advertising S.A. is a subsidiary of Spot Thompson, and is Greece's most profitable advertising agency.

Titan Cement Co. S.A. is the second biggest cement manufacturer in Greece. It exports in many countries, including the United Kingdom and United States. It was the first company in Greece to introduce a social report.

Notes

1. An MBA student (an engineer by training) of one of the authors described accounting as follows: 'If physics is the science of the approximate, accounting is the science of the exact.' In our experience, this view is very common among people with an undergraduate or MBA-level education in accounting.
2. For an extensive description of the status of auditors in Greece, see Ballas 1994.
3. The plan makes provision for the computation of standard cost as well.
4. R & D expenses are split into those that relate to long-term projects, which are capitalized, and the rest, which are transferred to the profit and loss account. The depreciation of capitalized R & D expenses is a determinant of production cost.
5. To do justice to the Accounting Plan, we should add that all companies felt that it substantially improved financial accounting information and record keeping in general.
6. The rest of the responses were complaints pertaining to financial accounting.
7. This represents a significant increase since the early 1970s, when, in a similar survey, the corresponding percentages were 44% and 20%.
8. The rest were not willing to provide information in detail, which was a prerequisite for the methodology used in this study.
9. The authors acknowledge that this methodology is potentially open to a different communication problem: viz. how managers' words are translated from Greek into English. For this reason, we opted for the most direct, hence neutral, translation possible.
10. Strictly speaking, since the sample was not random, statistical tests would not be valid anyway.
11. Taking effect from January 1995.
12. The description is necessarily vague here, in order to preserve the anonymity of the company.
13. This is in addition to cost computations required for financial reporting purposes.
14. Excluding forecasts about the Greek economy or the industry.
15. Two firms computed standard cost for materials only.
16. Efficiency improvements in the mind of the Greek public are associated with lay-offs and salary caps.

References

Ballas, A. (1994), 'Accounting in Greece', *European Accounting Review*, 3: 107–21.

Hellenic Management Association (1972), *Management in Greek Companies* (Athens: H.M.A.) (in Greek).

—— (1986), *Management in Greece* (Athens: H.M.A.) (in Greek).

—— (1993), *Survey Regarding the Hellenic General Accounting Plan* (Athens: H.M.S.) (in Greek).

Hofstede, C. (1980), Culture's Consequences (Beverly Hills, Calif.: Sage Publications).
Venieris, G. (1991), 'Management Accounting: Theory and Practice', paper presented at the 14th Annual Conference of the European Accounting Association.

7
Management Accounting in Italy
Evolution within Tradition

Maria Bergamin Barbato, Paolo Collini, and Alberto Quagli

Introduction

The evolution of accounting theory in Italy has played a crucial part in the development of management accounting. The relative lack of acceptance of new accounting techniques is largely due to past achievements in accounting theory, both in financial reporting and in cost accounting. Putting modern accounting in a historical and cultural context represents an appropriate way to understand its stages of development and potential future changes.

This chapter starts from the debate on financial accounting between the two major schools of thought at the beginning of this century, and traces some of the major changes the country witnessed in its attempt to tie changes in the economic environment to accounting change. Today, many of the innovations in management accounting are derived largely from American accounting techniques, but, as in the past, the specifically Italian tradition and the economic situation played an important role in shaping management accounting and the way it is still largely used by managers.

It is argued in this chapter that Italian cost accounting has been affected by two major factors over the last 90 years: the characteristic financial accounting tradition and the lack of keen market competition.

Italian accounting tradition stems in large part from the works of Fabio Besta and Gino Zappa, two of the main thinkers. Besta laid down the foundations of modern financial accounting, and saw the integration of cost accounting into accounting. Zappa[1] was later able to advance Besta's accounting conceptual framework. The prevalence of Zappa's theory over his predecessor's[2] in the first half of this century has had a strong influence on academics in the field of management accounting.

The low level of market competition until the late 1970s has driven companies' attention partially away from the issue of cost efficiency, with an effect on the way management accounting has been used and designed.

We believe that these factors provide some explanation of the relative lack of Italian methods in management accounting over the past several decades, with the consequent adoption of American accounting techniques. However, we believe that this has also contributed positively to the way academics and managers face the challenges of modern cost accounting at a time of dramatic change, which Italy is presently undergoing.

In this chapter, some factors that have shaped management accounting are explained, and the peculiar characteristics of Italian cost accounting are highlighted. In addition, in the last section, some of the predicted trends in the fields are described.

Italian Accounting Tradition and its Impact on Management Accounting

During the first part of this century the accounting debate in Italy mainly focused on financial reporting. The then new Zappa accounting conceptual framework was named *sistema del reddito* (income-based accounting) to differentiate it from Fabio Besta's generally accepted accounting system known as *'del patrimonio'* (patrimonial accounting, or asset-based accounting). The dispute between the two approaches drove a large part of accounting work in academia at the time. Zappa's approach became 'the only approach' accepted by regulators when Italian civil law imposed Zappa's income statement form on all incorporated firms.[3] Zappa's stand against Besta's approach and his success in both academia and practice drove academic accountants later to consider Zappa's conceptual approach as the principal framework for any accounting concept.

Zappa paid special attention to computing product costs, and criticized the then common practice of showing in the income statement gross margins by single products and operations.

In addition, in accordance with Besta's approach, financial accounting and cost accounting were, before Zappa, jointly kept within the same book. Zappa propounded the need for keeping two separate books. In his view, the two accounting systems should pursue different goals, and therefore represented different assumptions. Consistent with this approach to financial reporting, Zappa warned against the danger of adopting an income statement form where costs and margins of individual products or operations are shown. He held that management can only be appraised as a whole, because of the strong relations between different products and different operations within organizations.

Moving away from Besta, Zappa asserted the need to calculate income independently of the value of invested capital. Accordingly, in Zappa's view, financial accounting should be applied only to calculate total income. For Zappa, the value of capital shown in financial reporting is not directly related to market value of assets and liabilities: it is a consequence of the need to calculate period incomes. The assets' accounting value is derived from the need to split the cost of long-term assets over several administrative periods (Zappa 1950), and the value of capital investments shown in the balance sheet is a consequence of income determination. For example, the book value of an asset is the difference between its original value (cost) and total depreciation, where depreciation is based on the contribution of the asset to the production of income and is independent of the asset's current market value.

In addition, Zappa strongly insisted that calculations of profit or margin figures that do not refer to the whole company's activity have no meaning. He observed the growing complexity in business in his time. The Italian economy was moving from an agriculture- and trade-based economy towards an industrialized one. In agriculture and trade, different parts of the business (products, specific deals, etc.) are largely independent of one another, and linkages between different operations can be ignored. However, in manufacturing, different products and different operations are closely connected, and it becomes impossible to separate clearly costs and revenues of one segment of activity from those of another (Zappa 1950). For Zappa, all operations performed within a company and all decisions taken by management related to one another, and it is impossible to distinguish the financial consequences of one activity (operations and decisions) from those of another.[4] Only the total income can be computed, and specific margins of individual segments of the whole activity are considered misleading. Therefore, they do not represent fairly the firm's financial performance.

According to Zappa's view, figures in financial accounting are exclusively based on the market values set in the transactions between the company and other economic entities. Any accounting value not deriving from monetary transactions with external entities is a 'deviation' from economic reality and an abstraction. Abstraction, in this sense, means a subjective evaluation of economic measures without any reference to actual market transactions. For Zappa, reference to market prices guarantees unbiased financial reporting. Conversely, both costs and revenues that are internally differentiated among different objectives are seen as the cause of poor financial reporting. Following this approach, all costs and revenues are measured on the basis of the amount of financial resources exchanged with other entities when materials and services are acquired or products are sold.

For Zappa, the period income, identified in the economic flow generated by management, is given by costs and revenues, where both are derived from market transactions. This reverses the previous approach: for Besta, income was the result of variations in capital investments' value related to current market prices. By contrast, for Zappa, the assets' value cannot be affected by current market prices. They must be kept fixed, in order to measure only the 'economic flow' generated by management. For Zappa, the reliability of income calculation is crucial in the design of his accounting theory, therefore only market transactions are the basis for accounting bookkeeping. Accordingly, the freedom of accountants to split values among different objects weakens the reliability of income statements. Zappa's approach was seen by academics as the most objective method of preparing balance sheets and income statements in a going concern.[5]

Finally, for Zappa, all values originate from market transactions. Values that do not originate in market transactions (e.g. estimated current repurchasing prices or current market values) cannot be included in income calculation.[6] According to this view, income is not the sum of the margins of a firm's operations: it is the result of the whole company's activities. Consistent with this approach, Zappa developed form of income statement where expenses and revenues are shown without allocating them to any object (products or operations).

Zappa's crucial point: correlation among different events in a complex organization.

Zappa realized how the complexity of businesses affected the practical possibility of tracking costs to different objectives. According to him, the costs of different products and processes are strictly related to one another, and it is impossible to identify the contribution of each individual factor to the whole result (profit) (Zappa 1950: 338). The following quote clarifies Zappa's thinking on the issue: 'All costs of a company in its whole lifetime are related to one another, they all affect one another in their variation' (Zappa 1957: 2. 825).[7]

It is worth noting that this position was based not only on the recognition of the high level of overheads that is now normal in manufacturing. The 'communality' of costs, in Zappa's thinking, referred to an invisible connection between any kind of decision and the final goal of producing value, in terms of profit in the long run, for the company as a whole.

A good example of this position can be seen in product policy. Often companies sacrifice one product's profitability in order to achieve some strategic results that will make other products more profitable in the long run (i.e. market penetration of one existing product to open the way for other new products). A firm cannot consider costs and revenues of the individual product in order to make decisions: costs and revenues of other products, both at present and in the future, have to be taken into account in order to evaluate overall profitability of the strategy, because they are all dedicated to achieving a common goal. In the same way, in Zappa's view, all products, all decisions, and, more generally, all economic events (both resources consumption and revenue generation-related events) in a firm are related to one another.

This theoretical position led Zappa to strongly reject the possibility of calculating the real costs of anything other than those of the company's activities as a whole (Zappa 1950). This position was taken to its extreme, and the same concept has been applied to income calculation: 'Income arises from the whole complex of operations.' 'Income is seen as the result of the total systematic co-ordination of a firm in a view in which assets, factors, and elements lose their individual identity' (Zan 1994: 290). Zappa adopted a totally unitary view over time and space for all economic consequences of management activities.

Finally, Zappa was absolutely convinced that it did not make any sense to calculate product costs. According to him, companies cannot make any sensible decisions on the basis of misleading cost calculations. In fact, he warned several times about the risk of using product costs and margins instead of referring to the company's global financial position as stated in the form of income statement he supported.

Cost Accounting within Zappa's Conceptualization

Zappa's speech at the commencement of the academic year of 1926–7 at the University Ca'Foscari in Venice marks the definition of modern management studies in Italy. The speech (Zappa 1927) defines the object and the methods of a new discipline named '*economia aziendale*'. Zappa stated the need to consider all management studies (accounting, organizational studies, strategic management, business finance) as elements of a single field devoted to explaining a firm's conditions of existence and its economic (or financial) equilibrium. In a general sense, Zappa considered accounting as part of management.

Starting from this point, some of his academic followers saw the possibility of measuring costs of individual segments of business operations without contradicting Zappa's conceptual position. They stated that, in spite of the fact that product costs do not exist in reality (because of internal operations' complexity), it is 'logically' feasible to calculate some cost figures in order to achieve some specific management goals. In other words, product costs can be calculated only if the purpose of the specific cost information is stated and considered in designing the measurement system. In addition, these figures make sense only within the boundaries imposed by the specific purpose for which they have been calculated.

In addition, consistent with Zappa's theory, financial accounting and management accounting must be kept separate, because they belong to different frameworks. They are designed within the boundaries set by their specific set of combinations of 'purpose/cost' allocation.

Theory and Practice of Italian Management Accounting

As stated at the beginning of the chapter, we believe that a historical analysis of managerial accounting development will aid in understanding current Italian management accounting and its differences from other European countries. In our analysis, we distinguish between three periods, whose time frames are defined by historical events relevant to economic activity. The first is a 'pre-industrial age', lasting from Italian national unity (1860) to the Second World War, in which agriculture was the prevailing economic activity, and industry was only slowly beginning to develop its structure. Second is an 'industrial age' (from the Second World War until the early 1970s), a time of strong industrialization due to post-war Western policies. Third is the current age, during which the country has had to face dramatic economic changes. Each of these periods had a different effect on the evolution of management accounting in Italy.

The Pre-Industrial Phase

The Italian economy fundamentally has its roots in agriculture. At the beginning of this century, there were very few industrial firms, and production output and worker resources were largely defined in agricultural terms.[8] Relative to other Western countries, Italian firms of that period were small-sized,[9] and ownership was concentrated in the hands of a few families running different activities (industrial and trading), but fundamentally based on large agricultural possessions.

These factors reduced the need for advanced financial markets; a small number of people owned firms' equity, and often created owner-managed businesses; the lack of shared property gave little pressure to improve management and short-term outcomes. In addition, at that time, Italian firms ran their businesses in favourable market conditions, given protectionist governmental policies imposing custom duties on imported goods, fixed prices for some largely used agricultural commodities, and intensive financial support of major national firms. Moreover, the government became the main customer for the production of large industrial firms, fixing high prices and adopting a policy of large advance payments (Dewerpe 1991).

Under these conditions, competitive pressure was weak, and there was no pressure to focus management efforts on cost control and reduction. In addition, wages were low, due to the large availability of workers moving away from agriculture. The level of mechanization and development of equipment in manufacturing processes was less intensive than in other Western countries. Under these circumstances, there was little interest in efficiency control and improvement.

Moreover, the 'steady state' economy did not encourage firms to undertake programming and planning. It was assumed that past trends would continue into the future, so there was little need to forecast costs and revenues. In this context, the standardization of costs and the implementation of budgetary controls had to wait for many years.

The role of cost accounting

In the pre-industrial period the main purposes of cost accounting were price setting and inventory evaluation for financial reporting.[10] Cost accounting was used for price setting, since competitive pressure was relatively low and the government guaranteed easy markets. Firms could easily transfer their costs to the customers through products' prices. At the time, prevailing accounting theory (Besta's theory) asserted that the evaluation of finished goods should use estimated market prices, but the difficulty of measuring these induced scholars and practitioners to accept the use of full production costs (Besta 1921).

On the other hand, cost accounting did not play an important role in making long- and short-term decisions, due to the steady evolution of business activity and reduced investments in machinery and equipment. In regards to efficiency control, as pointed out, there was weak commitment to reducing input/output ratios. At the same time, the small size of firms and strong family control constrained the development of differential managerial roles within organizations, as well as the development of what would later be identified as 'responsibility accounting'.

Nevertheless, the need to compute costs for pricing led to important consequences. Product prices were set by mark-up methods on full cost. Then, for determining prices, the forecasts of both overhead and production volume began to spread out. Thus, managers also had a way to compare actual with estimated costs and to draw information on the quality of management.

The use of cost accounting in that period had a formal role, however, due to the concept *Ragioneria*, 'the science of administrative control', in which 'control' meant 'constraint' rather than 'guide'. A fundamental role of both financial and cost accounting was the recognition of administrative operations and their evaluation in terms of assessment of personal responsibilities. Cost accounting helped monitor adherence by middle managers to the 'rules' established by top managers. In addition, accounting was the basis for the calculation of workers' wages. Firms used incentive pay and piecework methods, and therefore analytical records of finished goods, scrap, works in progress etc. were needed.

For the afore-mentioned factors, managers and scholars of that period believed in a 'true cost' concept, which was used for all purposes. This was to change radically of course under the influence of Zappa's theory. During the pre-industrial period, however, scholars thought that true cost was difficult to calculate, but not impossible.[11] The role of accountants was to work on estimating this unknown cost.

The structure of production cost

Full costing was seen as the most consistent cost structure, with the purpose of calculating the 'true cost' for price determination and inventory evaluation. Direct costs (labour and materials) were directly traced to product cost on the basis of actual quantity used in different productions. Overheads were classified into fixed and variable. Variable overheads (energy, maintenance, indirect labour) were grouped by organizational units or machine groups, and then traced to products through a single-basis system. The allocation driver was selected from a group of volume-based possible parameters like direct labour cost, manufacturing direct cost, or machine hours. Fixed overheads (machinery and tools depreciation, administration and financial expenses) were traced to products as a proportion of units manufactured. The negligible nature of this expense justified the use of such a simple method. Overall, the volume-based allocation system was seen as simple and reliable by managers.

From around the 1920s, the growing complexity of production processes led to a search for more precise techniques. More sophisticated methods were being studied by academics. Scholars began to distinguish among production centres at different levels inside factories (branches, departments, single machines). For each one, cost-allocation procedures used different bases, depending on the nature of the elements which had to be attributed. For example, there were machine hours for depreciation, direct labour hours for indirect labour costs, etc.[12] Nevertheless, business practices were not much affected by this method. Companies continued to use single-basis cost-allocation methods. The gap between theory and practice has continued to be characteristic of Italian accounting.

The development of management accounting after the Second World War forms the basis of modern management accounting in Italy. Although many of the factors that shaped management accounting during that time have changed recently, the structure of the costing systems still used in many firms was laid down at that time. We argue that the understanding of the key factors affecting accounting at that time is fundamental to understanding the path of progress of accounting in Italy.

The Industrial Phase after the Second World War

In the post-war period the Italian economy grew quickly, and manufacturing became the most important activity of the country.[13] Many factors affect this growth. Basic influences included the initial aid from the Marshall Plan, the surge of low-cost workers as a result of internal migration, the need for converting war industry to a peace economy, and more international trade exchange to replace the pre-war closed economy policy.

The first effect was the development of heavy investments in infrastructures, equipment, and machinery,[14] allowed by a growing demand which was able to absorb the increasing production volume.[15] Therefore many firms expanded, with a consequent impact on organizational structures and the development of managerial roles. This occurred slowly, however, because Italian firms were still characterized by strong family ownership, fundamentally unwilling to delegate their decisional power to professional managers. This also constrained willingness to seek capital on stock exchanges. Thus, even though economic power lay with large-sized firms, small companies continued to play an important role in the economy.

The growth of fixed investments led owners and managers to look to long-term horizons. Consequently, conditions became favourable for systematic planning and budgeting. Other factors were also important, including the increasing presence in Italy of multinational firms, which led to a gradual diffusion of well-tested American managerial techniques such as standard costing, budgeting, variance analysis, management by objective, etc.

The growth of production volumes resulted in an integration of production processes in many firms, so as to attain scale economies in specific manufacturing phases. With a policy of gradual diversification, there was also increasing correlation between production processes. This trend led to greater complexity in calculating product or production phase costs, given that the development of internal relationships meant a reduction of special costs though an increase in overhead or 'common' costs.

Cost calculations began to be sought for many more decision areas than had previously been the case. Owners put questions to accountants about the benefits of decentralization and out-sourcing specific manufacturing phases, as well as about widening product ranges and substituting variable factors with fixed investments, etc. Academics and accountants began to ponder more extensively these problems.

The role of cost accounting

Zappa's theoretical framework characterizing the industrial period contrasts with the increased need for more information from cost accounting at the time. We thus discuss the role of this managerial tool in supporting economic control, managerial decisions, and balance-sheet evaluations.

With regard to the use of cost accounting as an economic control tool, in the industrial period it is possible to distinguish two phases. In the first phase, academics stressed the risks of the use of responsibility accounting based on standard costs and management by objectives. With increasing acceptance of Zappa's theory, the assignment of single responsibility risked decomposing the holistic view of the firm. Moreover, this did not take into account the interrelationships among different departments and production processes (Zappa 1950). Further, standardization of economic measure seemed opposed to the growing environmental changes which affected firms. Zappa saw standardization as a burden on management attempting to exploit a firm's competitive potential and confront a continuously changing environment. This was mostly due to the structure of the Italian economy with its few large-sized firms,[16] generating, with some exceptions (Coda 1969), little trust by academics as to the use of standard costs and budgeting.

In the second phase, these positions gradually changed. On the one hand, the broader the use of these techniques among firms, the more relevant the demonstration of their effectiveness. In addition, the first consulting firms which began working in Italy in the 1960s and the Italian branches of multinational firms played an important role in spreading the use of these techniques. Academics quickly recognized the importance of such management tools and tried to justify them, without going against Italian tradition, in an attempt to forecast the 'economic equilibrium' of firms (Amaduzzi 1949; Giannessi 1958) and to identify firms' distinctive competencies.[17]

Concerning the use of managerial accounting to support short-term decisions, academics exhibited caution in assigning meaning to the resulting information. Initially, the risks of using profitability measurements of individual parts of a business, instead of considering the business as a whole, limited the diffusion of standard costing and budgeting in academic books. Academics preferred to deal with theoretical analyses of cost variability or accounting record problems rather than the normative, practical usage of managerial techniques for decision support (such as job-order acceptance, sensitivity analysis, break-even analysis, product profitability analysis). Consequently, the development of handbook literature on these subjects, which was extensive in the United States, came later to Italy, around the 1970s, when the need to support practitioners overcame the theoretical constraints, leading to a broader diffusion of these calculation tools.

With regard to the use of cost accounting for financial reporting, many factors, both operative and theoretical, contributed to reducing its influence. By excluding internal operations from financial accounting, as ruled by Zappa, accountants had to design and implement an 'autonomic' cost accounting system, since there was a need to evaluate inventory. In relation to inventory evaluation, Zappa considered the product cost and the presumed market value as two limits within which the value of finished goods had to be set. Neither product cost nor market value is easily determinable. Consequently, the determinism of the previous period, in which scholars believed in the 'true value of the goods' (true cost, true price) diminished. Because of the need for judgement in the evaluation process, product costing lost appeal for academics.

Another influence in this regard stemmed from the Italian legal context.[18] Italian law protected the interests of creditors by imposing a very conservative regime on inventory valuation, rather than requesting a 'true and fair view' of the economic and financial position of firms. Thus, from 1942 to 1991, Italian law ruled that inventory be evaluated at an amount between the production costs and the estimated market value; in other words, it permitted the under-estimation of inventory cost. All these factors weighed against a 'strong' use of cost accounting in inventory evaluation.

The structure of production costs

Following the relativism of Zappa's theory, each purpose of cost accounting calculation demands specific configurations of cost elements. Thus there is no single production cost configuration applicable for all purposes.

Theoretical studies underlined the relativism of the distinction between variable and fixed costs because of the influence of the time frame of the analysis. Scholars also highlighted the relativism of the distinction between direct and indirect costs due to the influence of the scope of the considered 'cost object'. These considerations undermined the 'true cost' concept, which had been very important for the preceding generation of scholars. A true cost does not exist if the internal measures are subjective, empty of autonomic meaning, and if the structure of cost production changes according to different purposes. Thus, in cost accounting there are many costs, but none of them is the true one. This change in cost accounting theory eliminated the 'true cost' concept, and introduced the concept of 'rational cost', whereby the rationality depends on the nature of objects to be considered and on the purposes of calculations.

In terms of overhead allocation, the 'functional principle' represented an important step forward in Italian management accounting. It is based on the definition of production cost as a monetary measure of the consumption of the services provided by labour, materials, and production means. Consequently, the cost of an object (i.e. production phases, organizational units, products) is the measure of services absorbed by the object itself. Thus, the cost-allocation process must respect a *functional principle* (*or criterion*) according to which indirect costs of an organization unit are absorbed on the basis of the function performed for other units (or cost centres).

This theoretical principle is very rational and still valid, since it looks at the overhead allocation problem as a question of measuring the services absorbed by 'cost objects'.[19] The problem arises in practical terms when accountants have to select the measures able to implement the functional principle. In practice, the functional principle has favoured the use of multiple overhead cost application bases. According to the method of multiple overhead allocation, the bundle of overheads is split into different pools. Each pool is characterized by a specific cost driver which is able to measure the services consumption due to production. The selected drivers are often, but not necessarily, related to volume, measured in terms of inputs or outputs. Thus a typical structure of overhead cost pools considers, among others, the following allocation drivers:

specific machine hours for the depreciation, maintenance, and energy costs of industrial machinery;
hours of direct labour for the indirect industrial labour;
amount of handled materials for storage costs;
amount or revenues from the goods sold for selling costs.

From these considerations, some important effects have been noted. First, academics have pointed out the absurdity of allocating overhead when no measure of the services provided is available. Without any rational consumption measure, all the suggested measures (e.g. direct labour hours) could be correct and incorrect at the same time. Second, cost drivers could be different, depending on the way processes are designed; therefore, there is no single 'cost model' suited to any firm. In addition, in theory, production volume was only one possible cost-allocation basis, but in practice it remained the most important driver, since the production of Italian firms was still not very diversified.

The computation of product costs was based on different phases. The first phase entails recording and classifying cost elements, depending on the nature of each resource used (labour, materials, services). The second phase involves allocating costs to organization units (cost centres). Finally, there is the allocation to products. In these last phases, the functional principle, with its multiple overhead allocation basis (mostly volume-based), regulated the allocation process.

The role of the accounting profession and of education in shaping a modern Italian cost accounting approach

Italian education played no role in shaping Italian management accounting until the early 1970s. Only very rarely was cost accounting taught in universities as a specialized topic, and very little time was spent on it in general accounting classes. This was a direct consequence of the academic stance against cost calculation drawn from Zappa's theory. Only in the 1970s, with the then emerging degree in management, alongside the more traditional degrees in economics and business, were specific classes on management accounting given. This has had a direct impact on the accounting profession. Certified accountants received an education based mainly on financial accounting, taxation, commercial law, and bankruptcy regulation, with virtually no cost accounting training. Consequently, public accountants (named *commercialisti*) take care of financial reporting, with a strong emphasis on taxation. In fact, there is very little involvement by public accountants in management in a broad sense. Often firms are more interested in the opportunity to reduce income taxes, due to a very complex taxation system and public accountants have characterized themselves as experts in helping companies to manage taxes.

A totally different role has been played by consulting firms, often subsidiaries of large American firms. They have focused almost exclusively on management tools like cost accounting and management control systems, and they can be credited with having contributed to the diffusion of American approaches to accounting among Italian firms.

Italian Management Accounting in Recent Times

The 1970s did not see any change in Italian companies' custom of discounting the relevance of management accounting and control versus other critical success factors. In spite of the fact that the market (degree of competitiveness, state subsidies, national 'undeclared' protection against foreign competition) had begun to change, moving towards a more competitive, efficient one, major changes in this direction only became evident by the mid–late 1980s.

Due to the economic downturn that followed the oil shock of the early 1970s, the proportion of companies that were government-owned and run grew to almost 50% of the total economy. The crisis had no effect on the distribution system, which remained very inefficient and in the hands of either a few large corporations or thousands of small, low-volume, high-price and high-margin, family-owned stores. The control of distribution channels, besides the capability of obtaining subsidies from central and local government (tax breaks, free workers' early retirement, low-interest mortgages for investment, etc.) were among the critical success factors for enterprises. In addition, the high inflation rate (about 20% per year) was making accounting unreliable and corporate finance a major management issue. The combination of high inflation rates, unstable exchange rates, and low-interest mortgages offered by governmental institutions had the effect of making financial management more relevant than cost management.

At the same time, inventory control, cash-flow management, budgeting, and capital budgeting, which were extremely important to the overall profitability of firms, were (and still are) directly linked to management control. As such, cost efficiency was not seen as very reliable or relevant to profitability, but management accounting was still a fundamental tool for the tight control of resources.

Under these circumstances, management accounting became more a management control tool than a 'cost model' focusing on simulating cost consequences of decisions and anticipating future products' profitabilities. Consistent with this view, the debate between direct and full costing was largely won by the supporters of direct costing. According to the literature at the time, the best way to control resource usage, at least in the short term,[20] was to measure responsibility by direct costs, without 'polluting' cost figures with uncontrolled allocated overheads (Bergamin 1983). Full costs do not make sense in evaluating responsibility centres' performance. This approach gained ground, in contrast to the traditional Italian academic view that since there is no such thing as a 'true neutral cost' and accounting has to be shaped by specific management needs, the most appropriate cost figure for management control is direct cost. In addition, direct costing provided a satisfactory approach for academics, who shunned arbitrary overheads allocation. According to a research project involving 66 Italian manufacturing and service firms (MIP-Politecnica di Milano 1991), direct costing is today adopted as a single approach by 33% of firms (versus 38% using full costing). In addition, the degree of acceptance of direct costing tends to increase steadily with firm size.[21] It is thus generally the case that, today, direct costing is largely deployed in management accounting systems used by Italian firms.

At the same time, the Italian economy still depends heavily on small family-owned firms in which the low level of organizational complexity does not lend itself to the extensive use of management control tools. Many of these firms are run by family members, who are motivated in their managerial activity by personal interest and loyalty. Under these circumstances, managerial accounting is not used to control resource consumption within organizations, and this was particularly true in the 1970s. Most of the small companies are not managed by professional managers, but by self-made individuals, often former blue-collar workers without any specific business education. Their management skills come from experience, and they lack an understanding of the potential of management tools.

Special consideration must be given to the influence of taxation on the diffusion of management accounting. As indicated earlier, financial reporting and management accounting are independent of one another in the Italian context, and taxation should therefore not be considered as affecting management accounting. However, taxation does have an influence on the decision to keep track of costs, since many small firms prefer to under-represent income and attempt to reduce their tax liabilities by bookkeeping adjustments. Such practices need to be hidden from government agencies, of course, so, as a consequence, a management accounting system cannot record actual financial flows. Clearly, it does not make any sense to have a management accounting system that does not represent accurately the business process. However, many small companies prefer to avoid taxation charges through 'black' business activities rather than achieve a higher degree of potential efficiency by adopting management accounting tools requiring and producing accurate, relevant data. This factor has affected the diffusion of management accounting among small firms in Italy, a country where small firms have been, and still are, an important part of total economic activity.

The role of cost accounting

Italian academia, breaking somewhat with a strong tradition, has partially adopted American management accounting theory as a reference for management accounting thinking. The debate has centred particularly around direct versus full costing, and the issue of overhead allocation has been shaded as a result. In Zappa's theory there is little concern that direct costing does not represent the real economic value of resources used because, for Zappa, neither direct nor full costs are capable of representing the complexity of a business's economic reality. Therefore, it may be argued that direct costing has found relatively easy entry in Italian academic circles because of the national accounting tradition.

In medium-sized and large corporations, management control is the main function of cost accounting. In the academic literature, American management-control systems are largely studied and explained (Brunetti 1979; Bergamin 1983). There has, however, been little consideration (until the 1990s) of the use of cost accounting either for pricing products or for making strategic decisions; market forces set prices, and the future cannot be forecast through accounting data. Nevertheless, many small firms have been growing in size and complexity (in terms of the extension of product lines), and the issue of control within the organization is starting to emerge. Thus, management control is the main reason for studying (in academia) and implementing (in the business world) management accounting in Italy in the 1970s and 1980s.

Taking the recommendations of academia, companies have been integrating direct costing, with some overhead allocation on the basis of the 'functional principle': allocation of overhead costs must be consistent with the actual usage of indirect resources in the production process. This has led to a multiple-basis allocation method. In the firms sampled by MIP-Politecnica di Milano (1991), less than 20% of firms use a single allocation basis,[22] and these are mainly small firms.[23] According to the functional principle, indirect resources used in some production-related areas with a measurable output (internal services provided to other decision centres) are allocated to production centres as a proportion of the amount of output they have requested during the period of time (see Figure 7.1).

The management control approach adopted by Italian firms is directly derived from an early American control model (Anthony 1965), with responsibility centres classified as 'profit, investment, revenues, cost and expenses centres' (Vancil 1973). Accounting systems are designed to monitor resource usage in organizational units rather than to compute product costs. Power and responsibility are organized by functions, organizational units, departments, offices, etc., and resources are managed at those levels.[24] Therefore, resource control needs to focus on where resources are used (responsibility centres), not on the 'reason' for which they are used (to make products). This view has allowed academics to develop management-accounting approaches while adhering to Zappa's views on the unreliability of product costs and focusing on production phases instead of products. Phases are often identified with organizational units or machine groups (responsibility centres).

However, many small firms are still concerned largely with product profitability, with some 'cultural' difficulties in using direct-cost figures instead of full-cost ones. In this context, there is little leeway for arguing that full costs have little meaning, as managers need to know the cost of their products to support decision making in establishing product policies. Small firms use product costs mainly for evaluating product profitabilities, and tend to adopt the simple overhead allocation method (MIP-Politecnica di Milan, 1991). In this context, costs are used to set prices either for standardized products or for 'customized' products in workshop manufacturing.

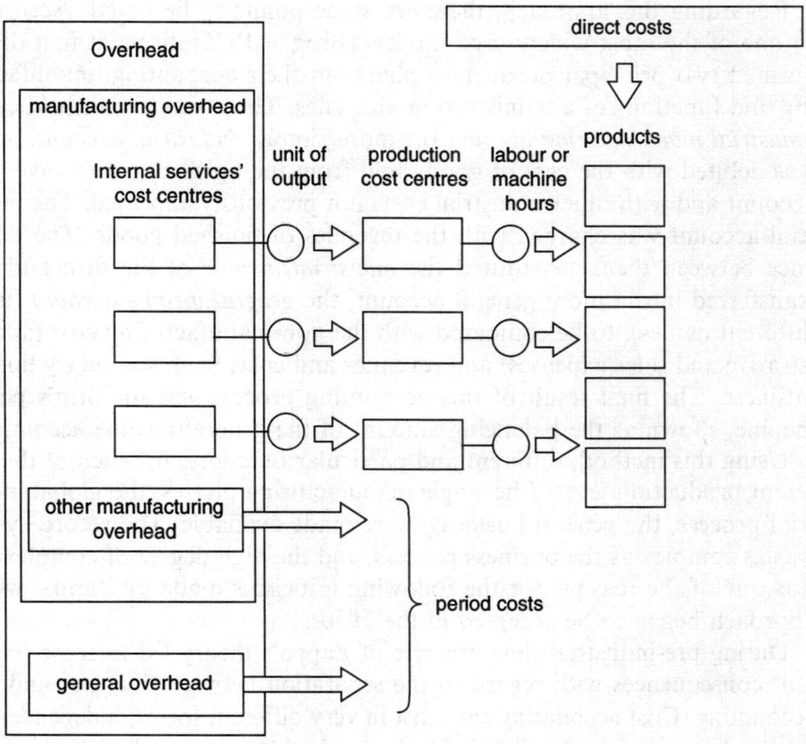

Fig. 7.1. Overhead allocation structure

The cost model is quite simple. Direct costs are directly traced to products, and overheads (factory overhead, selling and administrative expenses) are grouped in a single pool, and allocated to products on the basis of a single coefficient based on either labour or machine hours. Often costs are not calculated by an accounting system; instead, *ad hoc* calculations are performed *una tantum*, in order to have a general understanding of products' costs.

Management Accounting Bookkeeping

In what we call the pre-industrial phase, there was a single bookkeeping system for cost accounting and financial accounting. This use of a single book had some advantages (e.g. perpetual inventory), and arose from the adoption of the the 'true' cost concept. If production costs have only one 'configuration'—the 'true' one—useful for all purposes, then the accounting system must only have one structure.

Regarding this approach, there are some points to be noted. According to one of the most widely used models (Broglia 1925), firms at first distinguished two principal production phases in their accounting: manufacturing and functions of administration and sales. There was an account called *industrial manufacturing account* or, more simply, *industrial account*, which was debited with the cost of goods sold from the finished goods' inventory account and with other industrial costs not previously allocated. The industrial account was charged with the revenues of finished goods. The difference between them constituted the *industrial income* of the firm and was transferred into a more general account, the *general income account* (using different names), to be compared with the non-manufacturing cost (administrative and sales expenses) and revenues and costs from secondary lines of business. The final result of this accounting process was the firm's period income, shown as the balancing amount of the general income account.

Using this method, different and particular outcomes for each of the different production levels (the single manufacturing phases, the global industrial process, the general business) were made available. The record system was as complex as the business process, and the high degree of complexity[25] was one of the reasons for the following criticisms made by Zappa, whose approach began to be accepted in the 1930s.

During pre-industrial time, the rise of Zappa's theory led to some important consequences with regard to the separation between financial and cost accounting. Cost accounting can exist in very different forms, independent of financial accounting standards. The same double-entry method became one of the options for the cost-recording system; many scholars and practitioners preferred the use of 'non-accounting methods' (*approccio extracontabile*) (i.e. elaboration of statistical data, reports in different and specific forms). In many other cases, the separation from financial accounting led firms to give up cost accounting because financial accounting was imposed by law, but management accounts, being independent, were not compulsory. This was relevant to the future development of management accounting.

The structure of cost accounting included different kinds of accounts: *connection accounts*, which tied cost accounting to financial transactions; *cost centres accounts*, which recorded resource allocation to the organizational units; *inventory accounts*, which recorded inventory and *industrial accounts*, which compared the cost of goods sold with the corresponding revenue. The balance of the industrial account could be viewed as the industrial income for the period. The revenues from goods sold came into the industrial account from a *revenue centre account* or, more simply, directly from connection accounts.

This system could be used for either direct costing or full costing. The use of full costing involved passage of fixed cost through the cost centre accounts and the manufacturing phase accounts. Conversely, the direct-costing method demanded fixed costs from cost element accounts to pass directly to the industrial account. When a standard costing system is adopted, *variance accounts* are used in order to measure responsibility.

Recently, for medium-sized and large companies, distinctions in the structure of the accounting system have partially lost their meaning. Modern information systems are largely integrated, and they connect accounting with other operational information systems (e.g. the manufacturing scheduling system and manufacturing requirement planning). Expenses and revenues are classified with different codes (by nature of resources, responsibility, organizational unit, product, market, distribution channel, activity, and so on), and the structure of the accounting system does not affect the 'structure of costs' used for different purposes. In particular, this flexible approach to accounting is perfectly consistent with the idea of using different cost figures for different purposes.[26]

Current Problems and Trends of Italian Management Accounting

The fast growth of the Italian economy in the 1980s and the economic crisis in the early 1990s have created several managerial problems for both large and small firms. Large firms have had to face dramatic changes in both market structure and competition. Firms are experiencing something analogous to what happened in the United States in the early 1980s, with the invasion of Japanese competitors and the decline of national competiveness, in both internal and global markets. Traditional management accounting and control approaches have been roundly criticized for their inability to support management's action in competing in the market (Johnson and Kaplan 1987). This claim is less pertinent in Italy, because of the small role played by management accounting. However, several criticisms of management accounting have been made recently. Direct costing is no longer perceived as a practical way to overcome the problem of misleading allocation of overheads; in manufacturing today, overhead costs are often above 50% of the total expenses of the firm: to neglect their influence on product profitability or to ignore the relations between production and overhead means, very often, that efforts at control are focused on the least important part of resources.[27] Controlling overheads is often perceived s the key problem of managers in dealing with accounting.

At the same time, small firms have grown in size and become more international in marketing their products. As reported in the North American literature, product lines have expanded, and traditional cost methods have revealed weaknesses. Further, traditional cost-accounting systems have been designed to suit the needs of manufacturing industry (Kaplan 1984) and are unsuited to the emerging service sector.

Italian firms take these challenges seriously, and have started to consider some of the new American accounting methods. However, compared with their American counterparts, Italian firms show some peculiarities that affect the way they consider new approaches. These are as follows:

1. Italian academics have helped companies to understand why it is unrealistic to look for an accounting system suited to all management needs. Zappa's view of costs as a 'management fiction' is perfectly consistent with the idea of using different cost figures for analysing different situations (e.g. short- and long-term product profitability). Understanding the impossibility of coming up with a single, 'true' cost figure for all purposes makes it easier to consider new accounting systems as additional information systems, rather than substitutes. In other words, the idea that 'one cost system isn't enough' (Kaplan 1988) was part of the Italian management tradition before the development of new cost systems like Activity Based Costing.
2. Sometimes the use of new cost systems is inconsistent with existing financial accounting approaches in terms of financial representation of the overall business. The traditional separation of financial accounting from management accounting and the understanding of the different roles played by the two systems makes it easier to accept cost approaches that do not completely complement financial reporting.[28]
3. A relatively extensive use of direct costing for management control purposes has at times increased the sense of dissatisfaction with overhead allocation among managers. The shift from full costing to direct costing is based on the fact that the allocation of overhead on the basis of direct labour can be misleading in measuring management performance. This mind-set, often supported by academia (Bergamini Barbato 1983), might make it difficult to accept, in principle, full-cost systems like ABC, both for management control and for product profitability analyses.
4. Acceptance of the *functional principle* and the multiple-basis approach in allocating overheads renders criticism of traditional cost accounting less relevant and, at the same time, the innovative contribution of ABC more difficult to understand.[29] Many accounting academics claim that cost driver allocation is only a remake of what Italian accounting theory had previously developed with the idea of functional multiple-basis overhead allocation. This position has in part driven academic attention away from new approaches. Therefore, Activity Based Costing/Activity Based Management has been left in the hands of consultants and scholars who did not play an important role in its early development.[30]
5. The use of management accounting mainly for controlling operations[31] and the traditional caution with regard to considering product costs as a reliable figure have made companies, in line with the recommendations of academics, reluctant to consider sophisticated product-costing methods like ABC. However, companies were willing to consider the

implementation of more sophisticated cost-management approaches based on activities analysis (ABM).[32]

6. The striving for efficiency in many firms exceeds the desire to exploit the opportunity of a 'black economy'. Firms, both small- and medium-sized ones, are preparing themselves to compete in global markets where efficiency is more important than sporadic, irregular gains from tax avoidance.
7. In many family-run businesses second-generation managers with a college business education and a greater understanding of the potential of new sophisticated management tools are progressively taking over company responsibilities.

Given these factors, Italian firms have started considering new accounting approaches. There is no evidence of any firms having shifted from traditional accounting an ABC approach. However, Collini and Stefani (1994) found that more than 30% of the sample firms have adopted ABC of sorts. These findings, even though limited to a sample of large-sized firms, indicate that large Italian firms are open to the ABC concept in order to either improve overhead allocation, as a further development of multiple-basis technique, or support *una tantum* activities analysis (Activity Based Management) as part of cost-reduction efforts. The latter appears to be more popular in Italian firms than 'pure' ABC. ABC is often seen as a burden to administrators, because of the costs of running such a system, and as being inflexible in relation to the continuous changes arising from a dynamic business environment. Several large companies, both in manufacturing and service industries, have been experimenting with ABM under the guidance of specialized consulting firms,[33] but none appears, at this stage, to have implemented it as a management-accounting system for the whole firm. Often, ABC's applications are limited to specific management areas or are directed towards the solution of specific problems.

At the same time, there is little interest in Italy in adopting non-financial measures as part of performance-appraisal systems. Companies often keep track of non-financial measures (number of defects, customer satisfaction, delivery time, etc.), but do not seem to integrate them into a total performance-evaluation system.

Some Considerations Regarding the Future of Italian Management Accounting

The Italian accounting tradition has strongly influenced the application of management accounting. Initially, Zappa's view of costs as an 'accounting fiction' delayed the development of original cost accounting in Italy, and companies adopted American approaches uncritically. These approaches were mainly employed in large corporations, and implementation in small, family-owned Italian firms required adjustments. The lack of interest on the part of academics until the 1960s and the practical views of consulting firms were in fact obstacles to adaptation. At the same time, cost efficiency was not seen as a relevant factor in facing market competition, and managers focused more on other areas of business. Only in the 1960s did academics start to become interested in cost-accounting issues, especially volume-based allocation. The development of functional and multiple-basis allocation techniques was the first attempt to establish an original approach to cost accounting. However, companies were not ready to take academic theoretical recommendations into their actual business practices.

Cost accounting later became an important management tool, because management control systems were introduced in large corporations. The traditional caution in using product costs did not affect the use of costs to control operations and to measure management performance, but resulted in a low degree of interest in full product-cost figures. Direct costing, in conjunction with application of the functional principle, opened the way for sophisticated management control approaches in Italy. However, the 1990s show a concern for improving management control and the need for better decision support systems. Companies are beginning to look to management tools to enhance efficiency and effectiveness in management in view of the rising competitive pressures from operating in global markets.

Notes

1. Gino Zappa is credited with being the founder of *economia aziendale*, the modern Italian discipline of management.
2. Both authors held the Chair in accounting at the University of Venice, Besta from 1872 to 1919, Zappa from 1920 to 1950.
3. In Italy financial reporting is regulated by law. Recently the adoption of EEC directive on accounting in Italy (Law no. D.L. 127/91) has reversed this position by imposing an income statement form where value added and cost of production are stated, in contrast to Zappa's approach.
4. In Zappa's view, operations and decisions are linked to each other both when they happen in the same period of time and when they happen in different periods during the company's lifetime.
5. Exceptions are possible in the case of balance sheets prepared for special situations (merging, death of a firm, bankruptcy) or in the case of a one-time revaluation (on this issue see Masini 1970).
6. Zappa made it clear that this approach is based on the assumption that the currency keeps the same purchasing power over time.
7. Translation from Italian by the authors.
8. In 1861 people working in agriculture made up 70% of the total workforce,

while industrial activities employed had 18%; in 1914 the percentage of agricultural workers fell to 55% (Dewerpe 1991; Romano 1991).

9. In 1880, firms employed an average of 5 workers (Dewerpe 1991).
10. This paragraph concerns manufacturing firms primarily.
11. This was the prevailing opinion within firms and in academia. At the beginning of the century, there were some economists (e.g. Pantaleoni 1909) who believed that a true cost concept was absurd. They considered the difficulty in estimating the 'true' absorption rate of overhead expenses given the growing complexity of manufacturing processes. They perceived the relativity of cost calculations as depending on the informational purposes of the calculation itself. But their opinions were set aside until Zappa's theory emerged.
12. The theoretical validation of multiple overhead cost-application bases for the cost-allocation process became firmly established in the following industrial period with the rise of the 'functional principle', a distinctive point of Italian management accounting literature.
13. In 1951 manufacturing industry absorbed 32% of the work-force, in 1971 it rose to 45% (Romano 1991: 164).
14. In 1962 and 1968 investments showed a 12–13% growth (Sapelli 1991).
15. Government and public administration continued to play an important role in creating a demand for heavy investments, whereas private demand remained low compared to other Western countries (Sapelli 1991).
16. Small organizations have less need for controlling and a higher degree of flexibility relative to larger ones.
17. Between 1955 and 1970, many planning and budgeting books appeared. In 1967 the first studies on strategies were published.
18. Italian law has always adopted the most relevant accounting standards for balance-sheet evaluations. The function of private association of accountants has recently been integrated with respect to standards set by law.
19. In the Italian literature, cost objects are the objects to which costs are traced, such as products, production phases, organizational units, departments, etc.
20. This view has become obsolete in recent years, mainly because of the decline of mass-production approaches (Collini 1993).
21. In another research project on small successful firms (10 billion liras revenue and 50 employees on average), Farneti and Marasca (1992) found that 27% of the companies surveyed adopted direct costing, versus 55% using full costing.
22. This appears to be direct labour (hours of liras) in 90% of cases.
23. Similar results are shown in a survey of 22 large Italian corporations by Collini and Stefani (1994).
24. This approach was largely accepted by academics, regardless of the fact that it goes against earlier views of scholars on the use of standardized measures.
25. Accountants of that period were aware of the complexity of this system. Sometimes simplifications were suggested, such as the use of only one manufacturing account, which would receive input consumption for all the phases (Tognacci 1925).
26. Collini and Stefani (1994) found that about 30% of firms claim they use different cost measurements (full, direct, ABC) in different decision-making contexts. At the same time, 90% of managers claim that they are satisfied with their accounting system. However, in the MIP-Politecnico di Milano's survey (1991),

only 37% of managers claimed that the accounting system did not need to be changed.

27. The importance of overhead is not only linked to its percentage of the total expenditure of a firm. In terms of control, overheads are very important because the non-value-added activities are in the so-called *hidden factory* (Miller and Vollman 1985).
28. e.g. the concept of long-term variability of costs, adopted by ABC, might not be consistent with costs recorded for financial reporting.
29. It is quite common to find in the literature a sense of *dejà vu* when reading about the ABC costing approach.
30. In Collini and Stefani's survey (1994) the adoption of new accounting approaches stemmed from academic studies in only 4% of cases.
31. In Farneti and Marasca's (1992) research, 44% of firms adopted management accounting for controlling operations and costs, 26% for profitability analysis, and 14% for long-term planning.
32. In the MIP-Politecnica di Milano survey (1991), companies rated overhead control as their first priority in improving management accounting, while product-cost reliability ranked only fourth out of five.
33. Among others, Alenia (aerospace), COIN (retailing), Glaxo (pharmaceutical), and Zanussi (electric appliances) claim to have successfully experimented with ABM.

References

Amaduzzi, A. (1949), *Il Systema dell'impresa nelle condizioni prospettiche del suo equilibrio* (Rome: Signorelli).

Amodeo, D. (1941), *I costi comuni nell'aspetto funzionale* (Milan: Giuffrè).

Anthony, R. (1965), *Planning and Control System. A Framework for Analysis* (Cambridge, Mass.: Harvard University Press).

Bergamin Barbato, M. (1983), *Il controllo di gestione nelle imprese italiene* (Milan: Etas Libri).

Besta, F. (1921), *La ragioneria*, vol. 2 (Milan: Vallardi).

Broglia, G. (1925), *L'azienda industriale* (Turin: Mercurio).

Brunetti, G. (1979), *Il controllo di gestione in condizioni ambientali perturbate* (Milan: Franco Angeli).

Collini, P. (1993), *Sistemi di rilevazione contabile per gli ambienti produttivi avanzati* (Padua: CEDAM).

—— and Stefani, A. (1994), 'Sistemi di controllo in Italia un ruolo in via di definizione. Alcune evidenze da una ricerca empirica', unpublished report 1994. A revised version is available in the working paper series (3/95) of *Dipartimento di Economia e Dirizione Aziendale—Università Ca' Foscari di Venezia* (Venice, 1995).

Coda, V. (1969), *I costi standard nella programmazione e nel controllo della gestione* (Milan: Giuffrè).

Dewerpe, A. (1991), 'Verso l'Italia industriale', *Storia dell'economica italiana. L'età contemporanea un paese nuovo*[3] (Turin: UTET).

D'Ippolito, T. (1958), *I costi di produzione e di distribuzione*, vol. 3 (Palermo and Rome: Abaco).

Farneti, G., and Marasca, S. (1993), 'I sistemi di contabilita analitica nelle aziende marchigiane di successo', in Farneti and Marasca (eds.), *Nuove metodologie per la determinazone del costi di prodotto* (Ancona: Clua).
Giannessi, E. (1958), *Il Kreislauf tra costi e prezzi come condizione determinamente per l'economicità aziendale* (Pisa: Cursi).
Innacconne, P. (1906), *Il costo di produzione* (Turin: UTET).
Johnson, T., and Kaplan, R. (1987), *Relevance Lost. The Rise and Fall of Management Accounting* (Boston: Harvard Business School Press).
Kaplan, R. (1984), 'The Evolution of Management Accounting', *Accounting Review*, 59 (July): 390–418.
—— (1988), 'One Cost System Isn't Enough', *Harvard Business Review*, 69 (Jan.–Feb.): 25–42.
Masini, C. (1970), *Lavoro e Risparmio—Economia d'azienda* (Turin: UTET).
Massa, G. (1907), *Trattato completo di ragioneria* (Milan: Massa Editore).
Miller, J., and Vollman, T. (1985), 'The Hidden Factory', *Harvard Business Review*, 66 (Sept.–Oct.): 72–94.
MIP-Politecnico di Milano (1991), *A Survey on Cost Accounting in Italian Manufacturing Firms* (Milan).
Pantaleoni, M. (1909), 'Alcune osservazioni di valori in assenza di formazione di prezzi di mercato', in *Scritti vari di economia*, vol. ii.
Romano, R. (1991), 'I fattori della produzione', *Storia dell'economia italiana. L'età contemporanea: un paese nuovo*[3] (Turin: UTET).
Sapelli, G. (1991), 'Dalla periferia all'integrazione europea', *Storia dell'economia italiana. L'età contemporanea: un paese nuovo*[3] (Turin: UTET).
Tognacci, G. (1925), *La contabilità del costo industriale* (Milan: UTET).
Vancil, R. (1973), 'What Kind of Management Control do you Need?', *Harvard Business Review*, 54, no. 73213 (Mar.–Apr.): 28–38.
Zan, L. (1994), 'Towards a History of Accounting Histories/Perspectives from the Italian Tradition', *European Accounting Review*[3], 3: 92–109.
Zappa, G. (1950), *Il reddito d'impresa* (Milan: Giuffrè).
—— (1957), *Le produzioni nell'economia della imprese* (Milan: Giuffrè).

8

Managing Costs in The Netherlands

Past Theory and Current Practice

Tom L. C. M. Groot

Introduction

This chapter considers in broad terms aspects of Dutch management accounting theory and practice. Some peculiarities of Dutch accounting have their origins in past academic debates, which are discussed briefly while necessarily omitting extensive details. One especially important debate to Dutch accountants is that surrounding the use of current value versus historical cost accounting. This debate provides a starting-point for considering the extent to which theoretical debates have generally shaped current practices in Dutch management accounting. In dealing with this question, empirical data about Dutch accounting practice provided by surveys conducted during the last 10 years in The Netherlands will be discussed.

In The Netherlands, there is no tradition of carrying out surveys of management practices. Information about accounting practices is gathered infrequently and inconsistently, making it difficult (if not dubious) to make generalizations from different survey results.[1] The results presented in this chapter therefore provide only a very approximate picture of Dutch accounting practice and point only broadly to answers to specific questions. Another issue which I have tried to address here is the extent to which existing Dutch cost accounting practices reflect those presented in modern management accounting textbooks. Writers on modern management accounting techniques (Bromwich and Bhimani 1989; Kaplan and Atkinson 1989; Cooper and Kaplan 1991; Yoshikawa *et al.* 1993) assert that market circumstances have changed dramatically in recent years, such that customers today require larger product ranges (leading to increased product diversity), shorter delivery times, and improved customer services. At the same time, markets are becoming more competitive. Firms can meet these challenges by using new product designs and advanced production systems, which permit a large variety of products to be produced at high speed while reducing

I gratefully acknowledge the helpful comments of Alnoor Bhimani and Willem Biujink on earlier drafts of this chapter.

spoilage, waste, and production errors. According to some writers, these developments lead to changed cost structures.

Using the results of some recent surveys of a large number of Dutch firms, widely disparate in terms of size and industry, this chapter considers this question for the Dutch industry. The following points are addressed: the market factors confronting Dutch enterprises, the role played by modern production systems, the current cost structure of the 'average' Dutch firm, the types of cost-allocation systems currently being used, and how divisional performance is measured.

Historical Developments in Dutch Academia

Although 'general economics' was taught in Dutch universities[2] from the beginning of the eighteenth century, the first chair in business administration was created in 1909 at the Technical University in Delft, and this chair was named '*Bedrijfsleer en Boekhouden*' (business doctrine and bookkeeping). The first occupant was J. G. Ch. Volmer, who is considered the patriarch of Dutch business administration (Polak 1934; Slot 1979). The name *bedrijfsleer* (business doctrine) was borrowed from the German *Betriebslehre*, which referred not to a theory in the literal sense of the word, but to a loosely structured amalgam of pragmatic knowledge aimed at resolving practical problems in business enterprises. This pragmatic knowledge was derived from analyses of practical experience, using common sense and *ad hoc* reasoning. The introduction of *bedrijfsleer* was very much favoured by Dutch commercial firms, which played a key role in the establishment of several new business schools in the first decades of this century (Schreuder 1979; Dijksma 1992). Volmer's chair in Delft emerged as a result of the desire of Dutch engineers to start a programme called 'social engineering', in which attention would be paid to issues related to health, safety at work, and relationships between managers and subordinates (Dijkgraaf 1993). In his work, Volmer paid much attention to the ideas of the scientific management movement.

In 1913, certain Rotterdam firms and trading companies initiated the founding of the Nederlandsche Handels-Hoogeschool in Rotterdam (present-day Erasmus University). The main chair-holders were N. J. Polak, N. W. Posthumus, J. Goudriaan, and J. G. Ch. Volmer (who changed positions). The two-year curriculum consisted of courses in general economics, business doctrine, law, history, finance, bookkeeping, and statistics. This curriculum was partly inspired by the German tradition, especially the *Handelakademien* in Cologne and Berlin (van Stuijvenberg 1963). In 1921 the University of Amsterdam founded the *Handelsfaculteit* (in 1935 renamed the Faculty of economics), and its first chairman was N. W. Posthumus who came from the Rotterdam Nederlandsche Handels-Hoogeschool. The leading Amsterdam academic, however, turned out to be Theodore Limperg, who criticized the *bedrijfsleer* for not providing a solid scientific-theoretical basis to knowledge about business phenomena. Limperg attempted to develop a scientific way to structure and analyse the practice knowledge traditionally taught by the *bedrijfsleer*. He found a well-suited paradigm in the *economic motive*: in economic theory this is the rational striving towards greater welfare and towards lessening the gap between wants and means. Limperg studied organizational behaviour, and built a coherent theory called *bedrijfseconomie* (translated 'business economics') through a strict form of deductive economic reasoning. In this theory of business phenomena, he developed economic principles for *explaining causal relations*, aimed at *understanding* business behaviour. At the same time, by strict deductive reasoning, he managed, with compelling logic, to derive *clear prescriptions* for business administrators in their attempt to increase the welfare of their firms. In this sense, Limperg's *bedrijfseconomie* was intended not only to better understand business behaviour, but also to provide administrators with *normative-prescriptive* theories in order to improve the economic conduct of the firm (Limperg 1946, 1964).[3] This 'strength' of his *bedrijfseconomie* was at the same time its weakness. As a normative-deductive theory, the *bedrijfseconomie* permitted analyses and interpretations of phenomena in and around business enterprises only from the perspective of the economic motive. Phenomena that could not be related to this principle were ignored, and this gave Limperg's *bedrijfseconomie* its characteristic narrow focus (Camfferman and Zeff 1994). He was apparently influenced by the German *Betriebswirtschaft* as developed by Frits Schmidt, professor at the University of Frankfurt-on-Main[4] (Clarke and Dean 1994).

Limperg has had a great influence in Dutch business administration (which is still called *bedrijfseconomie*—business economics) and in Dutch accounting theory. Yet, the contents of the curricula have broadened significantly since Limperg introduced *bedrijfseconomie*. Limperg's great influence is still present in contemporary Dutch curricula for *bedrijfseconomie*, because Dutch universities still prefer to combine business administration (comprising finance, accounting, marketing, organization, statistics) with general economics. Limperg has also had a notable influence on Dutch accounting theory and practice. In order to assess the impact of his ideas, I now turn to his contribution to accounting theory

Economics and Accounting Theory

When Limperg developed his economic theory in the 1920s, he became aware that economists at the time had difficulties analysing and understanding the nature of enterprises' internal operations. Dutch enterprises at that time were rapidly growing in number, size, and internal complexity. They had developed their own managerial language and accounting systems for describing the internal operations. Limperg considered *bedrijfseconomie* a sub-discipline of economics which, for reasons of efficient specialization of academic work, is especially concerned with the study of organizational phenomena (Limperg 1946; Dijksma 1992). In the development of *bedrijfsseconomie* he made us of two sources, the first of which relates to the scientific management movement in the United States. He saw scientific management not as a science, but as a '*kunstleer*' (in German '*Kunstlehre*', a term best translated as 'artificial theory'; Limperg contrasted the '*kunstleer*' with the 'scientific theory' which he felt characterized *bedrijfseconomie*), which is merely a collection of 'rules of thumb' and practical knowledge derived from studying real-life situations.[5] The second development was the '*kunstleer*' of bookkeeping: in Limperg's eyes, the bookkeeper possessed the appropriate tools for observing (internal) organizational conduct which the economists were lacking. In Limperg's opinion, both *artificial theories* could be synthesized into a *scientific economic theory* of organizations if one accepts that the basic issue for both types of theories is that of the *economic motive*. He was convinced that the contribution of public accountants was decisive for this process of synthesis: they were able to provide information about a large number of different organizations, while, at the same time, their societal position permitted them to combine information about organizational behaviour with information about macro-economic phenomena. The synthesis of the two artificial theories into a scientific theory was, according to Limperg, the direction in which 'continental European theory in business economics' was developing.[6] He perceived this development to be clearly different from the Anglo-Saxon tradition (Limperg 1964: i. 40). Limperg's desire to transform the *bedrijfseconomie* into the mature academic discipline of *bedrijfseconomie* was originally shared by others like Polak, Goudriaan (both from the Nederlandsche Handels-Hoogeschool in Rotterdam, the present Erasmus University), and Cobbenhagen (from the Roomsch-Katholieke Handelshoogeschool in Tilburg, the Catholic University of Brabant nowadays). It also matched developments in Germany, propounded by Schmidt (1921; see also Clarke and Dean 1994) and Schmalenbach (1925; see also Potthoff and Sieben 1994). His theory evolved into what Dutch academics today refer to as the 'Amsterdam school'. This school consists of a group of scholars with H. van der Schroeff, A. Meij, and S. Kleerekooper as prominent leaders.

Narrow normative-deductive reasoning is no longer accepted in The Netherlands, although most faculties still maintain an economic orientation. Alongside the Amsterdam school, a Rotterdam school has emerged, advocating a more pragmatic (business administration-like) approach to the study of business phenomena (Bindenga 1990). From the 1960s onwards, the Anglo-Saxon literature became a dominant factor in Dutch business economics and business administration. Within the accounting discipline, however, Limperg's contribution remains significant and recognizable. This is partly because of his ideas concerning current-value accounting.[7] His theory of current value accounting is therefore considered briefly in the next section.

Current Value Accounting

In Limperg's vision, company costs arise from the multiplication of the quantities of producer goods which are technically necessary for production (excluding spill-overs, waste, and defects) and the *replacement value* or *current value*[8] of these goods. Valuation of producer goods by their current value was based on the idea that the economic value of a good is best assessed by the price a manufacturer would have to pay to replace the good if the need arose. Inherent in this reasoning is the axiom of 'continuity' of production. Limperg supposed that economic subjects are willing to process (manufacture or trade) goods only if they can be reasonably sure that the potential revenues from transferring these goods to customers will be sufficient to satisfy their own needs. This requires *continuity of production*, which becomes even more compelling when a firm makes use of fixed assets. These assets contain productive potential for a period to come, thereby placing greater stress on the importance of 'continuity' in the use of fixed assets for productive deployment (Limperg 1964: i. 60–70). This issue was viewed as related to the determination of the *residual profit* to be claimed by the firm's owners. The residual profit was determined by the difference between income and (current) costs necessary to maintain the productive capacity of the firm. It represents the amount of money which could be withdrawn from the firm and distributed to the owners for consumption without endangering the continuity of the firm.

After the Second World War, a number of Dutch firms adopted current-value accounting for financial accounting purposes (either in the income statement alone or in both the income statement and the balance sheet). Philips was one of the leading companies in this respect (Goudeket 1960). Despite expectations that current-value accounting would come to predominate as a financial accounting method, publicly listed companies using current-value accounting have always remained a minority (Camfferman and Zeff 1994). Klaassen (1975) studied the practical application of current-value accounting in the financial statements of 200 publicly listed companies in The Netherlands during the fiscal year July 1971/2. Only 30 companies (14%) appeared to use current-value accounting, mainly for valuing fixed assets. Among these 30 firms, only 7 valued current assets at replacement costs as well. In the 1970s, probably as a result of growing inflation, current-value accounting for external reporting was adopted by slightly more firms, although it never became common practice. In 1977, only 15 out of 82 listed companies (18%) valued buildings, and only 18 out of 126 companies (14%) valued machinery at current costs (NIvRA 1979). Over the last decade, even Philips and Hoogovens have reverted to historical costs in their financial statements.

As will be demonstrated in the next section, this gradual diminution in the use of current-cost accounting for *financial reporting* does not appear to reduce the role of current cost-accounting in *management accounting*. Current-value accounting is probably still relevant for internal decision making. The main obligation of managers is to preserve continuity by making sound economic decisions aimed at increasing the economic value of the firm. Modern approaches, like 'shareholder value' and 'strategic cost accounting', also stem from (renewed) attention to the corporate mission of creating economic wealth. Research in the use of current-value accounting for internal decision making is briefly summarized and commented upon in the following section.

Current-Value Management Accounting

In 1983 and 1984, 52 publicly listed larger Dutch companies, co-operatives, and state enterprises (excluding banks and insurance companies) were interviewed on their views toward the use of current-value accounting for management accounting purposes (Faas and Klaassen 1984). The main objective of this investigation was to study the *reasons* for adopting or rejecting current-cost accounting for internal decision making. It was not intended to provide a representative image of the *use* of current-value accounting by Dutch firms. Nevertheless, the results give an indication of the relevance of current-value accounting for internal decision making in larger Dutch companies. A distinction was made between accounting for *investment appraisal* (capital budgeting), for *product pricing*, and for *divisional performance assessments*. In the case of capital budgeting decisions, only 8% of the firms stated that current costs were relevant because they explicitly considered the need to replace the assets at the end of the planning horizon (see left-hand side of Table 8.1). The majority of the firms used cash-flow calculations based on historical costs.

A significant difference exists in the case of product-cost calculations for pricing decisions,[9] where slightly more than half the firms used current-value accounting. This result is confirmed by another research study of 160 Dutch industrial and trading firms (see Table 8.2) (de With and Faas 1986).

Among the different reasons for using current costs, two are clearly significant. First, current costs give a better estimation of the minimum selling price of final products.[10] The second reason has to do with profit determination: according to the controllers using current-cost accounting for this

Table 8.1. Use of current value and historical costs for capital budgeting and performance evaluation

Capital budgeting (%)		Divisional performance evaluation (%)	
Historical costs	73	Mainly historical costs	44
Current costs	8	Mainly current costs	39
No clear decision model applied	17	Mixed system: balance sheet based on historical costs income statement based on current costs	17
No response	2	No response	0
Total	100	Total	100

Source: Faas and Klaassen 1984.

Table 8.2. Use of current product costs and historical product costs for pricing decisions

Faas and Klaassen 1984 (%) (*n* = 52 larger Dutch firms)		de With and Faas 1986 (%) (*n* = 162 larger Dutch firms)	
Historical costs fully applied	17	Material costs:	
Current costs fully applied	54	historical costs	34
Only depreciation at current costs	21	current value	66
Only materials at current costs	6	Depreciation:	
No response	2	historical costs	43
Total	100	current value	57

Source: Faas and Klaassen 1984; de With and Faas 1986.

purpose, current costs give a more realistic picture of the profits made by each of the products considered.

For purposes of assessing divisional performance, Faas and Klaassen found that firms used a wide range of formal and informal performance measures. Among the formal financial measures, firms used internal balance sheets and income statements. The latter were used significantly more frequently than the internal balance sheets, presumably because income statements are preferred for assessing economic performance of business units. In preparing internal balance sheets and income statements, 39% of the firms used mainly[11] current costs (see right-hand side of Table 8.1). Slightly more firms used historical costs, while the remaining 18% employed actual costs in internal balance sheets and current costs in internal income statements. Firms using mainly current costs prefer this method because it gives a more 'realistic' net profit, avoiding additional residual claims by owners if profits were to be determined by historical costs. Sometimes, firms use current costs for motivating business unit managers to replace fixed assets when necessary[12] (Boonzaaijer 1986). Firms using mainly historical costs, on the other hand, claim to do this for pragmatic reasons: there would be no material differences between the two approaches, while current costing would cause additional measurement problems.

The research findings presented here suggest the following: that while the use of current costs for financial reporting has decreased, it appears that it is still used for management accounting purposes. But different uses also need to be taken into account: for capital budgeting purposes, current costs do not play a significant role; whereas more than half the firms studied apply current costs while evaluating divisional performance and making pricing decisions. The importance of current-cost accounting seems to increase in situations where management assesses the *economic value* of specific products and divisions. In principle, these decisions are made without any specific planning horizon, hence the argument of *continuity* of production plays a role here. By contrast, while making capital budgeting decisions, a fixed planning horizon and specific use of fixed capital play a dominant role. Firms decide on (discounted) net cash-flow figures, since only the continuity of production within the planning horizon of the investment project has to be taken into account explicitly.

Contemporary Cost management

In this section, an attempt is made to outline some relevant aspects of contemporary cost management in The Netherlands. The following issues are considered specifically: the current market position of Dutch enterprises and their cost structures, systems for the allocation of indirect costs, and methods of performance evaluation. The information presented in this section is largely drawn from a recent survey of 406 companies representing a wide range of businesses, each employing more than 50 people (Boons *et al.* 1994).

In terms of market competition, one-third of the companies reported that the number of competing firms had decreased (especially in the food and tobacco industry); one-third reported no changes; and one-third reported an increased number of competitors. Over three-quarters of the companies (76%) adopted a strategy of increased product diversification, especially firms in the metallurgic (90% of the companies), rubber and synthetics (95%) industries. The strategy of product diversification seems to have a modest positive correlation with market share ($R^2 = 0.23$) and a relatively low correlation with sales ($R^2 = 0.15$). However, there appears to be no relationship at all between product diversification and profit ($R^2 = 0.02$). This suggests, among other things, that application of a product-diversification strategy seems to be fairly effective in gaining a market share. This does not necessarily mean that profit will increase; factors other than sales, like manufacturing costs, overheads, and other financial and organizational circumstances, influence the net profit figure as well. The influence of modern production systems, like *materials requirements planning* (*MRP*), *just-in-time production* (*JIT*), and *computer-integrated manufacturing* (*CIM*), on product diversification appears to be limited (Boons *et al.* 1994: 18–20).

Findings on the average cost structure for the Dutch firms investigated suggest no increase in the proportion of overhead costs relative to others: 68% represent direct labour and direct material costs, 11% manufacturing overhead, and 22% general corporate overheads.[13] Firms reported that most of the cost increases have occurred in direct labour and direct material costs. This contrasts with reports that the portion of indirect costs has increased in recent years.

Cost Allocation

For the allocation of general corporate overheads, 20% of the firms used labour hours, around 9% machine hours, 30% volume of production, 6% material costs, and around 35% applied 'different systems' (Boons *et al.* 1994: 35). This indicates that 65% of firms apply a simple volume-related system for overhead cost allocation.[14] In the 'different systems' category it seems likely that firms use more complex methods than volume-related cost drivers. This is plausible if we consider the systems which Dutch management accountants frequently use for cost allocation. A commonly applied tool is the *cost-distribution sheet* (in Dutch '*kostenverdeelstaat*'). This sheet permits the identification of cost pools which do not necessarily represent the organizational or responsibility structure within the firm. It therefore offers the possibility of tracing causal relations between overhead costs and cost objects while crossing departmental boundaries. This system stems from the German *Kostenrechnung*, which attempts to identify the microeconomic and technical relations between the general cost level and the levels of production and capacity utilization (see also Boons *et al.* 1991). In this sense, cost pools do not necessarily coincide with departments or responsibility centres, but are *accounting entities* representing a *function*. In the words of Schmidt, 'A cost pool [*Kostenstelle*] need not always be a room: it can also be *an activity* [in German, *eine Tätigkeit*], like housing or logistics' (Schmidt 1929; see also Groot 1993). The principal idea behind the cost-distribution sheet is the reconstruction of causal productive and microeconomic relations. This theoretical approach has led some Dutch management accountants to conclude that, for the most part, 'new' ABC systems have much in common with the old German–Dutch cost accounting perspective. Many contemporary Dutch management accounting textbooks do not capture these nuances in traditional cost accounting theory. Recent publications and discussions relating to ABC have renewed Dutch academics' and practitioners' interest in the original German and Dutch theorizing about cost allocation.

Accounting for Performance Evaluation

Recently, the management accounting field has increasingly stressed the relevance of accounting information for strategic decision making (Shank and Govindarajan 1993). In the Dutch survey, financial managers and controllers ranked their organization's nine most critical success factors in order of importance (see Table 8.3).

Table 8.3. Critical success factors considered most important by Dutch enterprises

Rank order	Critical success factors	Type of factors*
1	Product quality	NA
2	Reliability of service	NA
3	Selling price	A
4	Speed of delivery	eff
5	Product development	NA
6	Long-standing relationship with customer	NA
7	Diversity of products	NA
8	Market share	NA
9	Distribution channels	NA

* A = accounting-based success factors; eff = efficiency-based success factors (which are considered to consist partly of accounting and partly of quantitative measures); NA = non-accounting-based success factors.
Source: Boons *et al.* 1994.

The relative absence of accounting-based indicators may be explained by noting that most non-accounting factors in Table 8.3 represent *income-generating factors*, while accounting measures merely give a financial (or accounting) representation of the *performance* of these factors over a certain period of time. It has been argued, however, that managers should also monitor the critical success factors themselves, in order to enhance control of these strategically important income-generating factors (Merchant 1985; Anthony *et al.* 1992). In looking at the performance measures most frequently used, a significant contradiction emerges. Most performance measures appear to be related to traditional economic dimensions of performance, like costs, waste, and profitability per job or product. More strategically oriented performance measures, like product quality, reliability of service, producer–customer relations, and speed of delivery are not represented in the list of most widely used performance measures (see Table 8.4). These results are echoed in another recently conducted survey of 52 Dutch listed large manufacturing companies, trading firms, and service organizations (de With and van der Woerd 1994).[15] Almost all companies (90%) have at least one profit centre, while slightly less than half the firms surveyed (48%) have at least one cost centre. This study shows that the performance measures most widely used (most firms reported more than one performance indicator), are return on investment (69% of all firms), profit (54%), return on sales (40%), and residual income (14%). The most widely used performance measures are financial measures, followed at a distance by measures of customer satisfaction, innovativeness, and product quality.[16]

Table 8.4. Performance-evaluation indicators most widely used in The Netherlands

	Boons *et al.* 1994 (*n* = 406 Dutch firms)		de With and van der Woerd 1994 (*n* = 52 larger Dutch firms)	
Rank order	Performance indicator	Type*	Performance indicator	Type*
1	Budget versus realization	A	Return on investment	A
2	Product profitability	A	Market share	NA
3	Material use per job or batch	eff	Cash flow	A
4	Labor hours per job	eff	Profit	A
5	Quality of materials used	NA	Return on sales	A
6	Waste spoilage	eff	Productivity measures	eff
7	Selling price compared to competitors' prices	A	Customer satisfaction	NA
8	Reliability of service	NA	Innovative performance	NA
9	Machine hours per job or batch	eff	Quality of performance	NA
10			Residual income	A

* A = accounting-based performance indicators; eff - efficiency measures (which are considered to consist partly of accounting and partly of quantitative measures); NA = non-accounting-based performance indicators.
Sources: Boons *et al.* 1994; de With and van der Woerd 1994.

As suggested by Table 8.4, accounting-based indicators appear to dominate performance evaluation in Dutch enterprises. These indicators take precedence over efficiency-related monitors and non-accounting indicators. It should be noted that indicators for seven of the nine most important critical success factors, as presented in Table 8.3, are not represented. Some of these, however, could be used as proxy for some success factors, but a direct relation does not exist. This problem has already been perceived by Dutch managers, and it is likely that changes in performance-assessment systems in Dutch enterprises may occur over the coming years.

Conclusions

This chapter has attempted to provide an assessment of contemporary management accounting in The Netherlands. Current practices do not exist on their own, but arise from past practices and academic debates. Two academic developments have been viewed here as having had a significant impact: *bedrijfseconomie* as an academic discipline and the debate surrounding *current cost accounting*. The upshot is that, while current cost is not widely used for financial reporting, it is still used for managerial decision making. This is especially true in the case of decisions related to the determination of the *economic value* of products and divisions. In considering several surveys concerned with current-value management accounting, the following longitudinal picture emerges (see Table 8.5). Thus although in 1986, 54% of the firms used current-value accounting, the figure has fallen to approximately 30% in 1994, indicating that the importance of current costs for Dutch management accounting practice is diminishing.

Table 8.5. Principles of valuation used by Dutch firms in 1986 and 1994

Research projects	Faas and Klaassen 1984	de With and Faas 1986	Boons *et al.* 1994	de With and van der Woerd 1994
Purpose of valuation	Product costing (%)	Product costing (%)	Product costing (%)	Income determination (%)
Percentage of book value			11	
Historical costs	17	43	47	70
Current value	54	57	36	27
Current value partially employed	27*			
Otherwise/no response	2		6	3

* Only for determination of depreciation and costs of raw materials.

In looking at current accounting practices in The Netherlands, the major link with what modern cost accounting textbooks promote is that dealing with product diversification in improving market position. The cost structure of the average Dutch enterprise has not changed in the direction that has been advocated, and traditional performance measures are still widely used for evaluating divisional performance.

A final question remains: does something like a Dutch tradition in management accounting exist? Clearly, Dutch management accounting thought has historically affected the practices of enterprises and these are not themselves immune to foreign influences. If similarities with trends abroad are on the increase, a more apt question may well be: can a Dutch tradition play a part in shaping the future of management accounting in The Netherlands? My own opinion about this is clearly affirmative.

Notes

1. It is notable that most accounting surveys in The Netherlands have been conducted by researchers working at the Vrije Universiteit of Amsterdam.
2. Most of the professors were appointed in law faculties.
3. Nowadays, all six faculties of economics and business administration in The Netherlands use the term *bedrijfseconomie*. Although the contents differ somewhat between the faculties, all curricula try to combine business administration with general economics, but without the strictly economic framework of Limperg's *Bedrijfseconomie*.
4. Schmidt also studied organizational behaviour from an economic point of view. In his publication *Die organische Tageswertbilanz* (Organic Accounting) (1929) he tried to develop a theory in which the relations of values in business administration could be derived from the relations of values in the economy as a whole.
5. He literally states: 'The word "Scientific" [in the term "Scientific Management"] sounds too reckless to us [the Dutch audience], but the Americans like big words' (Limperg 1946: 25).
6. It seems that he was referring here to developments in Germany (Von Böhm-Bawerk, Schmidt, and Schmalenbach), Switzerland (Weyerman), and Austria.
7. Another significant contribution of Limperg's, which is not discussed here, is in Dutch auditing theory. In particular, his 'theory of inspired confidence' is still used in the education of professional accountants (Limperg, 1933, repr. in 1964, pt. VI; Camfferman and Zeff 1994).
8. The terms 'current value' and 'replacement value' are used interchangeably here. Although 'replacement value' is a literal translation of the original Dutch word *vervangingswarde*, preference is given to 'current value' in the remainder of this chapter, as being more in line with usage in the English-language literature (see also Camffermann and Zeff 1994). It emphasizes the notion that values which are known at the moment of valuation rather than future values should be used (see also van der Schroeff 1974).
9. It appeared that the firms interviewed used product-cost calculations for 29 different purposes, of which the most frequently mentioned were decisions on product pricing, determination of values and profit, and evaluation of (divisional) performance.
10. Here two related arguments come into play. A product's current cost can be seen as the long-term value a firm has to sacrifice in order to maintain its productive capacity (that is to say, to continue producing the product). If the selling price is lower *for a prolonged period of time*, then continuation of the production is at risk. A second argument deals with the competitor's point of view: a cost figure based on current costs gives a good estimate of the costs a newcomer to the market would have to pay. If a firm maintains a high gross

margin (i.e. a large difference between selling price and current costs) for a time, this may induce new competitors to enter the market.

11. The word 'mainly' here means valuing at least 50% of non-monetary assets at current value in the balance sheet and at least 50% of depreciation amounts and current expenditures at current value in the income statement.
12. Historical cost accounting sometimes provides managers with incentives to postpone necessary replacement investments.
13. These results are similar to those of a survey among a sample of 313 Australian firms, which is considered fairly representative for Australian industry (Joye and Blayney 1990: 17).
14. Comparisons with similar survey findings in the United States (Cohen and Paquette 1991) and Australia (Joye and Blayney 1990) confirm the impression that mostly volume-related cost drivers based on direct labour and direct material usage or costs are used for cost-allocation purposes. In both surveys, between 10 and 17% of the firms reportedly applied 'different systems'. These results should be interpreted prudently because of differences in size and composition of the survey samples. The survey questions were also stated slightly differently.
15. Banks, investment trusts, and insurance companies were excluded from the survey.
16. These results are quite similar to the outcomes of a survey of 313 Australian companies (Dean *et al.* 1991).

References

Anthony, R., Dearden, J., and Govindarajan, V. (1992), *Management Control Systems*, 7th edn. (Homewood, Ill. and Boston: Irwin).

Bindenga, A. J. (1990), 'De Rotterdamse School', *De Accountant*, 10 (June): 578–87.

Boons, A., Roberts, H., and Roozen, F. (1991), 'The Use of Activity Based Costing Systems in a European Setting: A Comparative Case Study', paper presented at the European Accounting Association Conference, Maastricht.

Boons, A. N. A. M., Roozen, R. A., and Weerd, R. J. de (1994), 'Kosteninformatie in de Nederlandse Industrie', in *Relevantie, methoden en ontwikkelingen* (Rotterdam: Coopers & Lybrand).

Boonzaaijer, G. (1986), 'Vervangingswaarde en Management Control', *Tijdschrift Financieel Management*, 3: 15–27.

Bromwich, M., and Bhimani, A. (1989), *Management Accounting: Evolution not Revolution* (London: CIMA).

Camfferman, K., and Zeff, S. A. (1994), 'The Contributions of Theodore Limperg Jr. (1879–1961) to Dutch Accounting and Auditing', in J. R. Edwards (ed.), *Twentieth-Century Accounting Thinkers* (London: Routledge), 112–41.

Clarke, F., and Dean, G. (1994), 'Fritz Julius August Schmidt (1882–1950)', in Edwards (ed.), *Twentieth-Century Accounting Thinkers*, 95–111.

Cohen, J. R., and Paguette, L. (1991), 'Management Accounting Practices: Perceptions of Controllers', *Journal of Cost Management*, 5/3 (Fall): 73–83.

Cooper, R., and Kaplan, R. S. (1988), 'How Cost Accounting Distorts Product Costs', *Management Accounting*, April, 20–7.

—— —— (1991), *The Design of Cost Management Systems: Text, Cases and Readings* (Englewood Cliffs, NJ: Prentice-Hall).

Dean, G. W., Joye, M. P., and Blayney, P. J. (1991), *Strategic Management Accounting Survey, Overhead Cost Allocation & Performance Evaluation Practices of Australian Manufacturers*, Monograph no. 8 (University of Sydney).

Dijkgraaf, H. (1993), *Orientatiecursus bedrijfs- en bestuurskunde* (Heerlen: Open universiteit).

Dijksma, J. (1992), 'Bedrijfseconomie, enkele beschouwingen over een der bedrijfswetenschappen', in *Oratie* (Nijmegen: Uitgeverij Dijkhorst).

Faas, F. A. M. J., and Klaassen, J. (1984), *Vervangingswaarde en Interne Berichtgeving* (Amsterdam: Limperg Institute).

Goudeket, A. (1960), 'An Application of Replacement Value Theory', *Journal of Accountancy*, 110: 37–47.

Groot, T. L. C. M. (1993), 'Activity-Based Costing', *Tijdschrift voor Bedrijfsadministratie*, 97/1153: 126–32.

Joyce, M. P., and Blayney, P. J. (1990), *Cost and Management Accounting Practices in Australian Manufacturing Companies: Survey Results*, Monograph no. 7 (University of Sydney).

Kaplan, R., and Atkinson, A. (1989), *Advanced Management Accounting*, 2nd edn. (Englewood Cliffs, NJ: Prentice-Hall).

Klaassen, J. (1975), *De vervangingswaarde: theorie en toepassing in de jaarrekening* (Alphen a/d Rijn: Samsom Uitgeverij).

Limperg, T. Jr. (1933), 'De functie van den accountant en de leer van het gewekte vertrouwen', *Maandblad voor Accountancy en Bedrijfshuishoudkunde*, 9: 17–20.

—— (1946), Het object der bedrijfshuishoudkunde, *Maandblad voor Accountancy en Bedrijfshuishoudkunde*, Sept.–Nov., repr. in 25 jaren MAB, Muusses, Purmerend, 1950.

—— (1964), 'Bedrijfseconomie', in *Verzameld werk van Prof. dr. Th. Limperg Jr.*, delen I–VII (Deventer: Kluwer).

Merchant, K. A. (1985), *Control in Business Organizations* (Cambridge, Mass.: Ballinger).

NIvRA (1979), *Onderzoek Jaarverslagen 1977*, NIvRA-geschrift no. 21, Feb.

Polak, N. (1934), *Can boekhouden tot bedrijfsleer* (Wassenaar: Delwel).

Potthoff, E., and Sieben, G. (1994), 'Eugen Schmalenbach (1873–1955)', in Edwards (ed.), *Twentieth-Century Accounting Thinkers*, 79–94.

Schmalenbach, E. (1925), *Grundlagen der Selbstkostenrechnung und Preispolitik* (Leipzig: G. A. Gloeckner Verlagsbuchhandlung).

Schmidt, F. (1921), *Die organische Bilantz in Rahmen der Wirtschaft* (Leipzig: G. A. Bloeckner Verlagsbuchhandlung).

—— (1929), *Die Organische Tageswertbelantz* (Leipzig: G. A. Gloeckner).

Schreuder, H. (1979), 'Economie (en) bedrijven', in E. A. Muysken (ed.), *Economische Wetenschappen: eenheid in verscheidenheid?* (Assen/Maastricht: Van Gorcum), 199–223.

Schroeff, H. J. van der (1974), *Kosten en Kostprijs*, 8th edn. (Amsterdam and Antwerpen: Kosmos).

Shank, J. K., and Govindarajan, V. (1993), *Strategic Cost Management*: *The New Tool for Competitive Advantage* (New York: Macmillan).

Slot, R. (1979), 'Winst', in *Reflecties op Limperg* (Deventer: Kluwer), 131–50.

Stuijvenberg, J. H. van (1963), *De Nederlandsche Economische Hoogeschool 1913–1963* (Rotterdam: Nijgh en van Ditmar).

With, E. de, and Faas, J. A. M. J. (1986), 'Het gebruik van kostengegevens t.b.v. de prijsstelling', *Bedrijfskunde*, 58/3: 303–11.

—— and Woerd, E. van der (1994), 'Prestatiemeting en -beoordeling bij grote ondernemingen in ederland', in C. Boneco, R. ter Hoeven, R. Spekle, and R. v. d. Wal, *fMA-kroniek 1994* (Rotterdam: Vakgroep Kosten- en Winstbepalings-vraagstukken, EUR).

Yoshikawa, T., Innes, J., Mitchell, F., and Tanaka, M. (1993), *Contemporary Cost Management* (London: Chapman and Hall).

9

Management Accounting in Spain

Trends in Thought and Practice

Angel Saez-Torrecilla, Antonio Fernandez-Fernandez, Joaquin Texeira-Quiros, and Mercedes Vaquera-Mosquero

Introduction

The emergence of management and cost accounting in Spain, in terms of both practice and research, has lagged behind that in other European countries. As a discipline, it began to be taught in universities at about the middle of the present century. Until then, instruction in cost accounting was imparted outside universities in industrial and work environments, without scientific rigour and content. Consequently, Spanish companies applied different cost accounting and pro-rating procedures (which were, and still are, named '*escandallos*'). Thus, in most cases, enterprises calculated their product costs using a variety of arbitrary and subjective methods. Nevertheless, teaching and research in management and cost accounting have had a considerable influence on practices in Spanish companies.

This essay is divided into three parts, which are closely linked. They are as follows: (1) research in cost and management accounting, (2) teaching in cost and management accounting, and (3) practices in Spanish companies.

Research in Cost and Management Accounting

Because of the diversity of channels through which research on cost and management accounting has spread, we highlight only the main means of diffusion relating to research concerned with practice and, in particular, the role of academics in this area. We have for this purpose analysed all the papers published in the area in the relevant Spanish journals since their inception. We have also included all those papers presented in the different national accounting congresses, workshops, seminars, etc., as well as in books on management accounting which have appeared in Spain since the 1960s. In addition, we have analysed all the relevant doctoral theses, as these represent an important portion of the research output. The time horizon embraces the period from 1969 to 1994. We have separated these aspects of research, as they play quite distinct roles in Spain. Ph.D. research, for instance, is more detailed and less avant-garde than professional journal articles.

Before discussing research, teaching, and practice issues, the methodological approach of the chapter should be considered. The following points are relevant. The information presented is separated into time periods (decades) to provide a perspective on progression and shifts. In addition, we have separated management and cost accounting into different categories, using the following classification:

1. Frameworks.
2. Integration of product-cost elements.
3. Models to calculate costs.
4. Accounting normalization in Spain.
5. Industry sector cost and management accounting.
6. Teaching in cost and management accounting.
7. Decision making: profitability and productivity.
8. Decision making: planning and control.
9. Organizational issues and human behaviour.
10. New trends in management accounting.

In Appendix 1, we have identified and elaborated the above points.

The Cost and Management Accounting Literature

It is important to note that in Spain there are no specialist journals in management and cost accounting (hereafter management accounting). The subject area is covered in generating accounting journals or those on management and business organization issues. For this study, we have selected those journals which regularly deal with accounting issues. In each case, we have analysed all existing issues and volumes. The journals covered are noted in Appendix 2.

Analysis of periodical publications evolution

To our knowledge, the first Spanish article published in the area of management accounting appeared in *Técnica Contable* in 1949. It dealt with standard costs. Its publication may be viewed as an oasis in the desert, as it was another three years before anything else was published in the general area of management accounting. During the 1950s, a total of ten Spanish articles dealt with the area. Table 9.1 analyses journals published since 1950 dealing with the general topic areas, including frameworks and new trends in management accounting, and gives the frequency of topic coverage in both absolute and percentage terms. It shows that in Spain, the field began to vastly expand in terms of publications only during the 1980s. Each decade since the 1950s has witnessed a doubling in publications. The table also suggests the following:

Table 9.1. Analysis of articles in journals published since 1950

Topic	Decade									
	1950s		1960s		1970s		1980s		1990s	
	No.	%	No.	%	No.	%	No.	%	No.	%
Frameworks	1	8.33	1	4.76	13	27.80	11	9.90	8	7.69
Integration of product-cost elements	1	8.33	0		4	8.33	7	6.31	1	1
Models to calculate costs	8	66.68	9	42.86	7	14.58	13	11.71	6	5.73
Cost allocation	0		0		1	2.08	7	6.31	2	1.92
Sector cost and management accounting	0		2	9.52	2	4.17	10	9.01	20	19.23
Decision making: profit and productivity	1	8.33	2	9.52	2	4.17	20	18.02	5	4.81
Organization in companies and human behaviour	0		0		3	6.25	4	3.60	4	3.85
Spanish accounting normalization	0		0		5	10.42	4	3.60	7	6.73
Planning and control	1	8.33	7	33.34	11	22.92	28	25.23	8	7.69
Teaching	0		0		0		0		0	
New trends in management accounting	0		0		0		7	6.31	43	41.35
Total	12	100	21	100	48	100	111	100	104	100

1. Until the 1970s, research in management accounting focused on models for calculating product costs and on planning and control for decision making and budgeting. Since then, researchers have expanded their areas of interest considerably.
2. Spain has also witnessed research interests paralleling those in Western countries. Interest in models for calculating product costs waned over the period in question, whereas interest in cost and management accounting for decision making, which includes decision making for profit and productivity and decision making for planning and control has seen accelerated growth since the 1950s. This we see as paralleling the development in the United States, with conditional truths giving way to user models.
3. The concern with normalization in cost accounting emerged in 1978. The level of interest differed between academic research, industry, and a variety of conferences paying special attention to the matter. Some interest in Spanish accounting normalization was evident again in the early 1990s, when the new general accounting normalization stipulations promulgated in 1990 abolished cost accounting normalization.
4. As appears to be the case with the management accounting literature in general, Spain has seen a spectacular growth in the number of articles concerning modern cost management. A small number of articles were published in the 1980s (representing 6.31% of total publications). The

average for the 1990s to date is 41.35%, though for 1993, it was 61%. It appears, however, that Spanish researchers have not yet addressed in practice the research challenge presented by Bromwich and Bhimani (1989) that particular account should be taken of enterprise-specific factors when adopting novel management accounting approaches. At this time no empirical work about the different implementation issues of new management accounting tools in Spanish companies has been published.

5. Among the different areas covered by the term 'new trends in management accounting', the area referred to as strategic management accounting has aroused the highest interest (35%), followed by new management and control systems in the manufacturing environment using flexible production, advanced technologies, and quality control (33%).
6. Finally, it is worth noting that during the last two decades, interest has been shown in the specific management and cost accounting application to public and service sector enterprises. This amounted to 9.01% in the 1980s and 19.23% in 1993. This surge in interest is partly to be explained by the growth of the public sector over the past 20 years.

Analysis of papers presented at congresses and seminar

Analysis of presentations and unpublished papers is delimited by the following:

1. Since we are concerned here with the evolution of research in Spain, the analysis is limited to national congresses, seminars, workshops, etc.
2. The first such meeting took place in Spain in 1981.
3. Most congresses and seminars cover all aspects of accounting, including financial accounting, audit, consolidation, and financial statement analysis, in addition to management accounting.
4. The first congress specifically about cost and management accounting was held in 1992, hosted by Valencia University. Since then, one other seminar has been held (at Alcala University). The papers presented at the two meetings were limited to those offered by invited speakers.

Table 9.2, showing the results of the analysis, suggests the following:

1. The four first meetings held in the period 1981–5, included only 6 papers linked to management and cost accounting issues.
2. Over the two decades covered by the table, the same spectacular growth in the general area was to be witnessed as with publications. It is noteworthy that 65% of the total of the decade's papers were presented in 1988.
3. Most participants in congresses during the 1980s were researchers and academics, hence conceptual aspects and management and cost accounting frameworks were of interest (25.45%). Many presentations were linked to decision making, with regard to profit and productivity as well

Table 9.2. Analysis of papers presented at congresses since 1981

Topic	Decade			
	1980s		1990s	
	No.	%	No.	%
Frameworks	14	25.45	13	9.29
Integration of product cost elements	1	1.82	5	3.57
Models for calculating costs	2	3.64	10	7.14
Cost allocation	1	1.82	2	1.43
Sector cost and management accounting	5	9.09	28	20.00
Decision making: profit and productivity	7	12.73	4	2.86
Organization in companies and human behaviour	3	5.45	8	5.71
Spanish accounting normalization	7	12.73	5	3.57
Planning and control	7	12.73	9	6.43
Teaching	5	9.09	5	3.57
New trends in management accounting	3	5.45	51	36.43
Total	55	100	140	100

as planning and control (25.46%). During the 1990s themes linked to new trends in management accounting comprised 36.43% of presentations.

4. During the 1980s, two other themes were important: accounting normalization (12.73%) and teaching (9.09%). Their significance diminished during the 1990s (to 3.57% each). As with papers published in journals, there was a growth of interest during the 1990s in issues relating to public and service sectors (20%).
5. Finally, Table 9.2 shows that of the general areas covered by new management accounting, research on measurement and control systems in the new productive and technological context is of particular concern (26%), closely followed by activity based costing (ABC) and activity based management (ABM) systems (22%) and environmental management accounting (20%). Aside from ABC and ABM systems studies, this is reflective of the trend in papers published in journals.

Analysis of Ph.D. theses

Without a doubt, this is the most representative measure of research trends in Spain. We include here all Ph.D. theses carried out in Spain which deals with any area of cost and management accounting. The first such Ph.D. thesis appeared in 1969 (we have included it in 1970s). Table 9.3 presents the findings structured to allow comparison with Tables 9.1 and 9.2.

Table 9.3. Analysis of Ph.D. theses since 1970

Topic	Decade					
	1970s		1980s		1990s	
	No.	%	No.	%	No.	%
Frameworks	1	7.14	5	18.52	1	8.33
Models for calculating costs	5	35.72	2	7.41	0	
Empirical cost accounting	3	21.43	2	7.41	2	16.67
Decision making: profit and productivity	0		4	14.82	0	
Organization in companies and human behaviour	0		3	11.10	1	8.33
Planning and control	5	35.71	11	40.74	5	41.67
New trends in management accounting	0		0		3	25
Total	14	100	27	100	12	100

An analysis of Table 9.3 suggests the following:

1. Relative to the 1970s, the 1980s saw a doubling of Ph.D. theses. The 1990s will probably see another doubling.
2. There is also a qualitative progression in terms of the topic areas researched. The 1980s represented a transition stage in Spain from classical cost accounting concerns to modern management accounting.
3. The average Ph.D. thesis takes between 3 and 5 years to complete, and therefore reveals a time lag in topics when compared to papers published in journals and papers presented at congresses.
4. There are nevertheless some parallels with other forms of research presentation. During the 1970s, the focus was on models for calculating costs (35.72%) and planning and control issues (35.72%). There was then less interest in decision making linked to profit and productivity, decentralization, transfer pricing, cost allocation in production environments, information economics, etc. During the 1980s, there continued to be interest in planning and control issues (40.74%) and to research emerging from the previous decades, including decision making linked to profit and productivity (14.82%), methodological and conceptual aspects (18.52%), and organization and human behaviour (11.10%). During the 1980s, little appeared in the area of 'new management accounting methods'. In the current decade, based on the first 3 years, there is some polarization of research around planning and control issues (41.67%) and new trends in management accounting (25%).

Other facets of research in management accounting

Although we have considered the main research areas of cost and management accounting, it is appropriate to discuss two other issues: the

Table 9.4. Research evolution in the different branches of accounting

Research areas	Journals* (%)				Congresses (%)		Ph.D. theses (%)		
	1960s	1970s	1980s	1990s	1980s	1990s	1970s	1980s	1990s
Financial accounting	37.09	31.72	34.98	37.97	58.49	21.22	60.00	31.51	34.48
Cost and management accounting	8.49	8.94	9.47	18.57	17.41	25.58	25.45	26.03	20.69
Financial statement analysis	7.47	7.97	10.46	10.38	7.53	16.37	9.19	26.03	22.41
Audit	14.88	25.63	24.70	18.93	5.10	20.35		12.33	13.79
Other areas	32.08	25.75	20.78	14.15	11.50	15.46	5.45	4.11	8.62

* Included here are the four accounting-based journals (see Appendix 2).

evolution of science and the influence of particular doctrines on Spanish research.

Table 9.4 presents evolutionary trends in various branches of accounting relative to the main research platforms (journals, congresses, and Ph.D. theses). Table 9.4 suggests the following:

1. Increased interest in management and cost accounting in Spain is generally evident over the time period covered. This is especially true of papers in journals. The papers presented at congresses in this area likewise increased. This gives the general area second place for research publication platforms.
2. It should be noted that many management accounting presentations appear in accounting-related journals. This points to the interdisciplinary character of the field since the 1960s. This has resulted in some specialist accounting platforms to allow dedication of space to related disciplines.
3. During the early 1990s, there has been an appreciable number of papers in journals and Ph.D. theses on financial accounting. This may be explained by the interest generated by the Financial Accounting Normalization Act of 1990.

As regards the second issue mentioned above, foreign research interest and trends have clearly influenced Spanish research over the whole time period covered. During the 1960s and 1970s, Spanish accounting research was considerably affected by French doctrines, particularly the French full-costing model and in relation to the problem of homogeneous sections and the role of management control and variance calculations. The French influence reached its height in September 1978, with the promulgation of Spanish cost accounting normalization guide-lines. This followed the effect in 1973 of the French normalization plan on Spanish financial accounting. Over the same time period, there has nevertheless been some

Anglo–American influence, especially with respect to direct costing, cost–volume profit analysis, methods of cost allocation, and the problem of joint products costs. Additionally, Spanish accounting has been affected, though to a small extent, by German accounting concepts.

During the 1980s, American influence had an unprecedented impact. In the first half of the decade, this was comparable to the French influence during the 1970s. By the late 1980s, French concepts had been eclipsed by American ones. This was particularly evident in the growing Spanish interest in agency theory, organizational decentralization issues, transfer pricing systems, and budgetary control concepts (this area is now showing signs of being influenced by UK-based research interest).

Finally, the current decade is characterized by a primary interest in ABC, ABM, total quality control (TQC), management accounting in the new manufacturing context, etc. The USA-based Institute of Management Accountants and the writings of Robin Cooper, Robert Kaplan, and Thomas Johnson have had a most significant impact.

Jointly with the above-mentioned influences, the 1990s have been marked by a growing awareness in Spain of British research interests. This is especially so with regard to writings on strategic management accounting and new management accounting techniques. In this light, reference in Spain is widely made to Chartered Institute of Management Accountants publications and to the writings of Michael Bromwich, Al Bhimani, Robert Scapens, and Kenneth Simmonds.

The Teaching of Management Accounting

In Spain, cost accounting was taught from the early 1950s as part of a broad programme of studies encompassing political, economic, and commercial sciences. Until then, teaching of accounting as part of commerce studies was by preference practical in nature and directed at the management of enterprises with a lack of scientific or theoretical grounding.

In this section, we look at the evolution of teaching material by grouping, according to publication time period and conceptual orientation. The broad categories are as follows:

1. Models to calculate cost.
2. Spanish accounting normalization.
3. Profit studies.
4. Budgets.
5. Organization and human behaviour.
6. New management techniques.

The Evolution of Conceptual Orientations in Management Accounting Teaching Material

Since 1965 approximately 30 books have been published (inclusive of edition updates). Table 9.5 shows changes over time in the conceptual orientation outlined above.

Table 9.5. Evolution of Spanish teaching texts

Orientation	Decade			
	1960s (%)	1970s (%)	1980s (%)	1990s (%)
Procedures	24.00	18.74	16.92	15.87
Models to calculate cost	44.00	57.65	42.61	54.91
Empirical cost accounting		6.45	7.30	3.35
Decision-making: Profitability and product	8.00	13.90	8.14	5.94
Spanish accounting normalization		1.60	9.53	1.00
Planning and control	24.00	1.66	15.42	9.36
New trends in management accounting				9.57
Total	100	100	100	100

Certain significant factors are apparent from the table. First, teaching of management and cost accounting in Spain has been based on four pillars since its beginnings. These, in order of importance, are models to calculate costs, elementary techniques, planning and control concepts, and planning and control and productivity analyses. Models to calculate costs have clearly been given prominence (even though we have included ABC under 'new trends').

Second, normalization of accounts has played a very significant role in teaching, at least in a number of Spanish universities. The topic has received little coverage in textbooks, however. It was only in 1979 that Spanish accounting normalization first appeared in textbooks, but with the reduced importance of cost accounting normalization, it is now rapidly being de-emphasized. Its place is being taken by new trends in management accounting, comprising nearly 10% of teaching.

Influential Doctrines in Management Accounting

Germanic concepts of industrial accounting as espoused by the German Professor Schneider had an important effect on cost accounting thought in

Spain until the 1970s. This considerably reduced and replaced the French model embedded in the Plan Comptable Général of 1957. Some Spanish universities began to stress the homogeneous sections perspective and the labour unit normalization as an approach to full costing. French normalization significantly shaped cost accounting normalization in Spain since 1978. It is therefore not surprising that the general discipline was termed 'analytical accounting' as per the French term.

During the second half of the 1980s, Continental European influences diminished, and North American perspectives gained importance (especially Charles Horngren's textbooks). Over the past few years, British researchers have made an impact on management accounting thinking in Spain, as stated earlier. This has also been the case at the teaching level (especially Colin Drury's textbooks). Indeed, it has led to 'management and cost accounting' becoming the firmly entrenched term to refer to the broad field.

Management Accounting Practices in Spanish Companies

We have presented above an overview of the evolution of cost and management accounting research and teaching. In this section we consider the impact on practice. It is to be noted that there has been very little documentation of Spanish management accounting practices. Our approach has been to undertake empirical surveys and field studies to address the question. Although these investigations are ongoing, we report here our preliminary findings.

Some preliminary observations about the environmental context in which Spanish companies use internal accounting information are appropriate at this stage. First, it is important to note that in Spain accounting normalization has changed the format of management accounting information. The evolutionary steps are shown in Figure 9.1. As can be seen, management accounting in Spanish companies has changed in each of the last decades, given changes in the significance of the normalization of cost accounting. During the 1970s, Spanish companies designed their own cost accounting, independently of accounting normalization. The 1980s saw the impact of financial accounting normalization on cost accounting. Finally, the 1990s have seen the revision of general accounting normalization, which now omits any reference to cost accounting.

Secondly, it is noteworthy that the Spanish commercial environment has changed enormously over the past 10 years, especially since Spain joined the European Common Market in 1986. In 1992, the Universal Exposition in Seville and the Olympic games in Barcelona affected the economy. The increased market penetration into Spain of multinational companies brought with it new business practices and technologies.

Thirdly, Spanish companies are always concerned about taxes payable on

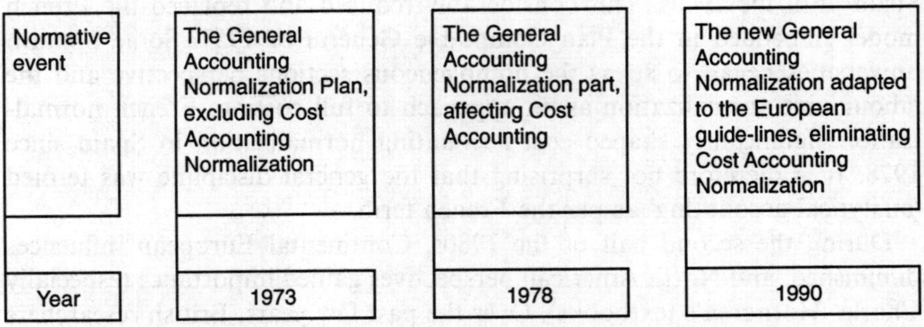

Fig. 9.1. The evolution of cost accounting normalization

income generated, which have seen major rises in recent years. Government spending has doubled over the past decade, and with the concomitant tax increases, financial management and accounting information has gained much relevance.

Fourthly, the recent economic recession has forced Spanish companies to look to new markets and to enhance their competitiveness. This has increased the role played by management accounting information.

Fifth, technological endeavours have affected the activities of all companies, large and small. The widespread use of computerized accounting software programmes with marketing and sales function linkages has altered the use of accounting information, which has become more management-oriented.

Different Systems of Costs and Management Accounting in Companies

Ongoing empirical studies are attempting to investigate costs and management accounting applications using the following methodologies: statistical surveys of different companies and company case-studies. Some studies focus on the implementation of techniques, such as activity based costing. Others concentrate solely on new accounting approaches developed by the companies themselves. It is essential to recognize that different companies use and react to accounting information in different ways. Any sample of companies must identify the different types of companies covered, as outlined in Figure 9.2.

The following should be noted. First, large companies are defined as those which have a sales volume of at least 3,500 million pesetas per year. In 1992 there were about 2,700 such companies. Second, medium-sized companies are defined as those with a sales volume exceeding 1,000 million pesetas per year, small companies as those with a sales volume below this amount. Third, public companies are usually large, whereas companies controlled by foreign capital tend to be medium-sized or large.

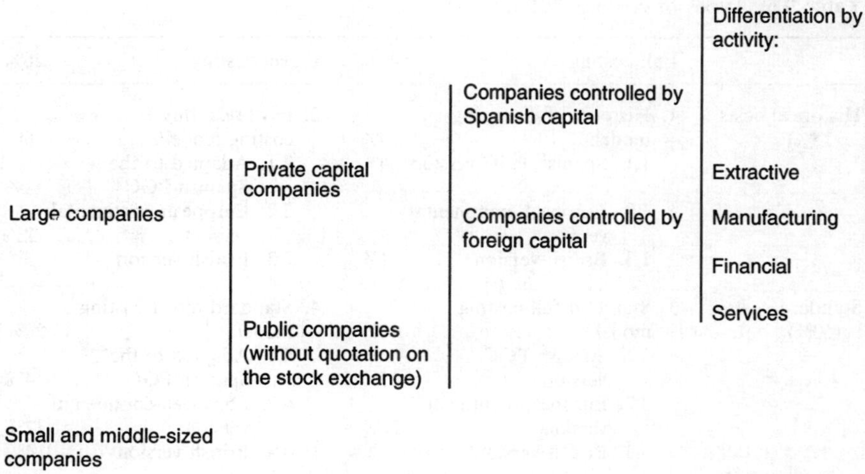

Fig. 9.2. Types of companies

Analysis of Management Accounting Practices

Large companies controlled by Spanish capital

There has been no empirical work on this group of companies. Consequently, we simply offer the results of partial studies and personal experience based on our research undertakings. Management and cost-accounting practices for this sector are as follows. All large companies of this type have an operational cost management accounting system. The costs found are presented in Table 9.6 (the information is based on publications and the preliminary results of ongoing research).

The following points are to be noted:

1. More than 50% of companies have implemented a standard cost system. Standard costing here includes any statistical or non-accounting approach to variance analysis, even where not all costs are covered. 'Standard cost system' also includes budgeted cost accounting models.
2. The Spanish accounting normalization introduced in 1978 was rescinded in 1990. Fewer companies now use cost accounts on this basis. Some companies have adapted them by grounding new approaches in this old model. We found 24% of companies still using the original model, but this percentage is quickly diminishing. We include in this category other *sui generis* models.
3. The companies using full-costing models are in the majority, by contrast with those that have implemented direct-costing models. However, the

Table 9.6. Types of costing systems

	Full costing	49%	Direct costing	26%
Historical costs (15%)	1. Historical full costing model:	9%	2. Historical direct costing model:	6%
	1.1. Spanish PGC version	4%	2.1. Adapted to the Spanish PGC	1%
	1.2. European-continental version	4%	2.2. European-continental version	2%
	1.3. British version	1%	2.3. British version	3%
Standard costs (60%)	3. Standard full-costing model:	40%	4. Standard direct-costing model:	20%
	3.1. Spanish PGC version	15%	4.1. Adapted to the Spanish PGC	4%
	3.2. European-continental version	20%	4.2. European-continental version	12%
	3.3. British version	5%	4.3. British version	4%
Other *sui generis* models (24.75%)				
Other posterior models (ABC, etc.) (0.25%)				

data distribution would be different if we considered just the full-costing models in very strict terms.

4. Very few companies are using ABC, and where they are, it is purely on a pilot basis. The factors influencing ABC experimentation are mainly professionals training with foreign parent companies. There is also some influence from large audit and consulting companies.

It is notable that the use of management accounting information for decision-making purposes is very limited. Where management accounting systems operate for decision making, managerial usage is in effect minimal. New management accounting techniques, including quality cost management, strategic management accounting, activity-based budgeting, and activity-based management systems have not been implemented.

Large companies controlled by foreign capital

Companies controlled by foreign capital can be separated into two groups: those controlled by multinational corporations (such as Coca-Cola and IBM) and those controlled by foreign companies without a multinational character. In such companies, the accounting system in use in Spain is usually determined by the parent company. In part, this is because the parent company needs to consolidate its financial accounting statements, which influences the cost accounting model in respect of valuations.

We will focus on the accounting system of one multinational company: Ford España S.A. has described Aspects of the basic structure of cost and management accounting at Ford España S.A. have been described by the company's general accounting and control controller, Mr Balada Ortega, as follows. As a result of cost system changes in the company over the past few years, cost responsibility now rests in Spain.

The accounting system at Ford is very comprehensive, and centralizes cost accounting information from 28 European plants.

The volume of information is structured into six 'macro' systems that make up the core accounting process. (These are a materials information system, a finished products information system, a system to calculate standard costs and deviations, a system of non-productive materials, a budgetary control system, and a costs and variance analysis system.)

Management accounting is based on a standard cost model. The availability of standard costs for each part of the production process enables variance calculations at different stages of production.

Indirect costs included as part of standard costs are applied using a rate proportional to labour input.

It is to be noted that the proportion of input decreases in relation to indirect manufacturing costs. This is also the case for inventories—both work in process and finished products.

Public companies not quoted on the Stock Exchange

Several factors affect the management accounting systems of public companies not quoted on the Stock Exchange. Company managers who report hierarchically to Public Administration authorities find it difficult to communicate resource management issues concerning modern accounting techniques. Public companies depend on subsidies, and any losses arising from debtors or bankruptcies tend to be absorbed by state funding. There is little doubt that costing and management accounting practices in these companies lag behind those of private commercial companies of similar size and activities.

Small and mid-sized companies

For this group of companies there is a need to differentiate between large- and mid-sized companies, intermediate-sized companies, and small companies. The group of small companies includes those with a sales volumes of 300 million pesetas per year if they are manufacturing companies, less if they are service companies with a larger value added. These small companies are often family-run, and the management style is personal. They apply elements of financial accounting only for tax reasons. The tax advisor typically performs all accounting functions which are not intended as information input for the management process. In many cases, even the tax accounting function is non-essential because of the categorization of small businesses into 'modules' for tax purposes. Computerized accounting programes are having some impact in many such companies, with some young managers choosing to undertake all accounting chores for the company.

The intermediate-sized companies have the following characteristics: the total amount of their assets is under 920 million pesetas; their net annual turnover is less than 1,920 million pesetas, and the number of employees is under 250. General accounting normalization requires income statements and balance sheets of companies which do not have the above characteristics to be prepared under different rules. Intermediate-sized companies sometimes use computer software accounting specially designed to allow analytical control of customers and suppliers and classification by geographic areas/business units.

Medium to large-sized companies tend to have cost accounting systems, though where such a system is not in place, detailed financial accounting is undertaken. As a result of the French influence on Spanish accounting models, this type of accounting is termed 'analytical operational accounting', or simply 'analytical accounting'. Questionnaire responses suggest little differentiation in the use of these terms.

Management and Cost Accounting Practices by Activities

In Spain management accounting systems differ according to company activities. For instance, car manufacturing and financial services companies use vastly different approaches. In the automobile sector, there is a high level of competition between major car-makers, including Volkswagen-Seat, Renault, Ford, Nissan, etc., all of which have well-developed cost management techniques. The banking sector is also highly competitive, though the lead companies are all Spanish, but there is little information available about their management accounting systems.

Conclusion

We have commented on cost and management accounting in Spain, focusing on research, teaching, and company practices. Research in cost and management accounting in Spain as documented and presented in journals, conferences, and doctoral dissertations shows evolutionary trends reflective of academic interest in the field principally in the United States and the United Kingdom. Research is also affected, however, by legislative and governmental changes in Spain. Presently, there is much interest in new management accounting approaches, including activity-based costing and management and strategic management accounting.

There is a great need for extensive empirical studies of cost and management accounting practices in Spanish companies. As has been suggested, internal accounting practices differ among companies, depending on the industry sector, and there are size-related differences. What is clear is that an increasing number of Spanish enterprises in different industry sectors perceive a need to enhance the role of cost and management accounting. Such a view is also shared by academic researchers, and is reflected in the increased emphasis given to management accounting in teaching institutions.

APPENDIX 1

Classification of Research Themes

I. Frameworks
1. Cost accounting concepts
2. Cost and financial accounting
3. Management and cost accounting
4. Manufacturing economy and cost accounting
5. Management accounting evolution and history

II. Product-Cost components
1. Raw costs
2. Labour costs
3. Amortization, financial and overheads cost

III. Cost allocation
1. Allocation process in cost accounting
2. Common and joint production
3. Cost-allocation models in joint allocation

IV. Models to cost calculation
1. General models of environment
2. Full-cost model
3. Variable-cost model
4. Rational-allowance model

V. Spanish accountant normalization
1. Group 9 from general accounting normalization
2. Spanish model to calculate the cost
3. Management accounting principles
4. Analysis compared with other normalization

VI. Decision making: profit and productivity
1. Profits and cost–volume–productivity analysis
2. Cost–volume–productivity analysis in uncertain situations
3. Efficiency and productivity excesses

VII. Business organization and human resources
1. Responsibility centres
2. Responsibility centres in decentralized companies
3. Transfer prices in decentralized companies
4. Agency theory

VIII. Planning, control, and information
1. Management accounting role in planning and control
2. Management accounting as management control tool
3. Productivity
4. Costs control

5. Standard costs system and deviations analysis
6. Budget

IX. Sector cost accounting
1. Applied management accounting
2. International aspects
3. Management accounting applied to public institutions
4. Information adaptations

X. Teaching of cost accounting

XI. New trends in management accounting
1. Management accounting in the new manufacturing context
2. Quality costs management
3. ABC, ABM and ABB systems
4. Environment costs
5. Advanced technology and management accounting
6. Strategic accounting

APPENDIX 2

Accounting-related Journals

Técnica Contable (Accounting Techniques). It began in 1949, and covers general accounting topic areas.
Alta Direción (Top Management). It started in 1965, and covers themes linked to company management and related accounting matters.
Revista Técnica del Instituto de Censores Jurados de Cuentas (Institute of Public Accountants Technical Journal). It started in 1967, and covers any research linked to auditing. It sometimes covers other accounting matters, such as management and cost accounting.
Revista Española de Financiación y Contabilidad (Spanish Review of Finance and Accounting). It was started in 1972 to deal with accounting matters only, but not to cover other areas linked with enterprise management.
Exit Market. It started in1976, and features any area of interest to business management.
Partida Doble (Double Entry). It was started in 1990, and covers general accounting matters.

References

Bromwich, M., and Bhimani, A. (1989), *Management Accounting: Evolution not Revolution* (London: CIMA).

10
Cost Management in Sweden
From Modern to Post-Modern

Urban Ask, Christian Ax, and Sten Jönsson

Introduction

The calculative practices in an economy can be described on several levels. Understanding may be enhanced by descriptive levels providing mutual support. One may distinguish between an institutional level, at which norms and standards are developed and argued for; a collective level, at which populations are described in terms of statistics on the use of different methods; and the level of individual organizations. Different factors explain changes on those levels. On the institutional level, growing strength of the unions, wars, free-trade agreements, or majority shifts in Parliament may generate conditions of opportunity. On the collective or industry level, corporatist arrangements may yield a committee that will seize the opportunity to focus attention on joint problem solving, or consultancy firms specializing in selling a 'package' or literature and conferences may drive diffusion. In the individual firm, specific contingencies may explain how practices have evolved.

A view of the evolution of practices over time seems necessary in order to be able to understand and evaluate current problems and rhetoric. Practices may be seen as the result of organizational learning, which may be experientially based as well as based on imported ideas. Generally accepted practices are supposed to satisfy functional as well as theoretical criteria; i.e. they work in the sense that they meet the practical requirements of user situations, and they are right in the sense that they satisfy the canons of rational discourse current at the time. There are good arguments for using a particular kind of costing method. In all kinds of settings, differences of opinion should be expected as to what extent functional and theoretical criteria are met. Authority and prestige may be expected to be called upon to settle such differences, which may concern what problems the calculative practices are supposed to deal with, as well as whether a certain technique is more instrumental for its purpose than others. The context in which influence over maintenance or change of practices is exerted is complex, whatever the level of description. In an economy that is fairly small, homogeneous, stable, and disciplined, it seems reasonable to aim for a more comprehensive approach to description and explanation than in an economy characterized by the opposite traits. We will focus on the industry level, and use the other levels of description as backdrop or illustration. We would thus expect competitive pressure, regulatory traditions, professional rivalry, and type of industry to be the external factors influencing how solutions to calculative practices are designed. The current theoretical discourse would determine the kinds of arguments used to justify or oppose proposed changes.

In this chapter we will first give an overview of the composition of Swedish industry and the institutional setting relevant to cost management in that industry. We will take special note of institutional changes that may have contributed to change or may have heightened the propensity to change. We will then account for some significant historical episodes in the evolution of cost management, and finally we will describe current practices in manufacturing industry and the rhetoric in support of change. This will provide the occasion for some conclusions concerning the correlation between rhetoric and practice.

Sweden, a Homogeneous and Internationally Oriented Economy

In describing Swedish industry, Porter (1990) pointed out the remarkable number of large, global companies for such a small country (The 17 largest companies are responsible for one-third of industrial employment, 40% of exports, and 60% of R&D expenditure (Government bill 1986/74).) He also identified clusters in forest products, metals (upstream industries), transportation, and power generation and distribution (industrial and supporting functions), but a relative lack of strength in consumer goods and services. Sweden's position in these clusters has been remarkably stable. The heavy transportation requirements of the forestry industry foster sophisticated buyers of heavy trucks which can function reliably on less than perfect dirt roads—hence, a strong position in heavy trucks. The generation of hydro-electric power in the northern rivers, with transportation of electric energy over long distances to southern population centres, energy-consuming forest, and ore-based industries, supports a competitive power generation and distribution sector.

It is reasonable to describe Swedish industry in these terms, but it can also be described as highly concentrated, with a strong tendency to concentrate in 'bank spheres', which were a result of the turbulent years of the 1920s. The small size of the domestic market is of significant. Many of the larger, trend-setting companies have less than 10% of their sales or production in Sweden. The flow of impressions from abroad has always been great, and the fact that large Swedish companies have been dependent upon niche strategies in foreign industrial markets for several generations of managers indicates a sensitivity and flexibility towards other cultures. It should also be noted that Sweden has long corporatist traditions, with a strong union movement and a tradition of solving institutional problems in tripartite negotiations (state, industry, unions). This corporatist trait is now in the process of dissolution, due to a weakening of the state since the oil crisis and a less prominent position for central union agencies. Industry has promoted decentralization of negotiations on wages and other benefits to the industry and firm, while the state has been unable to maintain its role as 'bondsman' in the structural change generated by wage settlements above what low-productive industries could carry. In the meantime, industry invested heavily in gaining strong market shares in niches through acquisitions in Europe and the United States. Dependence upon Swedish labour and Swedish authorities is thus minimal for big business, which was the darling of industrial policy-makers during the period of modernization.

State-Supported Modernism

The road towards this competitive position started during last century when industrialization came to Sweden. Before that, the location of industry was determined by the suitable combination of iron ore, forests, water power, and transportation routes, which led to the Bergslagen district becoming the industrial centre of Sweden, with Stockholm and Göteborg as export harbours. Imports of supplies also passed through these harbours, and generated an agglomeration of trading capitalists in those cities, with production facilities typically in the countryside. In Bergslagen the steel mills were large users of forests for charcoal, and as sawed timber took off as an export product, the trading capitalists moved north to exploit virgin forest. By the time the sawmill boom subsided during the latter half of the nineteenth century, pulp and paper production in small plants had caught on in southern Sweden, and was developed in almost complete separation from the wealth sawmill barons (Glete 1987). The forestry-based industry was ripe for restructuring, but the trading capitalists did not see the potential and did not put their company shares on the emerging stock market.

A period of mergers and acquisitions involving banks and financial capitalists was initiated. At the same time, a new generation of inventor-based companies were established around the turn of the century. Practical inventions like the milk separator and self-adjusting ball bearing were patented and exploited world-wide. The rather fragile financial structures that were erected during this time could not withstand the deflationary crisis of 1920–3. In the reconstruction of finances that ensued, the Wallenberg family's sphere of interest, including their Stockholm Enskilda Bank, was established alongside another sphere centred on the other major bank,

Handesbanken. Both banks were heavily involved as owners in the forestry-based industry, due to bad debts.

The towering figure in this period of financial speculation was Ivar Kreuger. He operated internationally, and when he fell in 1932, it was a numbing blow to the prestige of industry. The banks became deeply involved in clearing up the bankruptcy.

During the 1920s the union movement grew strong. The labour-intensive sawmills were in decline, and the rise of the modern capital-intensive pulp and paper industry provided arenas of confrontation. The recession and the fall of Ivar Kreuger provided a strategic opportunity for organized labour to take a firm stand. A coalition of Social Democrats and the Farmers' Party came to power in 1933, and the building of a strong welfare state with Keynesian management of the state finances and a full employment ideology commenced. An industry-friendly policy (e.g. free depreciation 1938–55) provided ample opportunities for self-financed growth. The fact that production facilities remained intact were the Second World War gave a head start, while the war in itself promoted a consensus mood under a self-sufficiency umbrella. During the 1960s, regulation of the financial sector was an instrument that directed resources towards expansion of the public sector and ambitious housing programmes.

The promotion of labour interests culminated in the early 1970s with the promulgation of a number of new laws, notably the Co-determination Act under the label 'economic democracy', which provided for participation and sharing of information between employer and union. Ever since the mid-1970s, with its energy crises, which had severe effects on the Swedish economy due to its cold climate and resulting reliance on imported fuel, the strong state, which had enjoyed the support of the Social Democratic party, has failed. A period of minority governments or unstable coalitions followed, during which the authority of the state as guarantor of a high living standard for all was undetermined. Entitlement programmes were reviewed, and uncertainty as to the omnipotence of a benevolent state spread. Adaptation to the EEC and international competition provided a background for tax reform and deregulation of the financial sector. In 1989, currency regulation was dismantled. Capital was again liberated, as labour had been 20 years earlier. A period of global competition and management had begun. Product costing for strategic decision making was made into a significant issue by Americans, and rapidly won an audience in Sweden. What was new? Did we really have problems with overhead cost-allocation methods distorting product costs?

Episode 1: Full Costing

These problems had been discussed by members of the scientific management movement, which became well established institutionally between the world wars. To some it sounded like the old rhetoric being repeated. The first time cost calculation was widely and intensively discussed was in connection with the establishment of 'Uniform principles of full costing' (E.P. 1937).

The issue of cost calculation had been put on the agenda in 1927 by the Royal National School Board, or rather, by one of its chief officers, Nils Fredriksson, who was in charge of occupational training. He had written to the Swedish Institute of Standards (SIS) asking it to take action to produce a uniform terminology for full costing to be used in schools. Fredriksson was also a prominent member of the Association of Technologists. That association had different sections for different engineering specialities, and for some time it has been discussing how to deal with a proposal to establish a new section for 'Industrial Organization and Economy', which would be the focal point for scientific management among engineers. The other sections resisted, because they would obviously lose members to this interdisciplinary, modern section.

Scientific management was already well established and institutionalized in industry. The Federation of Industries had set up a consultancy firm before the First World War, which was to become the biggest consultant dealing with rationalization projects. A committee appointed by the SIS had produced a draft standard terminology, and the Association of Technologists had been left behind, only to be asked if it wished to make any comments on the draft. Of course it did! The debate started.

The committee had largely followed a German standard from 1920. The procedure of full costing was described as consisting of three steps: (1) determination of cost elements, (2) allocation to cost centres, and (3) allocation to cost-carrying units. Overhead costs were defined as costs that are common to more than one unit of output. They were classified into materials overhead, production overhead, and sales overhead. Concepts like allocation base, burden, variable and fixed costs, a priori (estimate) and *ex post* calculus (costing), and prime costing were proposed.

Since two members of the committee, Liljeblad and Schultz (who were both engineers), represented ASEA, a heavy manufacturing company with thousands of products (machinery for generating, transmitting, and using electric power), it is not surprising that the proposal was strongly influenced by the terminology used by that company. Opposition came from SKF, a ball bearing company which had imported standard costing from its acquired subsidiary in the United States and later from Volvo (with the same costing tradition). After some years of intermittent discussions and revisions, an accord was reached, largely through the intervention of Professor ter Vehn (described below). This is the central event of this episode.

The point of decision for a standard on costing procedure was approaching. The standard on terminology had already been adopted. There was a clash between one camp, represented by ASEA and Ericsson, who wanted to integrate cost calculation into the cost accounting system in the German tradition, and another camp, represented by SKF and Volvo, who argued for standard costing and for keeping cost calculation and cost accounting separate, along American lines.

In this situation, Professor ter Vehn (1936) published a series of 7 articles in the leading professional journal of the time. *Affärsekonomi*, in which he described the costing systems of the four companies involved. By clarifying differences, he managed to diffuse the debate. The problem was that ASEA, which produced a very large portfolio of products, wanted to be able to measure efficiency in all its departments. Therefore it used internal prices that were regularly adjusted for price changes (of, e.g., copper). This was built into the accounting system, which could thus be described as 'calculatory'. SKF and Volvo, with mass production of standard products as their main activities, did not accept that unrealized price adjustments were included in inventory values, and maintained that calculation should be geared to the situation at hand and therefore kept out of the cost accounting system.

Ter Vehn (1936) used a neutral language, Schmalenbach's method of graphical representation of charts of accounts, and pointed out the strengths and weaknesses of both positions, and suggested that since good reasons existed for some types of firms to do cost accounting according to accounting principles and adapt calculations to the situation at hand, the committee should provide variants where practical reasonableness did not contradict what was right in principle. The issue was settled in line with the principle that a costing system must be able to produce various kinds of cost information ('different costs for different purposes'), and this was the leading principle when the standardization of cost systems entered a new phase.

This historical episode shows how costing practices were a constituent part of the scientific management movement, and how engineers conducted and guided the main aspects of the debate, which was very pragmatic and based on practical matters. When an accounting academic—another accounting professor, Sillén, had participated in early committee work—stepped onto the scene, it was to demonstrate that a costing system should be tailored to the calculative needs of the individual firm. In his view, the standard must allow for individual variations. The principle that systems should be able to meet different costing needs has been fundamental in the Swedish cost debate throughout the 'modern' period.

When marginal costing, the micro-economic idea from the London School of Economics, was introduced in 1949, another debate, spanning a number of years, took place. Again, academic intervention in the form of empirical mapping of practices informed solutions that advocated 'standards' which could accommodate different situations. This tradition in costing has been maintained by Professor Frenckner and his associates, who have worked closely with committees of industrial associations (Samuelson 1970; Frenckner and Samuelson 1984).

Episode 2: Computerized Systems

Another train of development started as a consequence of the settlement of the standard for costing procedures in 1936. It was thought that the next step in standardization of costing should be standards of charts of accounts to support the costing procedures. A number of industrial associations started committee work on such charts of accounts, and it was clear that Schmalenbach's graphical method of describing accounting systems was a great help and inspiration. The leading chart of accounts that came to be widely employed across a wide range of industries, and also, after minor adaptation, by municipalities, was the standard chart of accounts (the M-chart) of the Trade Association of the Swedish Mechanical and Electrical Engineering Industries, adopted in 1943. The war conditions no doubt affected the promotion of such standardization of accounting systems. The M-chart was a very useful framework for teaching introductory accounting at business schools, since it was built on a well-integrated set of cost concepts and contained provisions for variable- as well as full-costing systems. Not that variable costing was in much use during the first decades after the war. Swedish industry came out of the war with its production capacity intact and a surge in demand for industrial goods fuelled by the Marshall Plan. Since its cost-accounting problems were solved, industry focused on efficiency problems, time and motion studies, etc., to extract the most from available capacity.

When computerization came to industry, it was only natural that the industrial committee system took up a project in 1973 on how to adapt accounting systems to computer application. Conscious of the traditions of accommodating different costing needs, the positive aspect of this project was the attention it paid to the report-generation aspects of the systems. As a consequence of this tradition, Swedish software packages (EPOK and EPOS) with powerful and flexible report-generators were developed. However, little new was added to costing approaches.

The new project, called the RP project, was user-oriented (Samuelson 1989, 1990). It was also initiated in response to a belief, later documented in a survey (Östman *et al.* 1987), that accountants and controllers, accustomed to having access to standard solutions, lacked competence to design computer-based systems that could fulfil the high ambitions of flexible reporting. The methodology for designing accounting information systems built on specifying codes for report plans, register-holding plans, object plans, etc., to structure the accounting data so as to make them available for a number of different uses. The approach of the project was to work with individual companies which developed systems and use these practical examples as practical demonstrations of the principles involved. The problem was that interference from institutional changes in industry focused attention on one type of user, the headquarters controller in a large multinational firm.

Increasing problems with costs and wages in Sweden due to the oil crisis, government 'bridging' policies, and union victories in wage negotiations directed the attention of industry outward. The late 1970s and 1980s saw a surge of acquisitions and mergers in Europe and the United States for Swedish industry. Divisionalization and control by ROI calculation meant less interest in standardized costing and a focus on financial controls. The systems designed under the auspices of the RP project tended to take old costing systems on board in their previous form, due to approaching deadlines and exhaustion from designing the financial controls for divisions and subsidiaries. The link between the 'good' old costing traditions and the modern costing methods seems to have been loosened by the preoccupation with strategy and acquisitions by user groups. This in turn created the opportunity for post-modern salesmanship of Activity-Based Costing (ABC) and related techniques that was to be witnessed.

A Survey of Current Costing Practices

Research on cost accounting practices in Sweden has been limited. A few surveys have been conducted (Ahlberg and Sundqvist 1970; Frenckner and Samuelson 1984; and Olve and Samuelson 1989), but these are very narrow in scope and size. By far the most comprehensive survey is the Ask and Ax (1992) study which provides the focus for this section.[1]

Costing Methods

The question of whether full or variable costing should be used for decision making is a controversial topic in the literature. The survey findings show that it is not a matter of either full or variable costing. Full costing predominates, but there is also frequent use of variable costing on an aggregated level, i.e. exclusively and in conjunction with full costing (see Table 10.1).

An interesting finding is that of the companies using both full and variable costing, all but one use full costing as their primary method for calculating product costs. Variable costing is considered merely as a complement to full costing for special cost studies, mainly for product, market, and customer profitability analyses. The main argument for using variable costing is that it is considered much easier and flexible to use than full costing, while the main argument for using full costing is that it provides a solid basis for pricing and other product-related decisions.

Table 10.1. Usage of costing methods

Costing method used (*n* = 152 (no. of companies))	Number of employees (%)			
	50–99	100–499	500+	Total
Full costing	59.3	57.3	56.0	57.9
Variable costing	10.2	13.3	0	9.9
Full and variable costing	30.5	29.4	44.0	32.2

There are of course a number of situations in which product-cost information is being used, and the method preferred in specific situations differs among the companies. The respondents were asked to indicate which method they used in a large number of situations. The findings show that full costing is preferred by the majority of companies in all situations. Full costing is used with the highest frequencies for transfer pricing (87.5%), inventory valuation (88.4%), and R&D costing (81.6%); while variable costing was used most frequently for customer profitability analysis (32.5%), market profitability analysis (30.9%), and product profitability analysis (25.0%).[2] It should be noted that the proportion of respondents using full costing for these latter purposes was over 60% in all cases.

Interestingly, a number of non-traditional situations/cost objects are receiving increased attention. These include R&D, waste and defects, set-ups, marketing and sales strategy, analysis of transportation and distribution channel alternatives, and profitability analysis for different objects. Further, 44% of the companies also indicate a need to assign costs and revenues to more cost objects than just products. This suggests that companies are adapting to an increasing diversity and complexity of production, distribution, and service, and have recognized that costs are driven by factors unrelated to production volume.

A significant trend towards decreased use of variable costing and increased use of full costing was evident. The reasons given for changing methods were the increasing proportion of fixed costs, the inability of variable costing to address the higher degree of complexity in decision making, and a number of new decision-making situations which require a longer-term view of costs. Thus, the findings lend support to the view that in an advanced production environment the use of variable costing will decrease because of an increasing proportion of fixed costs. It also lends some support to the argument in the ABC literature for adopting a longer-term view of costing (i.e. ignoring the short-term distinction between fixed and variable costs).

Overhead Cost Allocation

The issue that has received the most attention during the past few years is overhead cost allocation. The message is that the conventional model of allocation distorts product costs, because it has not kept up with changes in the manufacturing environment. In order to make the allocation of overheads more accurate, several improvements based on the cause–effect criterion have been suggested (e.g. to make cost pools more homogeneous, increase the number of allocation bases, increase the direct traceability of costs, and introduce ABC).

Our findings, from a number of questions dealing with procedures for overhead cost allocation, show that a great deal of effort is put into making the assignment of overhead costs accurate. In most companies the allocation process is more developed and more finely tuned than in the 'horror' examples presented in the contemporary debate. The allocation process is complex, and it differs among the companies, as well as in different situations. The differences cannot easily be summarized, but some important characteristics of the process of allocation are the following:[3]

82.5% use a two-stage procedure for allocating overheads (there were also a few companies that used a three- and four-stage procedure).
16.1% use plant-wide rates for allocating overheads (1.5% use both a two-stage procedure and plant-wide rates).
No company applies a single plant-wide overhead rate.
The cost centres used are departments (60.6%), work cells (29.5%), groups of machines (18.2%), and single machines (12.9%).
Direct labour, direct material, machine hours, and number of units produced are the allocation bases most extensively used.
About 85% revise their cost pools and allocation bases annually.

The majority of companies consider overhead cost allocation a high-priority area. It is this area into which most companies that have made changes to their cost accounting have put a lot of effort. The changes included the establishment of more homogeneous cost pools, the development of alternative allocation bases, and a switch from applying overheads on the basis of direct labour and direct material to using separate machine-related overhead cost pools and machine hours to apply them to products.

The major reasons given for the changes were a desire to establish a more causal relationship between the consumption of resources and products, the view that labour and material have become inappropriate measures of the consumption of overheads, and the increasing proportion of overhead costs, decreasing proportion of direct labour, and increasing fixed costs.

The survey suggests that the allocation process in Sweden is more elaborate and more carefully carried out than in most of the 'horror' examples given in the literature. Further, the findings indicate that there is a high awareness of an increasing complexity in the allocation of overhead costs. 59.5% of the respondents stated that the most desirable change in their product costing system would be an improvement in their overhead allocation through development of allocation bases that better reflect the consumption of resources by different products. The second most desirable improvement would be to increase the direct traceability of costs to products (i.e. assign costs directly to products and thereby reduce the amount of costs to be allocated). This was the view of 51.9% of the companies. It is interesting to note that one area of major concern in the ongoing debate was not considered a high-priority improvement area. Only 6.9% of the companies considered treating direct labour as an overhead cost an improvement area.

Changes in Cost Accounting Systems

The companies surveyed were asked about any significant changes in their costing systems during the past 5 years. Significant changes were reported by 40.2% of the respondent companies.

31.1% of the companies had made changes to their overhead cost allocation procedure (see previous section).

Changes relating to integration and automation of different systems were reported by 26.7% of the companies. Of these, 8.9% had integrated their product-costing system with their accounting system. The reasons for this integration were related not to environmental changes but to a need to simplify internal reporting/routines. Another 11.1% had computerized their product-costing system. The reasons given for this were related to a need to produce more timely and up-to-date cost information. Also, 6.6% had implemented MRP systems. The main motive for this was not to improve product costing, but to improve production planning and control. However, the implementation also led to improvements in cost data collection and in the quality and timeliness of cost information for costing purposes.

11.1% had switched from variable costing to full costing (see previous section).

6.7% of the companies stated that they were currently running ABC pilot study projects, and that they were planning to adopt ABC if their experience of the pilot study proved positive.

Improvement Areas and Barriers to Change

Is there a need for improvement in cost accounting? What are the problems? The companies were asked to list the five areas in which they felt their cost-accounting system needed improvement. As many as 76.8% stated such needs. A total of 31 areas were mentioned, but the following emerged clearly as the areas indicating the greatest opportunity for improvements: development of alternative overhead allocation bases (70.3%), increasing direct traceability of costs (61.3%), cost collection (input data) (60.4%), assigning costs (and revenues) to more objects (60.4%), and introducing 'life-cycle costing' (35.1%).

The respondents stated that the major barriers to changing their systems were management priorities and policies (49.6%), habit (27.8%), lack of understanding of other options (26.1%), and lack of relevant data (22.6%). The fact that management priorities and policies are the major obstacle for improvements suggests that cost accounting is not an island; nor is it perceived as a high-priority area. The second largest obstacle shows that cost systems are deeply rooted, and that 'this has always worked' reasoning is common. Accountants usually know what they have, but are sceptical about what they will get. Therefore it is not surprising that lack of understanding of other options was stated as a major barrier to change. The fourth barrier, lack of relevant data, shows that the cost information offered by management accounting systems in many companies, at least to some extent, are inadequate for costing purposes.

Modern Cost Management Techniques

During recent years, ABC has been the subject of much discussion. Even though the basic ideas underlying ABC were developed early, and have been available in the literature for decades, it is the Cooper and Kaplan version which has received attention from a wider audience. Earlier references to *activity*, *activity accounting*, and *activity costing* can be found in e.g. Kohler 1952; Staubus 1971; and Shillinglaw 1977. Ideas closely related to ABC can also be found in Scandinavia, e.g. *variability* (Madsen 1959; Madsen and Polesie 1981), *objective* (Polesie 1976), and *the step-by-step costing method* (Frenckner and Samuelson 1984). A number of other 'new' techniques have also been introduced in recent years. The most discussed are backflush accounting, throughput accounting, target costing, and strategic cost management and strategic management accounting.

In order to find out the extent to which these new techniques have been adopted, companies were asked to indicate if they were using, or planning to use, one or more of the new techniques in the near future. The result is overwhelmingly in favour of ABC and cost driver analysis (56 and 40% respectively), with value chain analysis attracting the least interest at 8%. These frequencies are for the larger companies (500+ employees). For the smaller companies the frequencies are markedly smaller. 'Modern' cost management techniques are of interest mostly to large firms, it seems, but only three companies reported on-going pilot studies, and no company claimed to have implemented ABC fully.

Summary of Current Practices

The findings show that traditional full-costing methods, based on standard costs, dominate, and there are few indications that they will lose their dominant role. Indeed, the findings suggest an enhancement of the Swedish full costing tradition. The companies are putting a great deal of effort into making overhead cost allocation accurate, and the allocation procedures are becoming more complex. Most companies use multiple overhead cost pools, and allocate overhead costs to products by applying separate allocation bases for each overhead cost pool. Thus, actual practice is far removed from the simplistic picture often portrayed in the contemporary debate.

Most of the changes made have focused on improving 'traditional' methods and techniques, rather than adopting 'new' ones. The major concern is overhead cost allocation, and the findings indicate that the companies are aware of the importance of adapting their overhead cost allocation to changing cost behaviour. There is little evidence in this survey that ABC or other 'new' techniques have been adopted by companies. However, some companies are showing interest in ABC. About one-fourth stated that they are planning to adopt or, at least, are willing to try ABC on a pilot scale. The interest in other 'new' accounting techniques is significant.

The Road to Post-Modernism

Earlier we described cost accounting development as an integral part of scientific management and thus of modernism. It was a debate between practitioners, based on experience that placed many issues on the agenda. Ordinarily academics would participate and promote differentiated solutions by conducting studies that illustrate principles and models. The link between pragmatic debate and academic research seems to have withered as researchers opt for international publishability and managers take an interest in strategy and governance structures. The void has been filled by consultants, who use strong rhetoric for change of the existing cost accounting practices and are leading actors in the diffusion process of ABC.[4]

The Rhetoric for Change in Cost Accounting

The rhetoric for change is almost identical to the message in the relevance lost debate (e.g. Johnson and Kaplan 1987; Berliner and Brimson 1988), i.e. that in practice, methods of product costing have not kept pace with changes in the manufacturing environment. The rhetoric is based solely upon a criticism of practice, not theory. In several publications, Cooper's (1987) symptoms characterizing an obsolete cost system, translated into

Swedish, have also been used to strengthen the rhetoric. The rhetoric is simple and straightforward, focusing on product costing as a rational, technical exercise designed to provide accurate accounting numbers to managers for decision-making purposes. The rhetoric is thus grounded in the tradition of managerialism.

Normally, the messages are delivered without putting the rhetoric for change into any wider context. The context is often implicitly included in the message, i.e. that 'conventional' and 'traditional' methods are obsolete, and therefore provide inaccurate numbers in the environment in which the companies are operating. In a few publications, however, increasing international competition is explicitly stated as a major pressure for change. The claim is that it is crucially important that companies become informed about the necessity to change their existing 'traditional' practices. Companies resisting change will not survive in global competition.

ABC as the Solution

The arguments for adopting ABC are similar to the rhetoric for change. There is a 'do or die' mentality in both. The dominant view is that elaborate management accounting techniques, leading to accuracy in the accounting numbers, are crucial for business excellence, and that these can give competitive advantage.

The basic underlying theme is that adopting ABC will lead to improved accuracy in the calculations. Improved accuracy will lead to a better basis for different product-related decisions, such as out-sourcing decisions, product-mix decisions, and product pricing. Hidden profit will be revealed, and it will be possible for managers to assess product, customer, and market profitability on a sound basis. The accuracy of ABC, it is suggested, will also improve the management of activities that produce the outputs. This includes how to perform the activities more efficiently, how to reduce or eliminate non-value-adding activities, etc.

The Leading Actors

Four different groups of actors can be identified as agents of change: a number of pioneering companies (early adopters of ABC), a few consultancy firms, the Association of Swedish Engineering Industries[5] (hereafter referred to as ASEI), and a few highly respected Anglo-Saxon academics. These groups are intertwined in a web of mutual relations, and form a complex pattern of interaction, which make it difficult to separate their individual contributions to the diffusion of ABC.[6] Still, the different groups have different major functions to perform in the diffusion process. The companies have an experience-sharing function, the consultancy firms a problem-solving and solution-providing function, ASEI a network-organizing and co-ordinating function, and the academics are used to attract participants, and have a status- and legitimacy-providing function.

The companies, on their own or through the consultancy firms, share their experience of implementing or experimenting with ABC. Hence, practical arguments are generated for practitioners. The experience is presented as case stories, and there are some twenty Swedish companies providing the empirical base. The companies are mainly, manufacturers, of which about 50% are large multinationals. Of these, three companies dominate: Volvo, Ericsson, and ASEA Brown Boveri (the same companies that were involved in the debate 70 years ago!). The Volvo and Ericsson stories are also included in three practice-oriented books on ABC, of which two were published by the leading ABC consultancy firm and one by ASEI.

It is of interest that a few large UK (e.g. British Aerospace and Lucas) and US (e.g. Apple, General Motors, and Hewlett-Packard) companies have voiced their support on several occasions, perhaps to give the calls for change an international dimension. It is also remarkable that many consultants from Britain and the United States have been presenters at several conferences.

The consultancy firms propose activity-based solutions to virtually any, possibly existing management-accounting problem. They portray themselves as leading experts in the field, with long-standing experience. The claims to expertise and experience are quite explicit in marketing publications from the leading ABC consultancy firm. When marketing the English version of its book on ABC, it states: 'The research for the report was undertaken by a firm of specialists in activity-based costing. . . . To draw on the best expertise and the most extensive knowledge in this field . . . order your copy.' It is solutions that are sold, irrespective of problems. Moreover, at least two consultancy firms explicitly take credit for having developed both ABC and ABM!

Another anecdote concerning expertise claims concerns the manner in which a consultancy firm described its activity-based analysis of the Kanthal Company, which gave rise to a Harvard Business School case. It tells how Robert Kaplan became very interested in the Kanthal analysis and how they, in close co-operation, developed the case, which became world-famous. There is an implicit claim that they transferred the knowledge to Kaplan and Harvard.

The academics give ABC the required legitimacy and status. Academic participation is twofold: either indirect, through mention in the publications, or direct, by participation at conferences.

ASEI serves a network-co-ordinating function. It gathers information from member companies on what problems they might have and their information needs. It keeps companies in the network up to date by passing around information. The association organizes conferences (open to the public) and network meetings (for network members only) on subjects proposed by the companies. In developing the contents for conferences and meetings, it mainly works in collaboration with the leading ABC consultancy firm and the multinational companies. The co-operation with consultancy firms may be characterized as bringing problems to the solutions (filling the 'garbage can', as it were).

Concluding Thoughts

The rhetoric surrounding modern cost management in Sweden is built upon a social construction of practice, which is divorced from actual practice. It draws heavily upon anecdotal evidence of management accounting practice, which forms the pillars of the 'Relevance Lost' debate (e.g. Young and Selto 1991). All the arguments are rooted in the US crisis perspective (see Bromwich and Bhimani 1989). It should be noted that the Swedish industrial sector has performed well, and that the stock market frequently presented new all-time highs during the period when the marketing of ABC began in Sweden. Thus, the same rhetoric seems to be valid around the globe. Irrespective of business conditions, there is a crisis that can be solved by ABC. In the marketing of ABC, one might note, only American, and no Swedish academics, are involved. Noticeable too is the absence of references to Japan in the arguments for ABC (e.g. for dramatizing the rhetoric).[7]

Empirical mapping of the product-costing practices uncovered by Ask and Ax (1992) shows a situation of slow evolutionary improvement and an intention to try ABC among larger companies. The most promising driving forces behind the improvement process include a number of projects aimed at lean production and time saving from order to delivery. These activity-oriented projects will no doubt affect costing practices in due time. One might also, to balance the picture, note that Volvo has decided to close down its Kalmar plant, the first assembly plant designed for team-organized work. This has been criticized by researchers as a short-sighted measure. There is little evidence that traditional assembly plants are more effective. Maybe the decision was based on inadequate cost information.

Among the most active companies today, we find the same companies, ASEA, Volvo, and Ericsson, that were leading actors in the costing debate and the establishment of a full-costing standard in the 1930s. Their involvement, then as now, is manifested by representation on the management control committee of ASEI. The significance of that committee work in the Swedish setting is evidenced by the fact that five out of the nine committee members have been actively involved with ABC projects in their companies. The leading ABC consultancy firm, which in turn works in co-operation with American academics, has been involved in most projects.

One might conclude that the involvement of domestic academics to support the development process has been replaced by consultancy rhetoric.

The new fad seems to be 'packaging' the message in global competition terminology and enthusiastic exhortations of cost management as a solution. It is notable that the first 'solution' to the costing terminology problem in the 1920s was imported from Germany, whereas now the country of origin is the United States. However, ABC is new only to practitioners, since the underlying concepts and ideas have been well known to Swedish academics and taught, albeit with insufficient enthusiasm, in business schools for 30 years. This may explain the relatively distant attitude towards ABC among academics in Sweden.

Notes

1. The objectives of the survey were to obtain a broad picture of traditional topics in cost accounting, to identify changes made, areas of improvement, and actual and planned use of modern cost-management techniques. From a population of 957 companies with 50 or more employees in manufacturing industry, a proportionate stratified random sample of 226 companies was drawn (i.e. 24%. A total of 152 usable questionnaires were returned (a response rate of 67.3%). For more detailed information on survey findings, questionnaire design, response rate, positions held by the respondents, and characteristics of the companies surveyed, see Ask and Ax 1992.
2. The percentages are based on the number of companies calculating each individual situation.
3. The percentages here are based on n = 137, i.e. the number of companies allocating overhead costs.
4. This section is based on data collected between 1988 and 1994. The data include programmes and documentation from seminars and conferences, and advertisements from professional journals and marketing pamphlets for seminars, conferences, books, and courses.
5. In 1992 the Trade Association of the Swedish Mechanical and Electrical Engineering Industry and the Swedish Engineering Employers' Association joined together and formed the Association of Swedish Engineering Industries.
6. There is no Swedish counterpart to, e.g., the Institute of Management Accountants (IMA) in the United States or the Chartered Institute of Management Accountants (CIMA) in the United Kingdom, i.e. professional bodies for management accountants which promote the profession by engaging in diverse activities. The historical odyssey depicted in the chapter shows that Swedish cost management is driven by industrial organizations in collaboration with a handful of multinationals, rather than by professional organizations.
7. Japanese cost-management approaches, such as target costing, Kaizen costing, cost tables, and functional analysis, etc., have not received any widespread attention as yet, either among academics or among practitioners / consultants. However, one might expect them to be placed high on the Swedish cost-management agenda in the near future.

References

Ahlberg, G., and Sundqvist, A-I. (1970), *Traditionella kalkylmetoder och linjär programmering* (Traditional Costing Methods and Linear Programming) (Stockholm: EFI).

Ask, U., and Ax, C. (1992), *Trends in the Development of Product Costing Practices and Techniques—A Survey of the Swedish Manufacturing Industry*. FE report 333, Department of Business Administration (Gothenburg: Gothenburg School of Economics and Commercial Law).

—— —— Bergevärn, L-E., and Jönnson, S. (1992), *Calculative Practices and Cost Accounting in Swedish Industry—Evolution During the 20th Century*, paper presented at Workshop on Cost Accounting in Europe—Past Traditions and Current Trends, Brussels, 3–4 Dec.

Berliner, C., and Brimson, J. A. (1988), *Cost Management for Today's Advanced Manufacturing. The CAM-I Conceptual Design* (Boston: Harvard Business School Press).

Bromwich, M., and Bhimani, A. (1989), *Management Accounting: Evolution not Revolution* (London: CIMA).

Cooper, R. (1987), 'Does Your Company Need a New Cost System?', *Journal of Cost Management for the Manufacturing Industry*, 2 (Spring): 45–9.

Enhetliga principer för självkostnadsberäkningar (*E.P.*) (1937) (Uniform Principles of Full Costing) (Stockholm: Federation of Swedish Industries and Swedish Standards Association).

Frenckner, P., and Samuelson, L. A. (1984), *Produktkalkyler i industrin* (Product Costing in Industry), rev. edn. (Stockholm: Trade Association of the Swedish Mechanical and Electrical Engineering Industries).

Glete, J. (1987), *Ågande och industriell omwandling* (Ownership and Industrial Development) (Stockholm: SNS).

Government bill 1986/7:74, *Näringspolitik inför 1990-talet* (Industrial Policy for the 1990s) (Stockholm: Ministry of Industry).

Johnson, H. T., and Kaplan, R. S. (1987), *Relevance Lost—The Rise and Fall of Management Accounting* (Boston: Harvard Business School Press).

Kohler, E. L. (1952), *A Dictionary for Accountants* (New York: Prentice-Hall).

Madsen, V. (1959), *Regnskabsvæsenets opgaver og problemer. I ny belysning* (The Tasks and Problems of Accounting in New Light) (Copenhagen: Gyldendal).

—— and Polesie, T. (1981), *Human Factors in Budgeting: Judgement and Evaluation* (London: Pitman).

Olve, N-G., and Samuelson, L. A. (1989), *Produktkalkylering i omwandling* (Product Costing in Transition) (Stockholm: Trade Association of the Swedish Mechanical and Electrical Engineering Industries).

Östman, L., Ewing, P., and Glader, M. (1987), *Ekonomisk styrning i förändring* (Management Control in Transition) (Stockholm: Trade Association of the Swedish Mechanical and Electrical Engineering Industry).

Polesie, T. (1976), *Ändamålsbudgetering* (Goal-Budgeting and Direct Costing—An Empirical Study) (Lund: Studentlitteratur).

Porter, M. E. (1990), *The Competitive Advantage of Nations* (London: Macmillan).

Samuelson, L. A. (1970), *Produktkalkyler i industrin* (Product Costing in Industry) (Stockholm: Federation of Swedish Industries and Trade Association of the Swedish Mechanical and Electrical Engineering Industries).

—— (1989), 'The Development of Accounting Information Systems in Sweden', *Scandinavian Journal of Management*, 5: 293–310.

—— (1990), *Models of Accounting Information Systems: The Swedish Case* (London and Lund: Chartwell-Bratt and Studentlitteratur).

Shillinglaw, G. (1977), *Managerial Cost Accounting* (Homewood, Ill.: Irwin).

Staubus, G. J. (1971), *Activity Costing and Input–Output Accounting* (Homewood, Ill.: Irwin).

ter Vehn, A. (1936), *Självkostnadsberäkningens standardisering* (The Standardization of Full Costing) (Stockholm: Norstedts).

Young, M., and Selto, F. (1991), 'New Manufacturing Practices and Cost Management: A Review of the Literature and Directions for Research', *Journal of Accounting Literature*, 10: 265–97.

11

Management Accounting in the UK
Reflections on Research, Practice, and the Profession

Alnoor Bhimani

The management accounting literature in Britain has recently documented calls for extensive changes. Exhortations to change management accounting systems echo those which, with a longer history, have aimed at altering enterprise management practices themselves. Thus, whereas company executives now deploy the language of management gurus ('de-layering', 'empowerment', 'right-sizing', 'multi-functionality'), accountants also increasingly appeal to the rhetoric of their avant-garde masters ('cost-drivers', 'activity-analysis', 'backflush', 'Kaizen costing'). As the interface between management and accounting ideals evolves, its potential for engendering management accounting change continues to be voiced. Management accounting practices, research, and the management accounting profession seem to be affected. Accounting practices in some organizations are being altered as novel prescriptions for accounting change emerge. But in other enterprises they remain highly organization-specific and even tradition-bound (Ezzamel *et al.* 1995). For some management accounting researchers, observed changes in management accounting practices and theorizing about normative management accounting approaches form important foci of interest, and open new possibilities for forging a more diverse research agenda in the field. The management accounting profession in the United Kingdom has likewise heeded calls for management accounting reforms, and espouses in the main a progressive outlook predicated on modern precepts for effective enterprise management.

If change characterizes management accounting in the United Kingdom, then it is worthwhile to develop questions about the nature of the forces underlying the observed changes. This is in part the intention here. What is principally sought in this brief exposé of management accounting in the United Kingdom, is a discussion of the emergence of the management

This chapter has greatly benefited from comments on an earlier draft by Thomas Ahrens, William Baxter, Michael Bromwich, Christopher Chapman, Jeremy Dent, Susan Dev, Colin Drury, Trevor Hopper, Anthony Hopwood, John Innes, Sue Llewellyn, Stephen Lyne, Peter Miller, Falconer Mitchell, David Otley, Cyril Tomkins, Martin Walker, and Richard Wilson.

accounting profession, past and present research in the field, and the variety of management accounting approaches deployed by enterprises, based on recent case-studies and surveys. The structure of the chapter is as follows. An overview of the rise of the management accounting profession in the United Kingdom is preceded by a short delineation of historical and current research trends in management accounting. This is followed by a review of surveys and case-studies of management accounting practices in UK companies. These observations enable questions to be posed as to the conditioning elements of change in management accounting research, practice, and the professionalization of the field.

Management Accounting Research in the United Kingdom

One of the first books on the British origins on cost accounting was *Factory Accounts*, published in 1887 and written jointly by Emile Garcke, an engineer, and John Fells, an accountant (see Edwards 1937 and Solomons 1952). The book highlighted the concern with allocating manufacturing costs thought to fluctuate with the cost of labour and material prices. Administrative and selling expenses, by contrast, were viewed as near constant and unallocable, since, at the unit level, they would decrease or increase with changes in activity. As Parker (1980: 263) notes, such a view shows 'some appreciation of the important distinction between fixed and variable costs'. Solomons (1952: 46) remarks that these authors 'clearly assert the futility of allocating "fixed" overheads, and must be counted among the founders of the "marginal cost" school of thought'.

Other early cost accounting books were also largely 'rooted in practice' (Dent *et al.* 1984: 236) until the 1930s, when a number of UK economists became interested in accounting issues. A small group of scholars in the LSE Economics Department in particular were 'interested in the relevance of orthodox accounting procedures to business problems and, in particular, to the usefulness of cost accounting to business decisions' (Dev 1980: 5). The principal issue was that traditional accounting relying on double-entry bookkeeping principles was concerned with records of past transactions, whereas businessmen looked to their accountants for figures to aid decision making. It was perceived that decision-makers required not just historical cost records, but also information on future consequences of alternative plans. These scholars sought to replace prevailing methods of costing based on the collection and allocation of historic costs by more economically oriented costing approaches (Baxter 1991). Gould (1974: 96) suggested that the rationale underpinning the LSE research in costing was that 'The traditional system of recording transactions, as extended to costing, was being asked to solve problems for which it has not been designed'. The 'London tradition in cost theory' (Buchanan 1973: 15) was effectively concerned with linking costs to choices to be made, relying on relevant information, and applying cost concepts to real-world business problems. As such, research sought to be pragmatic and of practical significance rather than theoretically insular and self-contained.

Not unlike the recent spate of North American writings by accounting scholars alleging the obsolescence of traditional management accounting principles in modern enterprises (Cooper and Kaplan 1987; Kaplan 1983, 1984, 1985; see also Kaplan 1994 for a review), papers published by LSE costing academics in the late 1930s 'showed that current cost accounting practices were quite inadequate for decision-making [and] laid foundations for improvements in the estimation and analysis of data for decisions' (Gould 1974: 106). Possibly, the 'London tradition . . . played an important role in releasing cost accounting from its historical shackles' (ibid.).

Similarly, not unlike the modern-day widespread influence of North American accounting commentators calling for reforms in cost accounting practices, the London costing tradition was to have an impact on cost accounting thinking. LSE graduates formed a readily available pool of potential accounting teachers, who filled positions opened up by the rapid expansion of the university sector during the 1960s. Hopwood and Bromwich (1984: 138) note that the stress placed on marginal, future-oriented, and opportunity costs in decision-making contexts was to provide an outline for a general approach to cost determination that 'had a major impact on subsequent accountancy research and university education in accounting in the UK'.[1]

Over a period of time, accounting researchers became more and more concerned with developing an economics-based frame of reference, which was increasingly limited to theory rather than practice. Much of what is now seen as 'conventional wisdom' (Scapens 1991), relying on simple economic models embodying the assumptions of profit maximization and costless information, was in place by the mid-1960s. Theoretical perspectives on the determination of costs for decision making were not the sole focus of research. For instance, British accounting academics became interested in divisional measurement problems, and the usefulness of the concept of residual income as a divisional performance measure *vis-à-vis* return on capital investment provided a focus of significant scholarly debate (Amey 1965; Solomons 1965; Tomkins 1973). Accounting academics began to apply quantitative methodological approaches to the study of what are now traditional management accounting areas, including the economics of information costs, decision choices under uncertainty, transfer pricing approaches, and standard costing for planning and control (see Arnold *et al.* 1980 for representative illustrations of then 'current UK academic thinking in management accounting' (p. vii). See also Hopwood and Bromwich 1984 and Scapens 1991 for excellent reviews of this research).

As the gap between management accounting concepts and practices grew, accounting scholars trained in sociology, organization theory, and industrial psychology started to provide views contrasting with those of theorists relying more extensively on mathematical reasoning and economic analyses. As Scapens (1980: 280) notes, during the 1970s, 'research into management accounting proceeded along two almost separate paths: the development of quantitative techniques and the use of behavioural analysis'. Hopper (1994: 7) remarks that 'the 1970s marked a watershed in British management accounting research with the advent of behavioural and organisational approaches'. Behavioural accounting research initially encompassed explorations of the forms and roles of accounting information in the functioning of complex enterprises and the effects on individual behaviour of using such information (Hopwood 1972). Studies in this field also focused on the contingencies between environmental elements and the design of accounting systems (Hopwood 1974; Otley 1978; see also Emmanuel *et al.* 1990). This strand of management accounting research subsequently became concerned with critical and socio-historical analyses of accounting and its wider conditioning factors. Sociological perspectives became of increasing interest to British management accounting academics (see Roslender 1990). Investigations of the interplay between power, rituals, social struggles, and organizational politics and the design and functioning of accounting systems were a growing part of the research agenda (see Hopper 1994 for an overview of this research and reasons for its emergence. See also Hopwood and Miller 1994 for a collection of early and recent studies). Within the last few years, this research theme has expanded into explorations of the linkages between internal accounting changes and social transformations, using a variety of methodological perspectives stemming from other areas of the social sciences. Although initially providing a research focus primarily for some British accounting academics, this strand of management accounting research is now attracting an internationally dispersed scholarship.[2]

There is a growing predilection among British management accounting researchers for case-study analysis. This is possibly a result of calls during the early 1980s to investigate accounting in action, and to focus on how and why accounting is used the way it is in different contexts (Burchell *et al.* 1980; Tomkins and Groves 1983). As Scapens (1990: 279) notes, 'In the UK, case studies are becoming an increasingly important part of management accounting research' (see also Llewellyn 1992; Scapens 1992; and Otley and Berry 1994).

Another notable development is that over the past decade, many UK scholars have turned their attention to management accounting perspectives which seek to directly influence practice. Early studies focused on the relationships between the use of high technology and management accounting changes (Coates and Longden 1989; Innes and Mitchell 1989; Littler and Sweeting 1989; see also Bromwich and Bhimani 1989 for a review of others). Presently, the professionally oriented accounting journals regularly feature topic areas such as strategic cost analysis, activity based costing (ABC), and throughput accounting, which also feature in scholarly journals. Moreover, the Chartered Institute of Management Accountants (CIMA)[3] assumes a knowledge base in these areas in its professional examinations. Whereas British academic interest in some of these areas may be tied to research interest trends in the United States, aspects of Japanese cost accounting also seem to 'have become integral to contemporary British research' (Hopper 1994: 16). In this light, growing areas of interest include target cost management (Bhimani and Okano 1995; Carr and Ng 1995; see also Bromwich and Bhimani 1994), functional cost analysis (Yoshikawa *et al.* 1995), and cost tables (Yoshikawa *et al.* 1993).

Today, management accounting research encompasses a diversity of methodological rationales and frames of reference adopted by UK scholars who publish their works in academic and professional journals, some British,[4] others foreign or international. But while management accounting research now contributes importantly to academic accounting thought in broad terms, the advancement of management accounting as an occupational expertise has itself also witnessed rapid growth, and presently makes a very significant contribution to professional accounting activities in the United Kingdom. The rise of the management accounting profession is briefly considered below.

The Rise of the Management Accounting Profession

Arguments have long been advanced as to the importance of the formation of professional accounting associations in successfully promoting the accounting function (Stacey 1954; Garrett 1961). The incorporation of the Institute of Cost and Works Accountants (ICWA) in 1919 is no exception. It has been argued to have emerged out of 'a need for controlling costs and prices, and for means of raising productivity and improving industrial efficiency' (*Management Accounting*, 1969, p. 91), at a 'time ripe for cost accountancy to assume its rightful place in the field of scientific management' (ibid.). Within 50 years, the ICWA was seen to have grown into 'a highly respected professional organization whose contribution to the national welfare and industrial efficiency is beyond doubt' (ibid. 95).

More recently, the Chartered Institute of Management Accountants (CIMA), in reviewing its '75 years of progress' (*Management Accounting*, 1994, p. 4) noted that its anniversary theme was to be 'the promotion of the practical role of management accountants in providing information for top management and applying it to turn business strategy into profits'. Over the longer term, CIMA sees part of its strategy as aiming 'to capture and hold the high ground of information management in industry and commerce by the sophisticated range and vision of its training'. The 'high ground' held by accounting information and financial controls has been a characteristic feature of many UK enterprises for some time, and a sizeable proportion of British managers are accountants by training. Granick's (1971) early study of managerial characteristics in different countries carried out in the late 1960s indicated a relatively high degree of importance accorded to accounting-based controls by British managers. Horovitz's (1980) investigation of top management controls in the late 1970s also suggested the comparatively high financial control orientation of British companies (see Lane 1989 for a review of this and other studies). Strange's (1991: 14) study of engineering companies also affirms 'the British view of management accounts as a key part of maximising the long-term value of the company, the mathematical reliance placed on management accounting figures for rewarding management and the perceived necessity to relate all decisions as directly as possible to share price'. He further notes that 'management accounts are taken very seriously at the expense of other sources of information' (ibid.). More recently, in reporting on a study of strategic issues involving 42 manufacturing companies in the United Kingdom and Germany, Carr (1995: 21) notes that while there is little evidence of any direct impact on short-termism, British companies' 'stronger financial orientation', and 'the indirect impact of strong financial control styles adopted by most UK companies (though very few in Germany) is very powerful indeed'. It is thus widely reported that, 'Compared with other professions . . . accountants and other financial specialists are prominently represented in the managerial hierarchies of British capitalism' (Armstrong 1987: 415), and that 'Correspondingly there is an emphasis on financial as against alternative means of control, especially at the higher levels' (ibid.).

What may be questioned is the basis for the predominant role played by financial controls and accounting information in UK enterprises, and indeed, whether the formation of professional accountancy bodies has had a bearing on this. To understand the widespread prevalence of accounting controls in British organizations, it is worthwhile considering Armstrong's (1987) discussion of the impact of statutory legislation on business activities and consequently on shaping the positioning of accounting expertise in the United Kingdom. Armstrong (1987) notes how the Companies Act of 1861 increased the volume of work for accountants who served as trustees or assignees for creditors. The following year, the Companies Act 'created the position of Official Liquidator for limited companies and in most cases a professional accountant was appointed' (Armstrong 1987: 42). This piece of legislation came to be known as 'the accountants' friend'. Various subsequent statutes also increased the accountants' role in auditing until the Companies Act of 1900 'provided for a compulsory annual audit for all registered companies and probably by that date the accounting profession possessed a monopoly of this function although this was not incorporated into law until the Companies Act of 1948' (ibid. 422). According to Armstrong

(1987), the accounting profession's growing power base allowed it, over time, to sponsor its preferred methods of corporate control, and thereby strengthen its position in British management structures.

With regard to the establishment of a management accounting profession, the president of CIMA, commenting on the founding of its precursor association, the Institute of Cost and Works Accountants (ICWA), has noted that 'The institute arose out of a recognised need to develop techniques for a more scientific approach to the measurement of costs and their nature' (McRae 1994: 4). But it has also been argued that a variety of historical circumstances underlie the beginnings of management accounting's professionalization. Thus, the institute's origins have been traced to a variety of wider social forces of change, and the essentialism accorded to accounting as part of the management task has been viewed as a peculiarity shaped by a diversity of conditioning factors embedded in past history. It has been argued that cost accounting, for its part, only became integrated into the main body of accounting knowledge incidentally, following the outbreak of the First World War. War legislation was passed to prevent profiteering by industrialists who assisted in the manufacture of munitions and contributed to the war effort. The legislation established a basis for setting contract prices for war material where there was no clearly identifiable market price. This was achieved by a new clause embodied in the Defence of the Realm Act in 1916, enabling costs to be ascertained by examining manufacturers' figures. The shortage of expertise for such an undertaking ultimately led cost accounting to be brought to the attention of manufacturers. Loft (1986*a*: 165) argues that 'The bringing of cost accountants and cost accounting "into the light" came as a virtually unanticipated consequence of the war-time legislation'. Thus, just as Armstrong (1987: 419) has indicated that during the last decades of the nineteenth century 'the future of cost accounting as a body of knowledge was at this time, open. It could conceivably have been incorporated into the knowledge base of the engineering profession[5] . . . Alternatively, it could have given rise to a profession independent both of engineering and accountancy', so Loft (1986*b*: 85) remarks that 'Costing in Britain became the business of accountants, this was not a necessary development'. Whatever view is taken as to the management accounting profession's origins, what is clear is that management accounting plays a significant part in the functioning of many British enterprises. The significance of this role is considered in the next section.

Current Management Accounting Practices

A considerable number of studies have been carried out in recent years in UK companies to investigate management accounting practices. Some surveys cover a wide span of accounting activities, while others focus on studying the deployment of specific management accounting techniques. Certain studies rely on questionnaires, others entail interviews, with a number of investigations reporting on the results of extended field studies. Type of industry, size of sample, and depth of analysis differ considerably between investigations, which inevitably reduces the possibility, as well as the significance, of attempts at comparative juxtapositions. Moreover, those who carry out research in the field of management accounting inevitably differ in their philosophical orientation and disciplinary background. Nevertheless, the results of relevant studies are discussed here, so as to permit broad-based comparisons of what has been researched, rather than to address the full range of approaches and techniques covered in the normative literature in management accounting.

In considering survey results, it is notable that the exhortations of critics of traditional management accounting practices espousing the use of novel approaches often result in change, though not necessarily intended. One outcome of calls to adopt innovative management accounting techniques is sometimes an enhanced search by enterprises for accounting-based visibility through further use, rather than disuse, of the allegedly redundant cost accounting approaches inherited from the past. Consider, for instance, the deployment of capital appraisal techniques by 100 large British companies over the 1975–86 period (see Table 11.1).

Table 11.1. Trends in capital appraisal techniques in United Kingdom companies

Appraisal technique	1975 (%)	1981 (%)	1986 (%)
Internal rate of return	44	57	75
Net present value	32	39	68
Accounting rate of return	51	49	56
Payback	73	81	92

Source: adapted from *Management Consultancy's* Industry Survey, October 1989.

During the 1970s and early 1980s, capital appraisal techniques which did not discount cash flows received much adverse press coverage in both academic and professional UK-based journals. As a possible consequence, the use of discounted cash-flow techniques became more widespread; but, paradoxically, so did accounting rate of return and payback, which many accounting commentators had discredited. Attempts to change what are considered outmoded practices often publicize form alongside substance so as to reinforce the orientation which some commentators would prefer to see companies abandon. Such effects may be subsumed in the results of investigations which are considered below.

The survey studies covered here to provide a glimpse of the *status quo* of management accounting practices in UK companies include only those documented since the start of the decade. The areas discussed are limited to overheads allocation and activity based costing, the use of costs for decision making, standard costing, non-financial performance measures, and capital investment appraisal. The brief review of survey results is followed by a consideration of case-studies.

Surveys of Management Accounting Practices

Overhead allocation and activity based costing

One of the most comprehensive recent analyses of management accounting practices is that undertaken by Drury *et al.* (1993), who presented the findings of their questionnaire survey, with responses from 303 individuals across 260 UK medium- and large-sized manufacturing companies. On the question of choice of overhead-allocation bases, the researchers distinguished between automated and non-automated production activities with the results shown in Table 11.2.

Table 11.2. Choice of allocation bases

Allocation base	Automated (%)	Non-automated (%)
Direct labour hours or costs	68	73
Materials consumed	30	19
Machine hours	49	26
Units of output	42	31
ABC cost drivers	9	7

An early study by Murphy and Braund (1990) based on 263 questionnaire responses from management accountants working in 'Hi-Tech' manufacturing industries indicated that 54% of companies use labour-based overhead allocation mechanisms and 16% employed machine hour-based rates.

The results of the Drury *et al.* (1993) study on the existing and future use of ABC are shown in Table 11.3. An earlier survey on ABC carried out by Innes and Mitchell (1991) based on a responding population of 187 orga-

Table 11.3. The existing and future use of ABC

Use of ABC	Percentage
Using ABC	4
Intending to use ABC	9
Consideration given to introducing ABC	37
Decided not to introduce ABC	5
No discussion has taken place regarding ABC	45

Table 11.4. The implementation of ABC

Use of ABC	Percentage
Considered and implementing ABC	6
ABC currently under consideration	33
Considered ABC and rejected it	9
ABC not considered	52

nizations in the manufacturing and financial services sector provided the results shown in Table 11.4

In a follow-up study, Innes and Mitchell (1992) investigated 30 of the 62 companies which had indicated the previous year that they were considering ABC. Of these 30 companies, 7 had now decided to implement ABC, 3 had rejected it, and 20 were still considering it. These results, by comparison with Drury *et al.*'s (1993), suggest a lesser inclination to consider or adopt ABC on the part of enterprises. The results possibly mirror the lesser publicity which ABC had then received.

A subsequent study carried out by Innes and Mitchell (1994) surveyed the ABC practices of companies listed in The Times–1,000. Of the 251 usable responses, the authors tabled the ABC adoption rates shown in Table 11.5. Innes and Mitchel (1994) found clear evidence that larger firms typically had a higher rate of ABC usage. They also report that ABC's 'cost management applications now outweigh the product costing attributes which were central to its initial development. In the UK, the cost reduction and cost control attractions of ABC have proved to be particularly popular' (p. 18).

This is confirmed by a study of the organizational consequences of implementing activity-based techniques carried out by Friedman and Lyne (1995). They investigated 11 companies that had attempted to implement some form of activity-based approach, and found a variety of different uses, which they broadly categorize as product costing, resource allocation, and cost management (see Table 11.6).

The authors of the investigation also note that the 'implementation paths' of activity-based techniques were far more varied than they had anticipated. The organizational consequences identified by Friedman and Lyne (1995)

Table 11.5. The adoption of ABC

Use of ABC	Percentage
Currently using ABC	19.5
Currently considering ABC adoption	27.1
Rejected ABC after assessment	13.2
No consideration of ABC to date	40.2

Table 11.6. Different uses of activity-based techniques in eleven companies

Uses	Current uses	Additional planned uses
Product costing	2	0
Pricing and bidding	6	0
Product-range decisions	3	0
Budgeting	5	4
Capital budgeting	1	0
Monthly accounting	0	4
Cost management/cost reduction	6	1
Make/buy decisions	3	0
Process changes	2	2

include significant behavioural problems emerging from formal programmes to classify activities into value adding and non-value adding, the rise of new ways of talking about enterprise affairs, and changes in attitudes and relationships between management accountants and operational managers.

On the question of popularity of novel cost management approaches, a survey by Davies and Sweeting (1991; see also Bright *et al.* 1992) of 677 manufacturers' management accounting practices confirms ABC's predominance. Their results indicated 'usage or planned usage' by late 1994 of the novel cost management techniques listed in Table 11.7. There is no other evidence of such levels of usage of emerging cost management practices in British manufacturing enterprises at this stage.

Table 11.7. Use or planned use of cost management techniques

Technique	Usage or planned usage (%)
Activity based costing	60
Cost of quality	52
Target cost planning	46
Strategic management accounting	44
Throughput accounting	40
Backflushing	24
Life-cycle costing	11

Use of costs for decision making

The Drury *et al.* (1993) study investigated the extent to which different costs are used for product-mix and make-or-buy decisions as well as for pricing purposes, with the results shown in Table 11.8. Drury *et al.* (1993) note that it is the larger, rather than the smaller, organizations which use variable

Table 11.8. Types of cost information used in decision making

Cost basis	Usage (%)*				
	Never	Rarely	Sometimes	Often	Always
Variable manufacturing	11 (21)	9 (11)	28 (27)	33 (18)	19 (23)
Total manufacturing	17 (22)	15 (10)	23 (16)	31 (27)	14 (25)
Total variable	23 (32)	18 (18)	26 (22)	25 (18)	8 (10)
Total cost	22 (23)	23 (19)	24 (11)	23 (22)	8 (25)

* Figures in brackets indicate the use of costs for pricing decisions.

costs in decision making (see Drury and Tayles 1994 for a fuller discussion). Murphy and Braund's (1990) study also indicated that a large proportion of companies (78%) made use of costs which included overheads for pricing decisions.

Standard costing

Drury *et al.*'s (1993) survey found that 76% of the 260 companies investigated used standard costing widely. Respondents viewed a number of functions as of either 'above average' or 'vital' importance (see Table 11.9). These results echo the findings of Puxty and Lyall's (1990) survey of 423 manufacturing companies, which also indicated that 76% use standard costing systems.

Table 11.9. Importance of standard costing systems for different purposes

Purpose	Percentage
Cost control and performance evaluation	72
Costing inventories	80
Computing product costs for decision making	62
As an aid to budgeting	69
Data-processing economies	43

Non-financial performance measures

The Drury *et al.* (1993) survey produced the results on the question of non-financial performance measures shown in Table 11.10. Murphy and Braund's (1990) survey of 263 companies reported 31% of the companies not using any system of reporting non-financial measures, while 34% reported on quality, 7% on supplier performance, and 24% on labour turnover. The Chartered Institute of Management Accountants commissioned a study which provides contrasting results on the usage of performance measures in the manufacturing sector (CIMA 1993). Part of the

Table 11.10. Extent to which performance is measured

	Never/rarely		Sometimes		Often/always	
	Smaller firms (%)	Larger firms (%)	Smaller firms (%)	Larger firms (%)	Smaller firms (%)	Larger firms (%)
Customer satisfaction/ product quality	22	2	11	7	67	91
Customer delivery efficiency	16	2	22	7	62	91
Supplier quality/delivery	16	4	32	15	52	81
Throughput times	33	6	24	20	43	74
Set-up times	59	32	19	22	22	46

Table 11.11. Performance measures to board and executives

	Board				Executives			
	SME		Large		SME		Large	
	Rank	%	Rank	%	Rank	%	Rank	%
Financial return	1	92	1	100	2	85	1	100
Working capital	2	80	3	88	3	80	3	94
General production	3	78	1	100	1	87	1	100
Demand	4	67	4	71	5	78	7	76
Customer	5	53	8	65	7	77	6	82
Labour	6	52	4	71	3	80	4	88
Process	7	48	4	71	8	68	7	76
Product	8	47	4	71	8	68	7	76
Lender security	9	33	10	24	11	22	11	24
Supplier	10	27	12	9	9	52	9	35
Innovativeness	11	25	9	41	10	28	9	35
Capital market	11	25	11	18	12	18	12	12

study entailed a questionnaire survey, which, on the basis of 77 usable responses, produced the results shown in Table 11.11.

The results differentiate between small- and medium-sized enterprises (SME) and large companies, as well as performance reports to board members and executives. The performance monitors include both financial and non-financial categories. Aside from a greater use of non-financial measures by large, as opposed to smaller, enterprises, the results suggest little size-related differential in behaviour, which contrasts with Drury *et al.*'s (1993) findings. What is clear is that the use of financial metrics predominates across all enterprises. Another survey of 150 companies (KPMG 1990) selected from *The Times* 1,000 Index, but excluding the top 100, gave results comparable to the Drury *et al.* (1993) and CIMA (1993) investigations. The study indicates that nearly a quarter of companies in manufacturing, distribution, and service sectors do not use non-financial monitoring. Of particular interest is that more than half the companies rely solely on financial yardsticks in appraising the utilization of new technology.

Capital investment appraisal

The results of the Drury *et al.* (1993) study with regard to the use of different investment appraisal methods in the 260 manufacturing enterprises surveyed are shown in Table 11.12.

Table 11.12. Use of different investment appraisal methods (often or always replies)

	All organizations (n = 278) (%)	Small organizations (n = 43) (%)	Larger organizations (n = 46) (%)
Payback (unadjusted)	63	56	55
Discounted payback	30	30	48
Accounting return on capital employed	41	35	85
Internal rate of return	57	30	85
Net present value	43	23	80

In a similar light, Lefley and Wharton (1992) carried out a survey of capital investment appraisal practices within the top 500 UK manufacturing enterprises. Their findings were based on 144 usable responses and focus on the appraisal of advanced manufacturing technology (AMT) projects specifically. The survey results are as shown in Table 11.13. These results contrast with those of Drury *et al.* (1993) for large organizations, in that payback is more popular than accounting rate of return, and IRR and NPV techniques are used to a lesser extent.

What emerges from this brief review of empirical surveys is that novel management accounting approaches are being implemented in many enterprises. However, the reaction of companies as to the necessity of adopting

Table 11.13. The use of different appraisal methods

Appraisal method	(%, rounded)
Payback	69
Discounted payback	54
Accounting rate of return	20
Internal rate of return	55
Net present value	52
Other DCF	5

prescriptive approaches, including greater reliance on non-financial performance measures or the use of sophisticated discounted cash-flow techniques or the application of activity-based costing concepts, varies. Generally, in companies where change in management accounting is taking place, it is not unidirectional. Those enterprises which do not report changes in their management accounting systems appear to have opted for no change following due consideration of the likely consequences of undertaking accounting-related changes. Aggregate surveys, as has been suggested, give only a partial picture of existing practices, and provide little information on processes leading to change. A small number of UK-based case-studies have been undertaken by researchers to investigate the implications of accounting system changes and the consequences of adopting emerging cost management techniques. Such studies allow an alternative appreciation of operationalization and organizational issues to that offered by aggregate surveys of company practices.

Lessons from Field Studies

In a study of 7 electronics companies undergoing management accounting change, Innes and Mitchell (1990) sought to provide a descriptive analysis of the process by which such change occurs. The types of changes included the adoption of market-oriented practices to enhance cost competitiveness, the simplification of costing practices, and the extension of performance measurement monitors. The authors suggest that change in management accounting practice is associated with organization-specific conditioning variables, including 'motivators' such as production technology, 'facilitators' such as the authority of accountants, and 'catalysts' such as new accountants. Effectively, they maintain that micro-level changes at the firm level need to be assessed to better understand alterations in management accounting practices.

In another study of a major company in the electronics industry, Kellett and Sweeting (1991) explored management accounting practices, including the influence of the 'contemporary debate' on the relevance of accounting techniques and practices in manufacturing organizations. The study suggests that practising accountants exposed to contemporary debates innovate, adapt, and implement advanced accounting approaches to meet perceived demands. They view an evolutionary approach comprising a mix of traditional and emerging accounting techniques as evident. Accounting practices are effectively reflective of a process of experimentation and reassessment of the use of particular techniques. Thus, 'accounting acted to shape the company and the people within it in a dynamic and mutually interacting way' (Kellett and Sweeting 1991: 25).

Gietzmann's (1991) study of the implementation of an activity-based costing system in an engineering components manufacturing company indicates how this technique can break down 'barriers between different functional areas' (p. 199). The sales personnel in the company had had significant input in developing the revised cost allocation methods, which, as a result, were 'no longer viewed as "blackbox" rules set by accountants' (ibid.). Bhimani and Pigott's (1992) study of the implementation of ABC in a pharmaceutical manufacturing company confirms a reverse observation of the same effect: 'sales managers did not understand or appreciate the reasons for product cost changes since they had not taken part in developing the ABC system. Their resentment nevertheless tended to diminish once the logic of ABC was explained and the rationale for cost changes indicated' (p. 131). The study also identified a variety of unanticipated organizational and behavioural consequences, including transformations in the 'managerial ethos of organisational players' and shifts in 'authority and power bases'. The authors of the study concluded that 'the array of changes caused by the altered accounting approach exceeded those which were presented as likely effects of adopting the ABC system and the configuration of these changes followed a pattern specific to the sequence adopted in installing ABC as well as the particular structural context of the organisation' (ibid.). Friedman and Lyne's (1995) recent field studies also reveal a variety of unanticipated organizational consequences following implementation of ABC.

Ways in which accounting practices and organizational processes can evolve out of the interplay of disparate influences and the intentional actions of organizational members have been investigated by Scapens and Roberts (1993) in a study of a company's adoption of a new accounting control system. They examined how failure to establish the legitimacy of a novel accounting mechanism and an inability to find a viable relationship between the languages of production and accounting in the company led to resistance to accounting change. Rather than identify generalizable factors stemming from their case-study, they report that 'an understanding of accounting change requires an understanding of various organisational and historical contingencies' (p. 30).

Jones *et al.* (1993) report on field studies of British companies' experiences with costing and investment appraisal and the perceptions of accountants, technologists, and production managers. They also suggest that the study of social relations between accountants and other managers is important. The details of accounting methods are less relevant than the relationship of accounting to other kinds of information and of accountants to other managers. They remark that what is needed is 'to study how accounting information can be used, ways in which accounting modes-of-thought permeate management, and to relate differences in these to specific organisational and societal contexts' (p. 134).

One major, 3-year investigation of 16 companies (King *et al.* 1991) suggested that the amount of management accounting information made available to managers is reflective of a wish to be 'over-informed', 'because there is a cultural value on "being informed" ' (p. 50). Moreover, the study concluded that, given that the ownership and control of information is a major source of power in organizations, there is a tendency for management accountants 'to be put under pressure to deliver increasing amounts, more rapidly and in different formats' (ibid.). A number of case-studies relating to the use of accounting-based techniques in capital investment appraisals point to the existence and primacy of *ad hoc* procedures (Currie 1994) and informal processes (Fincham and Roslender 1993; Sheppard 1990; Nixon and Lonie 1992).

These studies of management accounting practices across British companies in different industry sectors suggest that one cannot generalize about UK management accounting practices beyond affirming that, ultimately, accounting practices are contextually conditioned. They are reflective of the enterprise's ethos, its functional demarcations, its managerial preferences, and the strategic actions it pursues, as well as of other internal forces of change. A broader categorization of contextual factors, however, must include contingencies related to elements outside the organization. Exploring such wider conditioning variables may ultimately make possible the identification of strains of similarity across enterprises encompassing management accounting practices.

Conclusion

Management accounting research in the United Kingdom has undergone important transformations from its initial primary focus on concerns of practice to the present-day multitude of objectives underpinned by a diversity of methodological frameworks and philosophical positions. The existing variety of research in management accounting is likely to expand further still, as calls by British scholars continue to be made to forge ahead with renewed, if not alternative, perspectives. These exhortations include undertaking investigations of the growing complexity between the organization and management controls (Otley 1994), of the origins of changed agendas in sponsoring management accounting effects in specific contexts (Lapsley 1994), of developing understandings of management accounting practices within an 'old' institutional economics perspective (Scapens 1994), and of studying the interrelationship between management accounting and changing forms and media of communication (Hopwood 1994).

The evidence regarding trends in UK management accounting practices based on the surveys and case-studies considered here suggests clear signs of change in a significant number of enterprises. Many companies intend to undertake some form of change, while others seek to maintain their *status quo* following due consideration of options for change. Management accounting shifts within organizations seem to be contextually specific if context is taken to include both internal and external forces of change.

Certainly, for CIMA, the principal body representing UK management accountants, the pursuit of change is quite explicit. This professional institute has in the past changed both in name and in purpose. It continues to see the expertise to which it lays claim as undergoing fundamental shifts away from the traditional focus on process knowledge and towards more financial management and strategy-related conceptions of management accounting (Armstrong and Jones 1992). Such shifts, while converging with those broadly in evidence within emerging notions of effective enterprise management, will probably bring apace novel issues and challenges affecting the institute's image, purpose, and form.[6] The scope of activities seen to be relevant to the management accountant is ever widening, bringing with it questions as to how the profession will demarcate its territorial expertise and body of knowledge, and, more significantly, whether it will alter its relationship to other UK accountancy bodies.[7]

Change thus appears to be a pervasive part of management accounting research, the rise of the profession, and current enterprise management accounting practices in the UK. Little is known, however, as to how it comes about. This chapter permits a variety of specific questions to be fruitfully posed as to what is at play in effecting management accounting shifts. It might be asked in what ways management accounting research in British academia can be considered to have followed an evolutionary course of development while also having been affected by a variety of unforeseen and unintended factors. How far has the professionalization of management accounting been shaped by strategic pursuits coupled with accidental events embedded in history? How are organizations differently affected by forces of change which mould accounting in unanticipated ways? Is there an enabling logic of action which permeates management accounting practices across UK enterprises? More generally, how do dissipated, as well as more direct, forces of change converge to enable transformations in management accounting research, practice, and the professionalization of the field.

For its part, this chapter suggests in a limited way, and very tentatively, that an element of conceptual conformity between trends in research interests, the rise of cost accounting and its professionalization, and enterprise accounting practices exists to the extent that they seem to be tied to forces of effects which are only partially dependent on strategic intent. Research and practice in management accounting as well as the professionalization of the field exhibit *raisons d'être* underpinned by incidents, circumstances, and chance events affected to varying levels, by predefined logics of action-guiding pursuits. This does not in any sense negate the propriety of attempting to advance or operationalize management accounting ideals. But the implication is that any functional imperatives exhibited by management accounting are likely to be embedded within the situationally specific processes whose rationale they inhabit. Beyond this, given the rudimentary exposition of UK management accounting provided here, any proposition about management accounting change must remain speculative and open to further questioning.

Notes

1. It is notable that Sir Ronald Edwards, who joined the LSE costing scholars in 1935 and became Professor of Economics at the school in 1949 before taking up a post in industry, 'continued to influence the School until his death in 1976' (Dev 1980: 6). Professor William Baxter, who took up a Chair in Accounting at the LSE in 1947 until his retirement in 1973, relates that he had been 'impressed . . . by the application of economic theory to problems of commerce' (ibid.) by LSE accounting scholars under whom he studied in the mid-1930s.
2. The journal *Accounting, Organizations and Society*, founded in 1976 by Professor Anthony Hopwood, has played an important role in both sponsoring and publishing this type of research.
3. CIMA is the principal management accounting body in the United Kingdom. It was founded in 1919 as the Institute of Cost and Works Accountants. In 1972, it changed its name to the Institute of Cost and Management Accountants, and the name was again changed, to the Chartered Institute of Management Accountants, in 1986. In terms of membership, it is the third-largest professional accounting body with approximately 36,000 members and 57,000 students (*Management Accounting*, Mar. 1994, p. 4).
4. *Management Accounting Research* and *Management Accounting* are two UK-based journals publishing, respectively, academic and professional articles in the area.
5. Solomons (1952: 19) notes that: 'Perhaps the most important factor leading to a growth of interest in costing (at the end of the nineteenth century) was the increasing difficulty of price fixing in the engineering industry'. It is also of significance that the president of the ICWA in 1946 said of Alexander Hamilton Church, an English engineer, that during the last decade of the nineteenth century he 'probably did more than anyone, both directly and indirectly, to promote costing as it is now known' (Roland Dunkerley, cited in Solomons 1952: 25).
6. It is notable that CIMA's publishing arm, which aims principally to service the professional management accounting market, has, within a short period of time, undertaken a formidable expansion and diversification of its publications base. This now ranges from examination and technical cost accounting material to coverage of areas relating to quality, personnel, marketing, service, presentation style, and gender issues, among others. Likewise, CIMA's educational syllabus has been 'systematically directed towards management accounting as the integrated management of finance and those aspects of accounting which underpin strategic policy-making at senior levels of management' (Armstrong and Jones 1992: 72).
7. Discussions are currently going on between the Institute of Chartered

Accountants of England and Wales (the largest accountancy body in the United Kingdom) and CIMA on the long-standing question of amalgamating and whether there is 'a basis for merger' (CIMA's President Tom Glancy, cited in *Management Accounting*, 1995, p. 2) have recently taken place.

References

Amey, L. R. (1965), 'Divisional Performance Measurement and Interest on Capital', *Journal of Business Finance*, 2: 22–31.

Armstrong, P. (1987), 'The Rise of Accounting Controls in British Capitalist Enterprises', *Accounting, Organizations and Society*, 12: 415–36.

—— and Jones, C. (1992), 'The Decline of Operational Expertise in the Knowledge-Base of Management Accounting: An Examination of some Post-War Trends in the Qualifying Requirements of the Chartered Institute of Management Accountants', *Management Accounting Research*, 3: 53–76.

Arnold, J., Carsberg, B., and Scapens, R. (1980), *Topics in Management Accounting* (Oxford: Philip Alan), 277–95.

Baxter, W., (1991), 'Early Critics of Costing—LSE in the 1930s', in Oliver F. Graves (ed.), *The Costing Heritage* (Harrisburg, Pa.: Academy of Accounting Historians), 138–49.

Bhimani, A. (1993), 'Performance Measures in UK Manufacturing Companies: The State of Play', *Management Accounting*, 71: 20–2.

—— and Okano, H. (1995), 'Targeting Excellence: Target Cost Management at Toyota', *Management Accounting*, 73: 42–5.

—— and Pigott, D. (1992), 'Implementing ABC: A Case Study of Organizational and Behavioural Consequences', *Management Accounting Research*, 3: 119–32.

Bright, J., Davies, R., Doumes, C. A., and Sweeting, B. (1992), 'The Development of Costing Techniques and Practices: A UK Study', *Management Accounting Research*, 3: 201–12.

Bromwich, M., and Bhimani, A. (1989), *Management Accounting: Evolution not Revolution* (London: CIMA).

—— —— (1994), *Management Accounting: Pathways to Progress* (London: CIMA).

Bruns, W. J., and Kaplan, R. S. (1987), 'Introduction: Field Studies in Management Accounting', in W. J. Bruns and R. S. Kaplan (eds.), *Accounting and Management: Field Study Perspectives* (Boston: Harvard Business School Press), 1–17.

Buchanan, J. M. (1973), 'Introduction: LSE Cost Theory in Retrospect', in J. M. Buchanan and G. F. Thirlby (eds.), *LSE Essays on Cost* (London: Weidenfield & Nicholson), 1–18.

Burchell, S., Clubb, A., Hopwood, A. G., Hughes, J., and Nahapiet, J. (1980), 'The Roles of Accounting in Organizations and Society', *Accounting, Organizations and Society*, 5: 5–27.

Carr, C. (1995), 'Strategic Investment Decision Styles in Britain and Germany', paper presented at the Management Accounting Research Group Conference, London, LSE, 30 March.

Carr, C., and Ng, J. (1995), 'Total Cost Control: Nissan and its UK Supplier Partnerships', *Management Accounting Research*, 6: 347–66.

Chartered Institute of Management Accountants (CIMA) (1993), *Performance Measurement in the Manufacturing Sector* (London: CIMA).

Coates, J. B., and Longden, S. G. (1989), *Management Accounting: The Challenge of Technological Innovation* (London: CIMA).

Cooper, R., and Kaplan, R. S. (1987), 'How Cost Accounting Systematically Distorts Product Costs', in W. J. Bruns and R. S. Kaplan (eds.), *Accounting and Management: Field Study Perspectives* (Boston: Harvard Business School Press).

Currie, W. (1994), *The Strategic Management of Advanced Manufacturing Technology* (London: CIMA).

Davies, R., and Sweeting, B. (1991), 'Management Accounting: Industrial Revolution?', *Certified Accountant*, 45 (May): 44–6.

Dent, J., Ezzamel, M., and Bourn, M. (1984), 'Reflection on Research in Management Accounting and its Relationship to Practice: An Academic View', in A. G. Hopwood and H. Schreuder (eds.), *European Contribution to Accounting Research: The Achievements of the Last Decade* (Amsterdam: Free University Press), 233–54.

Dev, S. (1980), 'Accounting and the LSE Tradition', Inaugural Lecture, London School of Economics and Political Science.

Drury, C., and Tayles, M. (1994), 'Product Costing in UK Manufacturing Organisations', *European Accounting Review*, 3: 443–69.

—— —— Braund, S., and Osborne, P. (1993), *A Survey of Management Accounting Practices in UK Manufacturing Companies* (London: Chartered Association of Certified Accountants).

Edwards, R. S., (1937), 'The Rationale of Cost Accounting' in A. Plant (ed.), *Some Modern Business Problems* (London: Longmans), 101–27.

Emmanuel, C., Otley, D., and Merchant, K. (1990), *Accounting for Management Control* (London: Chapman and Hall).

Ezzamel, M., Lilley, S., and Willmott, H. (1995), *Changes in Managers and Managing Change* (London: CIMA).

Fincham, R., and Roslender, R. (1993), 'Information Technology and the Strategy Process: The UK Financial Services Industry', University of Stirling Discussion Paper, Mar.

Friedman, A., and Lyne, S. (1995), *Implementing Activity-Based Techniques* (London: CIMA).

Garcke, E., and Fells, J. M. (1887), *Factory Accounts* (Crosby, UK: Lockwood and Son).

Garrett, A. A. (1961), *History of the Society of Incorporated Accountants 1885–1957* (Oxford: Oxford University Press).

Gietzmann, M. (1991), 'Implementation Issues Associated with the Construction of An Activity-Based Costing System in an Engineering Components Manufacturer', *Management Accounting Research*, 2: 189–200.

Gould, J. R. (1974), 'Opportunity Cost: The London Tradition', in H. C. Edey and B. S. Yamey (eds.), *Debits, Credits, Finance and Profits* (London: Sweet and Maxwell), 91–107.

Gramick, D. (1971), *Managerial Comparisons of Four Developed Countries* (Cambridge, Mass.: MIT Press).

Hopper, T. (1994), 'The Development of British Cost and Management Accounting Research: A Personal View', Working Paper, University of Manchester.

Hopwood, A. G. (1972), 'An Empirical Study of the Role of Accounting Data in Performance Evaluation', *Empirical Results in Accounting, Supplement to Journal of Accounting Research*, 156–82.

—— (1974), *Accounting and Human Behaviour* (London: Prentice-Hall).

—— (1994), 'An Organisational Perspective on Current Developments', paper presented at the Management Accounting Research Group Conference, LSE, 21 Apr.

—— and Bromwich, M. (1984), 'Accounting Research in the United Kingdom', in A. G. Hopwood and H. Schreuder (eds.), *European Contributions to Accounting Research*: *The Achievements of the Last Decade* (Amsterdam: Free University Press), 133–63.

—— and Miller, P. (1994), *Accounting as Social and Institutional Practice* (Cambridge: Cambridge University Press).

Horovitz, J. (1980), *Top Management Control in Europe* (London: Macmillan).

Innes, J., and Mitchell, F. (1989), *Management Accounting*: *The Challenge of Technological Innovation*: *Electronic Firms* (London: CIMA).

—— —— (1990), 'The Process of Change in Management Accounting: Some Field Study Evidence', *Management Accountant Research*, 3–19.

—— —— (1991), 'ABC: A Survey of CIMA Members', *Management Accounting* (UK), 69 (Oct.: 28–30).

—— —— (1992), *Activity Based Costing—Problems in Practice* (London: CIMA).

—— —— (1994), 'A Survey of Activity-Based Costing in the UK's Largest Companies', Working Paper.

Jones, T. C., Currie, W. L., and Dugdale, D. (1993), 'Accounting and Technology in Britain and Japan: Learning from Field Research', *Management Accounting Research*, 4: 109–38.

Kaplan, R. S. (1983), 'Measuring Manufacturing Performance: New Challenges for Managerial Accounting Research', *Accounting Review*, 58 (Oct.: 686–705).

—— (1984), 'Yesterday's Accounting Undermines Production', *Harvard Business Review*, 65 (July/Aug.: 57–63).

—— (1985), 'Accounting Lag: The Obsolescence of Cost Accounting Systems', in K. Clark and C. Lorenze (eds.), *Technology and Productivity*: *The Uneasy Alliance* (Boston: Harvard Business School Press).

—— (1986), 'Introduction', in *Costing Accounting for the 90's*: *The Challenge of Technological Change Proceedings* (Montvale, NJ: National Association of Accountants), 7–12.

—— 1994), 'Management Accounting (1984–1994): Development of New Practice and Theory', *Management Accounting Research*, 5: 247–60.

Kellett, B. M., and Sweeting, R. C. (1991), 'Accounting Innovations and Adaptations: A UK Case', *Management Accounting Research*, 2: 15–26.

King, M., Lee, R. A., Piper, J. A., and Whittaker, J. (1991), 'W(h)iter Management Accounting', *Management Accounting*, 2 (Mar.): 46–50.

KPMG Peat Marwick Management Consultants (1990), *Information for Strategic Management*: *A Survey of Leading Companies* (London: KPMG Peat Marwick Consultants).

Lane, C. (1989), *Management and Labour in Europe* (Aldershot: Edward Elgar).

Lapsley, I. (1994), 'Responsibility Accounting Revived? Market Reforms and Budgetary Control in Health Care', *Management Accounting Research*, 5: 337–52.
Lefley, F., and Wharton, F. (1992), 'Capital Investment Appraisal of Advanced Manufacturing Technology', Working paper, University of Hull.
Littler, D. A., and Sweeting, R. C. (1989), *Management Accounting: The Challenge of Technological Innovation: High Technology Industries* (London: CIMA).
Llewellyn, S. (1992), 'The Role of Case Study Methods in Management Accounting Research: A Comment', *British Accounting Review*, 24: 17–32.
Loft, A. (1986*a*), 'Towards a Critical Understanding of Accounting: The Case of Cost Accounting in the UK 1914–1925', *Accounting, Organizations and Society*, 11: 137–70.
—— (1986*b*), 'Understanding Accounting in its Social Context: The Case for Cost Accounting in Britain 1914–1925', Ph.D. diss., London Business School.
McRae, D. (1994), 'A Message from the President', *Management Accounting*, 72: 4.
Management Accounting (1968), '1919–1969: Portrait of a Profession', Mar.
Metcalfe, Captain H. (1885), *The Cost of Manufactures* (London: Wiley).
Murphy, J. C., and Braund, S. L. (1990), 'Management Accounting and New Manufacturing Technology', *Management Accounting*, 68 (Feb.): 38–40.
Nixon, B., and Lonie, A. (1992), 'Technological Innovation and Management Accounting Control: Some Evidence from 13 Case Studies', University of Dundee Discussion Paper, Sept.
Otley, D. T. (1978), 'Budget Use and Managerial Performance', *Journal of Accounting Research*, 16: 122–49.
—— (1980), 'The Contingency Theory of Management Accounting: Achievement and Prognosis', *Accounting, Organizations and Society*, 5: 413–28.
—— (1994), 'Management Control in Contemporary Organisations: Towards a Wider Framework', *Management Accounting Research*, 5: 289–300.
—— and Berry, A. J. (1994), 'Case Study Research in Management Accounting and Control', *Management Accounting Research*, 5: 45–68.
Parker, R. H. (1980), 'History of Accounting for Decisions', in J. Arnold, B. Carsberg, and R. Scapen (eds.), *Topics in Management Accounting* (Oxford: Philip Alan), 262–76.
Puxty, A., and Lyall, D. (1990), *Cost Control for the 1990's* (London: CIMA).
Roslender, R. (1990), 'Sociology and Management Accounting Research', *British Accounting Review*, 22: 351–72.
Scapens, R. W. (1980), 'Overview of Current Trends and Directions for the Future', in J. Arnold, B. Carsberg, and R. W. Scapens, *Topics in Management Accounting* (Oxford: Philip Alan), 277–95.
—— (1990), 'Researching Management Accounting Practice: The Role of Case Study Methods', *British Accounting Review*, 22: 259–82.
—— (1991), *Management Accounting: A Review of Recent Developments* (London: Macmillan).
—— (1992), 'The Role of Case Study Methods in Management Accounting Research: A Personal Reflection and Reply', *British Accounting Review*, 24: 369–84.
—— (1994), 'Never Mind the Gap: Towards an Institutional Perspective on Management Accounting Practice', *Management Accounting Research*, 5: 301–21.

—— and Roberts, J. (1993), 'Accounting and Control: A Case Study of Resistance to Accounting Change', *Management Accounting Research*, 4: 1–32.

Sheppard, J. (1990), 'The Strategic Management of IT Investment Decisions: A Research Note', *British Journal of Management*, 1: 171–81.

Solomons, D. (1952), 'The Historical Development of Costing', in D. Solomons (ed.), *Studies in Costing* (London: Sweet and Maxwell), 1–52.

—— (1965), *Divisional Performance: Measurement and Control* (New York: Irwin).

Stacey, N. A. H. (1954), *English Accountancy: A Study in Social and Economic History 1800–1954* (London: Gee).

Strange, N. (1991), 'Accounting Decline: Management Accounting in Large Engineering Companies in Germany and Great Britain', INSEAD Working Paper.

Tomkins, C. (1973), *Financial Planning in Divisionalised Companies* (London: Haymarket).

—— and Groves, R. (1983), 'The Everyday Accountant and Researching his Reality', *Accounting, Organizations and Society*, 8: 361–74.

Yoshikawa, T., Innes, J., and Mitchell, F. (1995), 'A Japanese Case Study of Functional Cost Analysis', *Management Accounting Research*, 6: 415–32.

—— —— ——, and Tanaka, M. (1993), *Contemporary Cost Management* (London: Chapman and Hall).

INDEX

accountants:
  in Europe xix
  training of: Belgium 2–3; Greece 124–5; Italy 151; Netherlands 165–6; Spain 182, 184–5, 187–9; Sweden 203, 205
Accounting Act (Finland, 1973) 60, 62
Accounting Plan (Greece) 123, 128
accounting publications, Spain 181–2
accounting-based budgeting techniques, Belgium 3–4
activity-based budgeting, Belgium 15
activity-based costing (ABC):
  Belgium 14–21; activity-based costing 22, 25; barriers 21; case studies 16–21; and continuous improvement processes 18–21; implementation 14–16; light bulb manufacture 16–17; textile industries 17–18; use of 15
  Denmark 38, 42, 43, 44, 46, 49
  Finland 60, 62; application of 65; evidence on 66–7; survey of 63–4
  France: cost flow accounting 83, 95, 97; diffusion of 84–5
  Germany 104
  Greece 126, 132
  Italy 158–9
  Netherlands 172
  Spain 187, 188, 192
  Sweden 206, 207, 208, 210, 212–13
  United Kingdom 222, 226–8, 233
activity-based management (ABM):
  Belgium 15
  Finland 63, 64, 66, 68
  France 95–7
  Italy 159
actual costing, Germany 106–9
  cost-reimbursement contracts 107–9
  inventorial costs 107
Adam, D. 104
advanced manufacturing technology (AMT), Belgium 3–4, 11, 13
Agthe, K. 112, 114
Ahlberg, G. 206
Ahola, P. 59
Ahrens, T. xx
Amaduzzi, A. 149
Amey, L. R. 220
Andersen, Michael 31–53
Anthony, R. 154, 173
Armstrong, P. 223, 224, 235
Arnold, J. 220
Ask, Urban 199–217
asset-based accounting, Italy 141–2
Association of Swedish Engineering Industries (ASEI) 212–13, 214
Atkinson, A. 3, 164
audits, Spain 186
Ax, Christian 199–217

Ballas, Apostolos 123–39
batch level costs, Finland 58
batch production:
  Denmark 45
  Finland 63
Baxter, W. 219
Becker, H. P. 101, 105
Beischel, M. E. 92
Belgium 1–30
  accountants in xix; training of 2–3
  activity-based costing 14–21
  performance measurement systems 21–8
  strategic capital investments, evaluation 3–14
benchmarking in cost management, Denmark 48
Bergamin Barbato, Maria 140–63
Berliner, C. 41, 211
Berry, A. J. 221
Bescos, P.-L. 85
Besta, F. 140–1, 146
Bhimani, A. xx, 4, 20, 63, 164, 183, 187, 218–41
Bindenga, A. J. 167
Bjornenak, T. 44
Blayney, P. J. 45
Bohr, K. 104
bookkeeping:
  Italy 155–7
  Netherlands 167
Boons, A. 171, 173, 174
Boonzaaijer, G. 171
Braund, S. L. 226, 229
Bright, J. 228
Brimson, J. A. 41, 62, 211
Broglia, G. 156
Bromwich, M. xx, 4, 63, 164, 183, 187, 220, 221, 222
Bruggeman, Werner 1–30
Brunetti, G. 154
Buchanan, J. M. 219
budgets/budgeting:
  control, Denmark 35–6, 40

budgets/budgeting (*cont.*):
costs, Germany 109–15; direct product costs 110–12; indirect product costs 112–15; and optimum budgeting 109–10
Greece 128, 133–4
Italy 152
practices in CIM, Belgium 4–9
see also capital budgeting
Burchell, S. 221
Business Taxation Act (Finland, 1968) 60

Camfferman, K. 166, 168
capacity costs 34, 36
capital appraisal techniques, UK 225
capital budgeting practices:
in CIM 5–9
decision making in 7
Netherlands 169, 170
post-implementation audit 9
responsibility for exponent 9
risk analysis 8
capital investment:
Belgium: strategic evaluation 3–14; case studies 9–12; company goals and strategies 13; problem definition 3–4; quality of 12–13; strategic fit 12–14; survey 4–9
Finland 61
Spain, foreign 192–3
United Kingdom 231–2
Carlson, C. E. 59
Carr, C. 223
Chartered Institute of Management Accountants (CIMA) xx, 125, 187, 222–4, 229, 231
charts of accounts:
Greece 126
Sweden 205
Clark, J. M. 32
Clarke, F. 166, 167
Coates, J. B. 221
Coda, V. 148
Coenenberg, A. G. 100
Collini, Paolo 140–63
Commission Générale d'Organisation Scientifique (GECOS, France) 75, 76, 78, 80
Commission interministérielle de normalisation des comptabilités (France) 76
Companies Acts (UK, 1861, 1900, 1948) 223
computer-aided design (CAD) 5
computer integrated manufacturing (CIM):
Belgium 4–9; decision making in 7; investment evaluation in 5–9; responsibility for exponent 9; risk analysis 8
Netherlands 172
computer-aided manufacturing (CAM) 4–9
computerized management systems:
Greece 131
Sweden 205–6
connection accounts, Italy 156
Conseil National de la Comptabilité (CNC, France) 82
contribution margin principle:
Denmark 33, 36, 37, 44
Finland 63
Germany 118
Cooper, R. 187
on Belgium 14
on Denmark 38, 41, 43, 47
on Finland 58, 62
on Netherlands 164
on Sweden 210, 211
on United Kingdom 220
cost accounting:
activity-based, *see* activity-based costing (ABC)
Finland 55–6; survey 62–5
France: structured framework 79–88; cost analysis, framework for 80–1; cost flow 81–8; costs, characteristics of 79; framework for 80–1; and information systems 95–7; network for analysis in 79; purposes of 79
Germany 101–6; components 104–6; systems 101–4
Greece 132; cost management 135; management of 130–1; standards 134–5
Italy 141; and financial accounting 156; post-war industrial phase 148–9; pre-industrial phase 145–6; recent phase 153–5
Spain: research on 182, 184–5, 186; teaching of 187–9
Sweden 206–11; changes in 209; improvements in 209–10; methods 206–7; modern techniques 210; overhead costs 208–9
United Kingdom 219–20, 224
cost allocation:
Denmark, product costing 44–5
Germany, causation principle 100
Netherlands 172–3
overheads:
France 85–6; Italy 146–7, 150–1, 155; Sweden 202, 203, 208–9, 210; United Kingdom 226–8
Spain, publications and research on 182, 184–5
cost centres:
France 80–2
Germany 104–5, 116–17
Italy 156
Netherlands 172, 174
Sweden 203

cost control, Germany 115–18
by activity 116–18
methods and components 115–16
cost determinants (cost drivers)
Belgium 18–21
Finland 62
Germany 105, 113
Sweden 210
cost-distribution sheets, Netherlands 172
cost flow accounting, France 81–8
cost pools, *see* cost centres
cost-reimbursement contracts, Germany 107–9
cost variance analysis, Germany 106
costs:
divisibility of 36–7, 38
Finland, information use of 66
France, structured framework 79
current value accounting, Netherlands 168–71
Currie, W. 234
Cyert, R. M. 35

Davies, R. 228
Dean, G. 166, 167
decision making:
Belgium, budgeting practices 7
France, information system 92
Italy 146
Netherlands 173
Spain 182, 184–5; teaching of 188–9
Sweden 202
Dellmann, K. 120
Denmark 31–53
accountants in xix
cost accounting data recording 37–9
cost management practices 40–2; diffusion of 45–8
current practice, characteristics 37–40
development of accounting principles 35–7
foundations of accounting 33–5
product costing methods 42–5
Dent, J. 219
Dev, S. 219
Dewerpe, A. 145
diffusion of cost management techniques, Denmark 40–2
changes in accounting systems 46
manufacturing overheads in 45, 46–7
results 46–8; benchmarking 48; overhead costs 47; performance 47–8; target costing 48
survey population 45–6
Dijksma, J. 165, 167
direct cost accounting:
Greece 127
Italy 152, 154–5, 158
Spain 192
Sweden 210
discounted cash flow accounting:
Belgium 3, 4, 10, 13
United Kingdom 225
Dorn, G. 100
Drury, C. 189, 226–7, 228–9, 231

economics and accounting theory, Netherlands 166–71
Edwards, R. S. 219
Emmanuel, C. 221
Ernst & Young 15
European Community 62, 67, 189
Euske, K. J. xx
expenditure-income theory 59
Ezzamel, M. 218

Faas, F. A. M. J. 169, 170
Federation of Swedish Industries and Swedish Standards Association 203
Fells, John 219
Fernandez-Fernandez, Antonio 180–98
Financial Statements Act (Denmark, 1981) 33
Fincham, R. 234
Finland 54–73
accountants in xix
contemporary practice 61–7; changes in 61–2; interview evidence 66–7, 69; legislation 60, 62, 71; survey on 62–5, 70
full costing to variable costing 55–61; driving forces of 61; early developments 55–6; embracing full costing 56–7; financial accounting on variable accounting 59–60; and management accounting 57–8; and variable accounting 58–9
inventory valuation 62–3
variable costing to full costing 67–8
Finnie, J. 4
firms:
Greece 128–9
small: Greece 123, 128; Italy 145, 146, 153, 157; Spain 193–4; United Kingdom 230–1
Spain 190–1
Sweden 200
flexible manufacturing systems:
Belgium 9–10, 13; continuous dyeing technology 11; laser cutters in 10–11; robotics for 10; truck assembly 12
Denmark 45, 47
Fog, B. 43
Fox, J. 21, 28
France 74–99
accountants in xix

France (*cont.*):
accounting background 75–8; conceptual foundations 78; government, role in 76–7, 78; modern period 76
activity-based costing in 83, 84–5
full-cost accounting in 77, 78, 86
information system for monitoring performance 74, 78, 89–97; causal model 89, 92; integration 95–7; nesting of information in 94; targets 93–5
inventory valuation 78
structured cost analysis framework 79–88; accounting policies 86–7; allocation of overhead costs 85–6; cost analysis, framework for 80–1; cost flow 81–8; costs, characteristics of 79; interdepartmental cost transfers 87–8; purposes of 79
Franke, R. 104
Franz, K. P. 120
Fredriksson, Nils 203
Frenckner, P. 204, 205, 206, 210
Friedman, A. 227, 233
full absorption principle 33
full-cost accounting:
Denmark 43
Finland 56–9
France 77, 78, 86
Greece 132
Italy 146, 153, 156
Spain 191–2
Sweden 202–5, 206–7, 209

Garcke, Emile 219
Garrett, A. A. 222
Garvin, D. A. 3, 4
Germany 100–22
accountants in xix
actual costing 106–9; cost-reimbursement contracts 107–9; inventorial costs 107
cost accounting research 101–6; components 104–6; systems 101–4
short-term performance reporting 118–20; components 118; contribution margin accounting 118; methods 118–20, closes 119–20, open 118–19
standard costing 110–18; cost budgeting 109–15, direct product costs 110–12, indirect product costs 112–15, and optimum budgeting 109–10; cost controlling 115–18, by activity 116–18, methods and components 115–16
Giannessi, E. 149
Gibert, André 77
Gietzmann, M. 232
Glete, J. 201
Goetz, William 33, 36
Goldhar, J. D. 4
Goldratt, E. 21, 28
Goudeket, A. 168
Goudriaan, J. 165, 167
Gould, J. R. 219, 220
government:
France, role in 76–7, 78
Greece, price control 124
Spain, spending 190
Govindarajan, V. 173
Gramick, D. 223
Granlund, M. 55, 62, 63, 65
Greece 123–39
accountants in xix; status 124; training 124–5
accounting profession in 124–5
charts of accounts 126
cost management 135
Hellenic General Accounting Plan 125–7
interviews 130–5; budgeting and planning 133–4; costing 132; financial control and performance measurement 134–5; management 130–1
small firms in 123, 128
survey methodology 127–30; data collection 129–30
Groot, T. L. C. M. 164–79
Groves, R. 221
Gurnani, C. 8

Hansen, Palle 32, 33, 58
Harvard Business School 33, 42, 213
Harvey, T. R. 20
Hauer, G. 101, 105
Hautakangas, T. 59
Hayes, R. H. 3, 4
Hellenic General Accounting Plan (HGAP) 123, 124, 125–7, 132
Hellenic Management Association (HMA) 133
Henzel, F. 100
Hill, T. 4
historical costing:
France 79
Netherlands 170
Spain 192
Hoffman, H. 101
Hofstede, C. 130
Honko, Jaakko 57, 58, 61, 63
Hopper, T. 221, 222
Hopwood, A. 101, 220, 221, 234
Horngren, Charles 57, 77, 189
Horovitz, J. H. xx, 223
hurdle rates (opportunity cost of capital), Belgium 3, 5–6

income-based accounting, Italy 141, 142–3
industrial accounts, Italy 156
industrial development, Sweden 201–2

information system for monitoring performance, France 74, 78, 89–97
causal model 89, 92
and cost accounting 95–7
integration 95–7
nesting of information in 94
targets 93–5
Innes, J. 221, 226–7, 232
inspiration analyses 34, 37
Institute for International Research (Denmark) 42
Institute of Accountants (IDAC, Belgium) 2–3
Institute of Auditors (IBR, Belgium) 2
Institute of Cost and Works Accountants (ICWA) 224
interdepartmental cost transfers, France 87–8
internal rate of return, UK 225, 231
inventorial costs, Germany 107
inventory valuation:
Finland 62–3
France 78
Italy 149, 152, 156
Sweden 207
investment:
Belgium: pay-back periods on 5–7, 13; strategic, *see* strategic capital investment
capital, *see* capital investment
Italy, manufacturing 147–8
Israelsen, Poul 31–53
Italy 140–63
accountants in xix
accounting tradition 141–4
activity-based costing in 158–8
asset-based accounting 141–2
budgeting 152
cost accounting: conceptualization of 144; and financial accounting 156; post-war industrial phase 148–9; pre-industrial phase 145–6; recent phase 153–5
current problems 157–9
direct costing accounting 154–5, 158
full-cost accounting 146, 153, 156
future of 159–60
income-based accounting 141, 142–3
inventory valuation 149, 152, 156
overhead cost allocation 146–7, 150–1, 155
small firms in 145, 146, 153, 157
taxation in 153
theory and practice 144–57; bookkeeping 155–7; post-war industrial phase 147–51; pre-industrial phase 145–7; recent phase 151–5
training of accountants 151

Jantzen, Ivar 31
Jelinek, M. 4
job-order accounting, Denmark 46
Johnson, H. T. 43, 62, 157, 187, 211
Jones, C. 235
Jones, T. C. 233
Jönsson, Sten 199–217
Joy, M. P. 45
just-in-time techniques:
Belgium 9–10
Denmark 45, 47
Finland 63–4
Netherlands 172

Kaitila, I. V. 55, 56
Kaplan, R. S. 187
on Belgium 3, 4, 14
on Denmark 38, 41, 42, 43, 47
on Finland 58, 62
on Germany 101
on Italy 157, 158
on Netherlands 164
on Sweden 210, 211, 213
on United Kingdom 220
Kasanen, Eero 54–73
Kellett, B. M. 232
Kilger, W. 101, 105–6, 109, 112, 114–15, 117–18
King, M. 233
Klaassen, J. 168, 169, 170
Kleerekooper, S. 167
Kohler, E. L. 210
Kokinos, J. 128
Kreuger, Ivar 202
Küpper, H.-U. 101, 114

Laitenen, E. K. 55
Lane, C. 223
Lapsley, I. 234
Larsen, A. 42
Lassmann, G. 104, 106
Lebas, Michel 74–99
Lefley, F. 231
Lehmann, M. R. 100
levelled time in product costing 111
life-cycle accounting:
Finland 63
United Kingdom 228
Lilius, A. 55
Limberg, Theodore 166, 167, 168
Littler, D. A. 221
Llewellyn, S. 221
Loft, A. 224
Longden, S. G. 221
Lonie, A. 234
Löning, H. xx
Lücke, W. 115
Lukka, K. 55, 57, 59, 62, 63, 65

Lyall, D. 229
Lyne, S. 227, 233

Madsen, Vagn 33, 34, 35, 36, 37, 210
Majala, R. 59, 60
Malmi, Teemu 54–73
management control systems, Finland 61
managerial economics 33
manufacturing:
  Finland, overheads 63–4
  Italy, investment in 147–8
  product costing methods, Denmark 42–5; diffusion of 45–8; overheads (MOH) 45, 46–7
  United Kingdom 229, 231
  see also flexible manufacturing systems
March, J. G. 35
marginal costing:
  Germany 104
  Sweden 204
market competition, Netherlands 171
material requirements/resource planning systems (MRP):
  Denmark 45, 47
  Netherlands 172
  Sweden 209
McBeth, Douglas 89
McNair, C. J. 21
McRae, D. 224
Meij, A. 167
Mendoza, C. 85
Merchant, K. A. 173
Méthode des sections homogènes, see cost accounting, France
Mey, J. L. 1
Miller, P. 221
Mitchell, F. 221, 226–7, 232
multinational enterprises:
  Italy 148
  Spain 189, 192–3
  Swedish 200
Murphy, J. C. 226, 229

Nanni, A. J. 21
Näsi, S. 55–6
net present value:
  Belgium 11, 12
  United Kingdom 225, 231
Netherlands 164–79
  accountants in xix
  contemporary cost management 171–3; cost allocation 172–3
  economics and accounting theory 166–71; current value accounting 168–9; current-value management accounting 169–71
  historical developments 165–6
  influence in Belgium 1
  market competition 171
  and performance evaluation 169–70, 173–4
  training of accountants 165–6
network for analysis in cost accounting 79
  cost flow in 81–8
  framework for 80–1
Nixon, B. 234
Nordic Journal of Technical Economics (Denmark) 31–2

Okano, H. 222
Olve, N.-G. 206
opportunity cost of capital (hurdle rates), Belgium 3, 5–6
organization theory in accounting, United Kingdom 220–1
Östman, L. 205
Otley, D. T. 221, 234
overhead costs:
  allocation:
    France 85–6; Greece 132; Italy 146–7, 150–1, 155; Sweden 202, 203, 208–9, 210; United Kingdom 226–8
  in cost management techniques, Denmark 47

Panhellenic Accountants' Association 125
Panhellenic Association of Cost Accountants 125
Parker, R. H. 219
pay-back periods on investment, Belgium 5–7, 13
performance evaluation:
  Belgium 21–8; changes in 22; in pharmaceuticals 26–7; in plastics 24–6; in suitcase manufacture 27–8; in textiles 23–4
  Denmark, cost management techniques 47–8
  France, information system for 74, 78, 89–97; causal model 89, 92; and cost accounting 95–7; integration 95–7; nesting of information in 94; targets 93–5
  Germany, short-term 118–20; closed methods 119–20; open methods 118–19
  Greece 134–5
  Netherlands 169–70, 173–4
  United Kingdom, non-financial 229–31
Pigott, D. 233
Pihlanto, P. 57, 59
Plan Comptable Général (France, 1982) 74, 75, 79–80
Plaut, H.-G. 114
Polak, N. 165, 167
Polesie, T. 35–6, 210
Porter, M. E. 200

Posthumus, N. W. 165
Potthoff, E. 167
price determination:
  Denmark 42–3; and firms' cost structures 44; by market 43–4, 45, 67
  Finland: costing on 56–7; and variable costing 58–9
  France 77
  Greece, by government 124
  Italy 146
  Netherlands 169, 170
product costing:
  Denmark 40–2; allocation methods 44–5; calculation methods, change, need for 44–5, form of 43–4; price determination methods 42–3; in pricing and revenue/cost analyses 43–4; revenue segmentation methods 42–3
  Finland 58, 64
  France 74, 77, 78
  Germany: direct 110–12; indirect 112–15, 117
  Italy 144, 146
  Netherlands 169
  Spain 182, 184–5
  Sweden 202, 209
product life-cycles, Finland 63
production costs, Italy:
  post-war industrial phase 149–51
  pre-industrial phase 146–7
product-variable costs, Denmark 34, 36
  and price determination 44
  see also variable costing
profitability analyses in product costing, Denmark 44
Puxty, A. 229

Quagli, Alberto 140–63

Rasmussen, K. 40, 44
Rautajoki, P. 55
R&D costing, Sweden 207
relevant costing, France 77
return on investment (ROI)
  Belgium 5–7, 10, 12
  France 90
  Sweden 206
revenue segmentation in product costing, Denmark 42–3
Riebel, P. 36, 104, 117
Riis, H. C. 32
Roberts, J. 233
Rohde, Carsten 31–53
Roslender, R. 221, 234
Rummel, K. 100

Saario, Martti 57, 59–60
Saez-Torrecilla, Angel 180–98
Samuelson, L. A. 205, 206, 210
Scapens, Robert 187, 200, 221, 233, 234
Scherrer, Gerhard 100–22
Schmalenbach, E. 100, 167, 204, 205
Schmidt, F. 166, 167, 172
Schneider, D. 100
Schneider, Erich 31–2
Schoenfeld, H. M. W. 100
Schreuder, H. 165
Schroeff, H. J. van der 167
Schwab, H. 104
Schweitzer, M. 114
Seicht, G. 117
Selto, F. 214
Shank, J. K. 173
Sheppard, J. 234
Sheridan, T. T. xx
Shillinglaw, Gordon 77, 210
Sieben, G. 167
Simmonds, Kenneth 187
Simon, Herbert 35
Slagmulder, Regine 1–30
Slot, R. 165
Smith, F. R. 92
Solomons, D. 219, 220
Sorensen, Poul Erik 31–53
Spain 180–98
  accountants in xix; training of 182, 187–9
  management accounting practices 189–94; by activities 194; analysis of 191–4; different systems 190
  research in cost and management accounting 180–7; congresses and seminars 183–4; doctorates 184–5; literature 181–5; periodicals, evolution 181–3; teaching of management accounting 187–9; publications and research on 182, 184–5
Stacey, N. A. H. 222
standard costing:
  Germany 109–18, cost budgeting 109–15, direct product costs 110–12, indirect product costs 112–15, and optimum budgeting 109–10; cost controlling 115–18, by activity 116–18, methods and components 115–16
  Spain 191–2
  Sweden 203–4
  United Kingdom 220, 229
Staubus, G. J. 210
Stefani, A. 159
Strange, N. xx, 223
Stuijvenberg, J. H. van 165
Sundqvist, A.-I. 206
Sweden 199–217
  accountants in xix; training 203, 205
  activity-based costing 206, 207, 208, 210, 212–13

Sweden (*cont.*):
computerized systems 205–6
current practices 206–11; changes in 209; costing methods 206–7; improvements and barriers 209–10; modern techniques 210–11; overhead cost allocation 202, 203, 208–9, 210; summary 211
full costing 202–5
as homogeneous economy 200–1
post-modernism in 211–14; ABC 212; actors in 212–13; change 211–12
state-supported modernism 201–2
Swedish Institute of Standards 203
Sweeting, B. 228
Sweeting, R. C. 221, 232

Tableau de Bord, *see* information system
Takikonda, L. A. and J. R. 47
target costing:
Denmark 48
United Kingdom 228
taxation:
Italy 153
Spain 190
Tayles, M. 229
ter Vehn, A. 203–4
Texeira-Quiros, Joaquin 180–98
Tomkins, C. 220, 221
total quality control (TQC), Spain 187
total quality management (TQM), Finland 63–4
trade unions, Sweden 201–2
transfer pricing:
Sweden 207
United Kingdom 220
Turney, P. B. B. 62

unit costs:
Denmark 34
Finland 58
United Kingdom 218–41
accountants in xix
activity-based costing 222, 226–8, 233
capital appraisal 225
current practices 224–34; activity-based costing 222, 226–8; capital investment 231–2; decision making 228–9; field studies 232–4; non-financial performance 229–31; overhead allocation 226–8; standard costing 220, 229
management accounting profession 222–4
management accounting research 219–22

Vaivio, Juhani 54–73
van der Meer, J. B. H. xxi
Van der Schroeff, J. 1
Vancil, R. 154
Vaquera-Mosquero, Mercedes 180–98
variability accounting, Denmark 33–5
variable costing:
Finland 58–9; and cost drivers 62; diffusion of 61; driving forces of 61; financial accounting on 59–60; and inventory valuation 62–3; and market conditions 62, 67; opposition to 59; priority order 59–60
France 77
Sweden 205, 206–7, 209
Vatter, William 77
Venieris, George 123–39
Virkkunen, Henrik 57, 58, 59, 62
Virtanen, Kalervo 54–73
Volmer, J. G. Ch. 165

Waeytens, Dominique 1–30
Wartmann, R. 115
Wharton, F. 231
With, E. de 169, 170, 174
Woerd, E. van der 174
Worre, Z. 36, 37, 38

Yoshikawa, T. 48, 164, 222
Young, M. 214

Zan, L. 144
Zappa, G. 140, 147, 151, 156, 159
on cost accounting 144, 146, 148–9, 153–4
on costs 143–4
on income 141–4
Zeff, S.A. 166